TAOS TALES

Elsie Clews Parsons

DOVER PUBLICATIONS, INC.
New York

Published in Canada by General Publishing Company, Ltd., 30 Lesmill Road, Don Mills, Toronto, Ontario.

Published in the United Kingdom by Constable and Company, Ltd., 3 The Lanchesters, 162–164 Fulham Palace Road, London W6 9ER.

Bibliographical Note

This Dover edition, first published in 1996, is an unabridged republication of the work originally published as Volume XXXIV of *Memoirs of the American Folk-Lore Society* by The American Folk-Lore Society, New York / J. J. Augustin Publisher, New York, 1940.

Library of Congress Cataloging-in-Publication Data

Parsons, Elsie Worthington Clews, 1875–1941.
    Taos tales / Elsie Clews Parsons.
        p.   cm.
    Originally published: New York : American Folk-Lore Society, J. J. Augustin Publisher, 1940, in ser.: Memoirs of the American Folk-Lore Society ; v. 34.
    Includes bibliographical references.
    ISBN 0-486-28974-5 (pbk).
    1. Taos Indians—Folklore.   2. Tales—New Mexico—Taos Pueblo.   I. Title.
E99.T2P3   1996
398.2'089974—dc20   95-45565
                                                                                                            CIP

Manufactured in the United States of America
Dover Publications, Inc., 31 East 2nd Street, Mineola, N.Y. 11501

CONTENTS

iii

Preface

The January moon, not before, is the time of year at Taos to begin story-telling.[1] There is, as elsewhere, a taboo or quasi taboo against telling tales (*łatsi'ana*)[2] in summer. "If we tell stories in the summer time, they say that it will snow"—and the speaker added, "but I do not believe it." The more credulous assert that story-telling in summer would bring cold. The Isleta-Zuni-Hopi sanction against summer-time narration, that it attracts the snakes, appears unfamiliar.

As usual the evening is the favoured hour of story-telling. On winter evenings, when one of my middle-aged informants was young, grand-parents would assemble their relatives, in his case there might be twenty children. Each boy would bring with him two sticks of firewood. All would sit around the walls, and each in turn would tell a story. They liked to have the one with the biggest or longest story start; it might take half the night. Then, as they grew sleepy, others would tell short ones. As it grew toward daybreak if somebody was in the middle of a story, any one present who knew how would say, "Let's make him [the unending story-teller] *łamopölu'na* (fæces roll up)." Then they spread a blanket on the floor, put him in it and bundled him up, tying him in. Four or five would carry him out to the refuse heap, the heap of the dead, and roll him down. If he could free himself and catch somebody, that one in turn would be bundled down the slope, and the others would all run back to the house.

While taking the "bundle" out from the house they had a song to sing which they kept up until they got to the refuse heap:

> *pępapau'lu*[3]
> deer hair bundle
> *paxöy'fïalu*[4]
> pumpkin seed earring

---

[1] At Picurís the season is identified with the ceremonial period of staying still, while Earth is asleep (Harrington and Roberts, 293) and I surmise this is so also at Taos.

[2] l'aciana̦ (T). Tales are also referred to as *piuchaiana* (p₁iwc₁iay'ana, death talk. T.). "Dump telling," an informant translated. At Taos, as throughout early Pueblo territory, the dead were buried in the refuse mounds.

[3] p₁ę- p'₁o + ?, deer hair ? (T).

[4] p₁ox₁əp'ial'una (T).

I

The conclusive word in narration is *kǫiw'ękima,* you have a tail, or *tenkkǫiw'ękim,* so then you have a tail,[1] which is directed to the one whose turn is next and means "you must tell a story to take it off, so it won't freeze."

Tales open in characteristic Pueblo style by naming the personages and the place they live. Frequently the place name is *tuɫata,* at the cotton-wood.[2] Ruined towns are not referred to as in tales of other Pueblos.

Very striking although not unique among Pueblos is a combination of migration narrative and song. In a series of localities the tale personage repeats his song with slight variations. Virtually this is a conte-ballad.

Tale character or content partakes of Plains Indian type as well as of Pueblo Indian type. Yellow Corn woman and Blue Corn woman are, of course, Pueblo personages and several tales are variants of familiar Pueblo tales. There are a number of tale elements or incidents also which are characteristically Pueblo. And yet some of the tales most familiar among other Pueblos appear to be unfamiliar at Taos, e. g., the tale of the war gods and the stuffed bear (found too among Pawnee),[3] of the theft of lightning and thunder, of Coyote seeking salt, of Coyote's false tail. On the other hand Coyote bulks larger in the following collection than in any other collection of Pueblo tales. Both as trickster and culture hero or pseudo hero he takes the same place in Taos tales as he does in Plains tales. In particular the Plains tales of Rolling Skull and of the still more widely spread tale Coyote Tricks his Daughter stand out conspicuously as not having been recorded, with one exception, among other Pueblos. In view of the hypothecated early relationship between Tanoan and Kiowa, the five or six Kiowan parallels are of particular interest, although the parallelism may well be due to recent contacts, direct or through Apache.

Coyote Tricks his Daughter, Eye Jugglers, How the Deer Got their Spots, Bungling Host, Coyote Believes the World is on Fire, and the Spanish tales Holding up the Cliff, Cheese under Water, Coyote Kills his Wife, and Gum Baby are among the sixty-six tales of the Coyote cycle recently recorded by Dr. Opler among Jicarilla Apache. In view of the centurylong contacts of the Jicarilla with Taos and the intertribal

---

[1] kǫyxᵂ'ękimạ: kǫy = kǫwi - 2d person sg. prefix kạ- + - wi- narrative prefix; xᵂ'ę-na, tail; k'imạ, it has been placed. teng for t'engạ, then, so then (T). Same nominee in Isletan and Picurís tales.

[2] t'uɫoto, cottonwood-at (T). Possibly a reference to Cottonwood-bird-pueblo-place (in Tewa, Tekeowinge), the place where in Tewa myth all the people lived after the Emergence and before they scattered (Parsons 4: 15 n.7). But see p. 30.

[3] Dorsey 2: 92.

loans it is surprising that there are no other tale parallels. Are we to infer that pottery technique, for example, spreads more easily than the folk tale? Since the early part of the sixteenth century Pueblo pottery has not been made at Taos, only Apachelike pottery (Mera).

In Taos culture there are many Apache-Plains traits or characters other than pottery or language: Bilateral descent and clanlessness; exclusion of women from the ceremonial life; marked separation of women from warriors; comparatively simple ceremonialism; comparatively indifferent craftsmanship; buffalo hunting; details in dress and headdress of men and of women; aggressive, self-assertive, comparatively individualistic temper or character. In physical characteristics also Taos people are said to approximate Plains type. Indeed, except for their houses, Taos people might well pass for Indians of the Plains. Other Tanoans have been more exposed to typical Pueblo culture but they too, Tewa and Towa, are quite well differentiated from Keres, Zuni, and Hopi. Perhaps the Tanoans did come down from the north, as Harrington asserts, from an area also occupied by their remote linguistic relatives, the Kiowa. At any rate in Taos different Indian cultural strains are quite apparent.

Mexican neighbors as well as Apache and Plains tribes have contributed to Taos lore. And, as elsewhere among Pueblos, the contributions are, so to speak, in different layers: there are stories which have been recently acquired and are comparatively unassimilated, and there are stories of an older acquisition, more assimilated. These stories are thought of as of Pueblo origin, although most of them are given a foreign setting, usually Apache. Apache chief will take the place of the king in the Mexican original. In the indubitably European tales of Faithful Wife and Woman Warrior the narrator was so convinced that the tale was Indian that he proffered the assertion that the medieval punishment of tying a criminal to the tail of a horse was the ancient form of Indian punishment.

In 1937 Dr. G. L. Trager took my manuscript with him to Taos and in the course of his linguistic work checked its terms, enabling me in many cases to make corrections or closer translations. The terms as recorded by Trager are given in footnotes followed by (T). The phonetic key is: a as French patte, e as in let, i as in police, o as in hot, u as in rude, ə as midback unrounded; ạ, ẹ, ị, ọ, ụ corresponding nasal vowels. Straight stroke *before* vowel 'a—main normal stress; lowered straight stroke ‚a—secondary normal stress; á—high tone; à—low tone. Consonants: b, c (as ch in chat), c', d, g, h, k, k', kʷ, l, ł (voiceless l), m, n, p, p', p', r, s, t, t', t', w, x (as German ch), x^w (like Spanish ju in Juan), y (as in yet), ? glottal stop (very weak).

I have also to thank Dr. Trager for versions of Gum Baby and Coyote Tricks his Daughter given in text in the Appendix.

Many years ago in recording tales at Zuni I learned the familiar fact that esoteric practices or terms are referred to or used freely in story-telling which would be withheld from a questioner. Similar attitudes are shown in connection with Trager's checklist. Trager's informant would not translate *łachi,* the term frequently given me for thunder and for kachina. (But Trager got the form nął̦acit''əotuna, thunder, ną— place prefix, łaci, and an unidentified element.) łaci (łatsi)[1] may be a variant of kachina or it may be the matrix term, a point bearing per-haps importantly upon the history of the kachina cult. Terms for med-icine man, for medicine bundle, and for supernatural power were also withheld from Dr. Trager, also terms for various supernatural beings, for the Scalp dance, for the "other world," and even for parrot, that bird of precious plumage. The younger Taos men have been very strictly trained, and undoubtedly they are more aware than their seniors of how much a single word may betray.

---

[1] The variation between the pronunciation ts and c (ch) is not significant in Taos, and Trager uses the letter c "for the single sound unit which may be one or the other or something in between, depending on the speaker."

1. The Kachina Suitors and Coyote

Those people were living at *tułata*, at Cottonwood, *iatsulekweama*,[1] Yellow Corn young woman and *iatsolekweama*, Blue Corn young woman.[2] In the cottonwood tree was living Nighthawk (*notakaiena*)[3] their husband. He was a great hunter. He would go out to hunt early in the morning and late in the evening he would come home with a whole deer which he had tied up by the legs in a bundle. Thus living, two boys were born to them. When they grew up old enough to know they asked their mothers (*inumk'anöma*)[4] who was their father. Their mothers told them that Nighthawk was their father (*inumt'âmöna*)[5]. Then they asked their mothers to make them bows and arrows. Their mothers said to them, "We can not make the bows and arrows, but you can go to your grandfathers (*manumtałułina*)[6]. They will give you bows and arrows. Go eastward (*töibuya*)[7]! That is where they live. There they will give you bows and arrows." So they went. When they got there, the watchman (*xina*)[8] came out, he asked them what they wanted. The boys told him that their mothers told them to come there to ask their grandfathers for bows and arrows. So he took them in. There they were sitting in the room. They all welcomed them by saying, "*Kimowaiina yiaŋyo maŋłai*,[9] our sons, here you two sit down. Why are you here, living at the cottonwood where your home is, your mothers being Yellow Corn woman and Blue Corn woman"?—"Yes, that is so. Our mothers told us that Nighthawk was our father and that our grandfathers were living here, at the Big House (*töłaai*)[10], in the Lake. So we asked our mothers if we could get bows and arrows from you here." Then all answered, "Yes,

---

[1] ìac'₁ulekʷ'iame, corn-yellow-young woman; ìac₁ǫlekʷ'iame, corn-blue-young woman. kʷ'iamena, archaic for young woman; łiw'ena, woman; kʷil'ena, girl (T).

[2] These two figure frequently in Hopi and Tewa (First Mesa) tales, also in the tales of eastern Tewa. For their representation as Hopi kachina in the Winter solstice ceremonial, see Fewkes, Pl. LX.

[3] n₁ut₁oke?'ena (T).

[4] ạnạmk'anemạ (T).

[5] ạnạmtǫm'ena (T).

[6] mạnạmt'ałułinạ (T).

[7] t'əybo?oyạ (T).

[8] x'ina (x'inemạ, pl.) (T).

[9] kim?ùwá?inạ y'ian?oy mạnł'oy (T).

[10] t₁əł'o?oy. See p. 20.

here we are, your grandfathers. You have found us. And you will get
your bows and arrows here." Then the guard (*p'o'watana*)[1] went into the
east room, he got the bows and arrows. Next he went into the north
room, he got a big mountain lion skin quiver (*hemłahaiklumuna*)[2] full of
arrows. Then he went into the west room, he got fruits (*p'ĕana*)[3] of all
kinds. In the south room he got some wild asparagus (*p'asiuna*)[4] and many
edible grasses. Then they packed up all those things, they said to the boys,
"Now you have what you desire. Take these fruits to your mothers!" Of
the corn they were told to husk the green corn to throw just outside of the
house for the people (*nałentaien*)[5] to see it. (They would be surprised,
it was winter.) So the people when they saw the husks, they wondered
how the green corn husks came there, the time being the middle of
winter, in the man moon (*sen pana*)[6] (January). Then the following
day the two boys wanted to go out hunting. Their mothers described
to them the prints of the animals—rabbits with small prints, jack rabbits
with larger prints, deer prints larger and split-foot, and elk prints the
same, but larger. Their mothers said to them, "There is only one way
you should not go in your hunt, that is northward (*tŏ'ota*)[7]." They went,
in the evening they brought in some rabbits. On the second hunt they
went westward. They got smaller game, like squirrels and other little
animals. They brought them to their mothers. Their mothers said to
them *inu·we'*![8] Next they went down south. They got some deer and
brought them to their mothers. They received them and said *inu·we'*!
Then they talked about going northward. Younger brother said to Elder
brother (*p'a'p'ana*),[9] "You remember that we were told not to go northward." Anyway, Elder brother decided that they should go and see for
themselves and find out what would be the outcome if they went
northward. Younger brother was unwilling to go, but he obeyed Elder
brother, saying, "It is naughty (*ha'p'anna*)[10], we are forbidden to go but

---

1   See pp. 25, 32. Not "recognized" by T's informant; possibly a ritual term.
2   x͜emłͺox͜oyłͺuom'ͧna, mountain lion-big-skin-arrow-bag (T).
3   p'ͺəo?'one, fruit, ripe seeds, ripe corn (T).
4   p'òs'iwnͣ, wild celery, watercress (?) (T). See Parsons 10: 24. See p. 10.
5   t''oynemͣ, people (T). The first part of the term, nałen, nałe, nała, which is used
    repeatedly, was not translated (T). I infer (see p. 20) the compound term means
    human beings in distinction to supernaturals, as Zuni would say "cooked people," or
    Spaniards, *humanos*. Cp. Athapascan *dine*, people.
6   s͜ͺəonp''ona (T). See Parsons 10: 83.
7   t'əwt'o (T).
8   Expression of pleasure used on receiving rabbits, deer meat, etc.
9   pͺop'ona (T).
10 p'ͺapaɪvámͣ (T).

you want to go anyway." Then Elder brother said, "Men should use their eyes and see what may come of it." So the next day they went northward. When they had gone half way, Scabby Fox (*hĕlwi tuʻwana*)[1] called them to come where he was, saying, "My younger brothers (*anumpaiyuwaina*),[2] let us talk as men (*sĕunchaanai*),[3] and then you will go on." So they went to him. And Scabby Fox said to them, "Why did you come up this way? Were you not living there in a good home at the cottonwood with your mothers, Yellow Corn woman and Blue Corn woman, and with Nighthawk, your father?" Then the two little boys replied, "Yes, that is the way we live, but we come out this way to hunt."—"So, my sons," said Scabby Fox, "Sleep with me tonight, then go in the morning." They did not want to stay, but Scabby Fox kept urging them to stay. After a long talk they consented to remain with him overnight. They went to bed and Scabby Fox watched them go to sleep. The boys slept and Scabby Fox got up and took off his scabby shirt and put it on the boys and took their clothing of fine buckskin. So Scabby Fox put on the clothing of the boys and at daybreak he went to a creek. He lay there to wait for Dogwood-of-the-Plains girls (*pata kwilenöma*)[4] to come down for water. These girls many young men had tried to induce to be their sweethearts (*piaaʼsina*),[5] but they would deny them. So Fox talked to the girls, he tried his best to get them to let him be their sweetheart, but it was impossible to get an answer from them. So the girls filled their jars of water and walked up to their house. They told their mother that down at the creek there was a nice young man (*uɬaɬaana*)[6], but that they did not listen to his talk. . . Later in the day the fox was taken up by the Dogwood-of-the-Plains girls to their house. There he became the husband of the Dogwood-of-the-Plains girls. At nightfall they went to their room to sleep. All night they teased and joked, he did not sleep. Towards daylight suddenly he went to sleep, very soundly. And the girls slept too. That morning the mother of the girls went down to the creek for water.

Meanwhile the two boys woke up. They were badly dressed and they were trembling. Their bows and arrows were made of ordinary wood.

---

[1] tͺuxʷˈana, fox, coyote: coyote is more specifically cʼùnˈena (as proper name, cʼùnˈe), but tͺuxʷˈana is also used; in Picurís, Sandía, Isleta, the words for coyote correspond to tͺuxʷˈana, not to cʼùnˈena. hĕlwi perhaps həol, sick (T).

[2] ąnąmpˈͺọywá ʔiną (T).

[3] sͺəoncͺiayá ʔi, men-let's talk-as (T).

[4] pɔ̀to, on the earth, plains, kʷˈəlenemą, girls (T).

[5] pͺiaʔąsˈine, heart-sweet ones; translation from English? (T).

[6] ùɬeɬę ʔˈena (T).

So they went out northward. As they were going along they came to a creek. Here they met the mother of the Dogwood-of-the-Plains girls. She asked them what had happened to them. They answered that Scabby Fox had played them a trick by giving them his scabby coat and taking their clothing, their bows, arrows and quiver. The old woman (*kliuna*)[1] said, "My sons (*anumukaina*)[2], that fox is not good." Then the woman took the boys up to her house. There she asked them again what had happened to them. And they told her what had happened to them and who they were. Then the old woman called out from the top of the house to the people (*naɫataine*) to gather. So they promptly came to her house. Then some men with clubs went in to the house where Scabby Fox was having his good time. So they clubbed him. He jumped, as he jumped he shit out all over, on the floor and to the walls, even to the beds and over the two girls. They threw their clubs at him, but missed him, he was too swift. He ran outdoors and out to the fields. Then he turned back toward where the crowd of people were, hollering and laughing at him and ridiculing the girls. Then he turned back and with his hand raised to his eyes, looking toward the people, he said, "So many young men (*uɫaɫanu*)[3] of the *naɫatain* have tried to be sweethearts to the Dogwood-of-the-Plains girls, but I am the first to be their sweetheart."[4]

Then the people sent the two girls to look for the two boys with the fox's scabby coat and to bring them up to the house. So the girls went down to the creek and brought them up. They wrapped them up in their best blankets, and the people went to work over them. They rolled a knife wheel (*chiatawena*)[5] over them in order to cut to pieces the scabby coats. When those coats were taken off there appeared two nice boys. So they made the two girls wash their heads and bathe them and dress them clean. Then the crowd of people made a surround to catch the fox. They caught him, and took the boys' clothing away from him and gave it to the boys. And the people gave back to the fox his own scabby coat. Then the boys went back to their mothers at Cottonwood. After they got there, their mothers said to them, "We told you not to go that way. You were a very long time away." Younger

---

[1] łiw ʔù ʔ'una, woman-little, the old woman (T).

[2] ạnạm ʔùk''oyinạ (T).

[3] ùłéłẹnạ (T).

[4] Compare Taos, Espinosa, 126-127; San Juan, Tesuque, Parsons 4: 147-148; Tewa (First Mesa), Parsons 4: 242-246; Hopi, Voth, 157-159; Wichita, Dorsey 1: 35.

[5] c̣iat''awanạ (T). A variant on the hoop to bewitch or restore, familiar in Pueblo tales.

brother said, "He is to be blamed. He urged me to go northward, and that is what happened to us through the fox exchanging his scabby skin for ours."

(How did you make out, our mother (*hi könapoa anumkana*)?)[1]

Variant

Yellow Corn young woman (*iatsulekwema*) and Blue Corn young woman (*iatsolekwema*) were living. They were very pretty. The boys came and asked them to marry them, but they did not want to marry them, even when they were *łachi söanenem* [2] (kachina men). Then Coyote put berries on his head and chokecherries around him and went to them. They took him to their house and spent the night. The people took the bows and arrows to shoot him. One man went in and saw Coyote sleeping between the two girls. Coyote heard him and jumped down the ladder and ran and hollered to them, "I am a friend of Yellow Corn girl and Blue Corn girl who would not take you. I am Coyote who knows them." Then the *łachina* sent hailstones (*iakane*)[3] which fell and struck him in the head and killed him.

2. Seed-marked Boy Destroys the Giant

At Cottonwood were living *tątöaöwia,*[4] Seed-marked boy,[5] and his grandmother. While living there the grandmother would go every day to bring in sticks of wood on her back. Every time she went she told her grandson not to go northward. The boy would play about the house. After a while the boy thought he would find out by going north why his grandmother told him not to go northward. So one day he went north-

---

[1] h'i kąnąp'uo ąnąmk'ana, how you disappeared (in sense of got through?) our (dual) mother (T). There were three of us present. I do not know whether the query referred to how I recorded the tale or to my trip which was secret and not quite safe.

[2] łˌacis'ɔonenem, ʔ-men (T).

[3] ˌi̯ek'ǫne (T).

[4] As is called the ear of corn which has a lightning mark on it, i. e. a red and white zigzag. See Parsons 10: 74 n. 8, 109. Tątöaöwia corresponds to the little war god who is represented as a corn kachina among the other Pueblos. The Lightning-Corn ear People or Water kiva People of Taos are associated with the kachina. Tątöaöwia is also Lightning. The War Brothers burn the giant who has tried to burn them, in various Keresan tales. Compare, too, Cochiti, Benedict 1:19. Compare Tesuque, Parsons 4:98; Hano, Parsons 4: 278-279.

[5] tˌątˌəʔ'ɔwyu (T). My informants translated Printed-red boy or Spotted Corn boy.

ward and found out that the giant (*toiłana,*[1] person big) was always around there. He learned that the people, men, women and children, never came back to their home because the giant was catching them and eating them up. So the people were diminishing all the time. They did not know what was becoming of them. Now Seed-marked boy was caught by the giant, and taken to his home. His home was *antoiłaenta* (ạnt̓ ͜ ͜oyło ʔl̥ent̓o, his-giant-feet-at). (It is a big, high, impassable rock.)[2] When he was taken there he was bound hand and foot. The giant went out to gather stumps, he laid the boy underneath and piled the stumps on top of him and set fire to the stumps for Seed-marked boy to cook. Then the old giant lay down alongside his blazing fire, waiting for the boy to be roasted to eat him. He sang,

tạ'töaö'wia tạ'töaö'wia

ạwi p'asiu[3] pa'okilku'yuma[4]

wild celery trickle nicely flowing

ạwi p'asiu pa'okilku'yuma

The giant heard the song. Giant said to himself, "Oh, you little thing, why does it take so long for you to be roasted?" Then the giant took his wooden shovel and opened up the burning stump. Then he got the boy out. He was not burned. So the giant got hold of the boy and said to him, "You are such a small boy you must have some kind of power; but I will see who is *łaiętuwaiemu,*[5] more powerful." So he took him up to the top of that precipitous rough wall of rock. Then he stood him up on the edge of the rock and said to him, "Here is the place from which you will never come back." Then he pushed him down. Down he went. Then he went back, hollering, and alit as a soft eagle tail feather on top of the rock where the giant was.[6] Then the second time the giant pushed him down. He said to him, "You are such a small boy, yet you know what to do!" Then he came back again, as a feather, hollering aloud. That was the second time. Then the giant pushed him down again. He came back again as the same feather, yelling and hollering. The fourth time he

---

[1] t'oyłona (T). In Apache tales Giant is Big Owl, and he is worsted by Slayer-of-alien-enemies. Compare, too, the early monsters killed by the War gods in Athapascan and Pueblo mythology.

[2] See Parsons 10: 111.

[3] p'òsịw- (T).

[4] ʔ + k'uyumạ, good, nice (T).

[5] ł̥ọy- more + ʔ (T). Obviously the rest of this term as well as the term below for medicine power informants would not translate. Compare Parsons 10: 83, for Isletan term for shaman, *toyide,* and for Kiowa terms, Parsons 6: 5 n. 1.

[6] Compare Kiowa, Parsons 6: 3.

pushed him down. He came back hollering. (That was where the giant threw down all the people he killed.) Then the boy said to the giant, "Now, it is my turn. We will find out who is more powerful." The old giant liked the trick of the boy. He said to himself, "Now, I will try it, too." He got hold of the giant and took him down to the place where he had been put to be burned. He gathered old cedar stumps, put the giant under the stumps, and set them afire. It made a strong blaze, the fire sounded as if it was boiling sss---s! And the stumps all burned down to charcoal. Nothing was seen of the giant, nor could his voice be heard, only the blazing of the fire sss---s! Until the charcoal burned away to ashes. So by his power (*tuwaiega*) he made a strong wind blow which blew the ashes away. The dead had been bound up by hands and feet, some sitting up, some lying down. Then by his power, he made all the dead come to life. They all exclaimed, "*Huwi,*[1] *kitamena*[2] (our father)! You are the man by whose power we shall see our world again." Then he looked for his grandmother and they went back to their home at Cottonwood. There they lived as before.

You have the tail now; if you don't take up your tail you will freeze.

Variant 1

Seed-marked boy was living at Cottonwood with his grandmother. He used to go out hunting. He said to his grandmother, "Grandmother, do not go out when I have gone out hunting." Grandmother thought to herself, "I wonder why my grandchild does not want me to go out. I will go out today." So she left off grinding and went out. When she went out, a giant came to her. He had a basket water jar (*t'öamuluna*)[3] and he told the old woman to get into it. He closed the mouth of the jar and carried the old woman on his back to his house. The giant lived far up in the mountain where nobody could go. When the boy came back from hunting, his grandmother did not come out to meet him. He thought to himself, "I wonder why my grandmother does not come running out to meet me." He threw down the deer and ran into the house and did not find his grandmother. The meal she was grinding was left there. Then he followed the tracks of the giant to *łakutuna*[4] (wood spoon). Wood Spoon called him and asked, "Where are you

1 h'uwi, y'uwi, whew! (T).
2 kitǫm'ena (T).
3 t'ͺͻodm'ulunạ, basket or pot shaped (T).
4 łͺok"utunạ (T).

going?" He said, "I am going to look for my grandmother." Wood
Spoon gave him a spruce seed (*k'uowaxöna*).[1] "This will help you to get
there," he said. "Cover this seed and it will grow." He took it and went
on. He came to Spider old woman. She said, "Seed-marked boy, why
are you around while you are living well at Cottonwood, with your
grandmother? A good hunter, why are you around here now?"—
"Yes, I live there well and happily with my grandmother and bring deer
to her all the time. But now the giant has taken her away, so I have to
look for her." Spider old woman said, "Your grandmother is far up in
the mountain where nobody can go. I know that Wood Spoon gave you
the spruce seed and now I will give something that will help you when
you get up there." She gave him some medicine and told him to put it
in his mouth and over his body so the giant would not kill him. Then
Seed-marked boy went to the foot of the mountain and he dug a hole
and, while he was putting in the seed, Squirrel came to him. Squirrel
said, "I will help you to make this tree grow fast." While the tree was
growing, he ran up and down the tree until the tree reached the top of
the mountain. Then he ran down and told the boy the tree was close
to his grandmother. So the boy climbed the tree and came to his
grandmother. She said to him, "Grandchild, why do you come here? I
am living with the giant. I know he will eat you up." As they talked
together the earth was shaking because the giant was coming. Grandmother hid him underneath the thatch of the hatch. Then the giant
came in and said, "I smell the blood of an Indian." Grandmother said,
"Who would come here? Nobody can come here."—"Yes, I smell, I
smell!" And he began to search. She said, "Yes, my grandchild came."—
"He thinks he is one to tame me; but he is not." Then he pulled him
out of the thatch. He did not cry, he hollered, "Hip! Hip! Hip! Hip!"[2]
Then the giant dug a fire and the giant put him there to roast. The giant
lay beside the fire waiting for him to roast. "He is so small, I think it
won't take long for him to roast," said the giant. The giant took down
his wheel and rolled it so the ashes would disclose the boy. Then the
boy jumped out hollering, "Hip! Hip! Hip! Hip!" The boy took the
wheel and rolled it to the giant and killed him. He had the people and
the *łachin* tied up (that is why it did not rain). So then the boy went and
untied them. He went to another place where there were piles of human bones and he put medicine on them and they all turned to life.
The women had the jars that they were carrying to get water when the

1 k'ˌuowox'əna (T).
2 As the men holler. (Women do not holler in this way.)

giant caught them and the men had on their backs the ropes which they used when they were going to get wood. "Now you go back to your homes," he said. When the *lachina* were set free, it began to rain, too.[1] He took his grandmother home and they lived happily.

Variant 2[2]

Long ago, when the pueblos were first where they are now, everything was wild. They were always on the lookout, they never made fire at night, they did all their cooking in the daytime. They went out in the daytime for firewood. Someone noticed that some people were missing, one or two every day. They wondered why. They did not know what became of them. The old men kept watch to see if it was enemies hiding. No one could find out for years what became of the missing persons. There was an old man then that went out after firewood. He made a bundle of wood to carry on his back. He started home. He came to a place where he rested. While he was resting he saw some kind of a human walking, but he looked *different*—kind o' naked, long hair on his body like an animal, big feet, hands, big muscle arms, big head, mouth. The man got scared. This creature came up and grabbed the man. It was a giant. The giant killed him and took him to his cave. It was late. The family missed the old man. The War captain and the officers went out to look for him. They came to where he had rested. They examined the place. They saw the footprints of the giant. They wondered what it could be. They tracked him to the foot of a hill—clear to the entrance of his cave. They saw blood on the edge of the cave. They finally decided it was a giant that had killed the man. They looked around. They found where the giant had thrown the bones and head. They saw lots of bones there. They did not know how to get the giant, but they were going to try to get him some way. Everyone who could carry weapons finally started out to fight the giant. They decided to cut brush and make a big fire at the mouth of the cave and smoke him out. The giant gnashed his teeth. He stuck his head out. The people stood back. Then the giant came out—furious. The people attacked him with bows and clubs. They could not kill him. Finally he ran away, angry.

[1] See the Zapotecan tale about Lightning killing the cave-dwelling devil who drives away the rain clouds (Parsons 9: 334). In Pueblo tales the War Brothers steal the kachina masks; but for a closer parallel to the Taos reference, compare San Juan, Parsons 4: 93-94.

[2] Recorded by Leslie A. White.

The people kept shooting. There were arrows sticking in his body, but he did not mind. They chased him, followed his trail of blood on the ground. They chased him to the north. He crossed Lucero river. The blood is still there, you can see it in the rocks and on the earth. He went on to Questa. Finally they surrounded him near Questa. He went into a cave and died. You can see that red line there now today.[1] The medicine men had helped on the last day of the fight. That is how they were able to kill him. It clouded up like a storm. There was a noise above [thunder]. Lightning killed him.

Variant 3

When at the Canyon of the Red Willows people (*iałapai'mu pahöatel t'ainemu*)[2] they first came to live, the giant came there. The people did not know he was there. All the men would go out for firewood, to carry in on their backs. Sometimes some were caught by the giant and carried up to his cave. He killed them. As the people, men, boys, women, would go out, he would catch them and carry them to his cave. For a long time they could not find out why these people were disappearing. They were not able to find out. So they went out to see what they could learn about these missing people. They kept searching in the hills and mountains. Finally they found the track of the giant, larger than men's tracks. They tracked him wherever he went. Sometimes they would lose the track on hard ground, and then they would find it in soft dirt. They kept tracking that way many days. Finally they found a fresh footprint and they followed and found where he had been sitting on top of the hill. His tracks led them to his cave. They saw him lying down asleep near his cave. The giant was a very big bodied man. So they went back to the village. They told the people to get ready to go and try to kill him. They went up there and began to shoot with their bows and

---

[1] The cannibal giant or giants appear to figure in some origin myth of Taos. In 1887 the Catholic priest at Taos related to Gatschet that about 700 years earlier the people came up through a lake in the Don Juan valley, New Mexico and travelled southward, reaching the canyon of the Rio Colorado, Taos county, ten or twelve miles from Taos. Here they built a stone village, *were attacked by giants* and forced southward, *leaving the canyon walls blood-stained*. They built another stone village on the Rio Lucero, on the flat-topped hill above Taos. Attacked again by the giants, they settled about 100 yards above Taos. After the Spaniards burnt this village, the people separated: one group went to the eastward, another to El Paso, and the remainder rebuilt Taos as it is today (American Anthropologist, V (1892), 191-192).

[2] ˌiało-p'ˌaymu-p'ʾöhɔot'ʾəl-t'ʾoynemą, willow-red-canyon-people (T), i.e. Taos.

arrows. He got angry and they could not kill him. Their arrows could not penetrate his hard body, they only scratched him where they hit. The blood was dripping from his body. He ran in to his cave. They poked at him with long sticks, and he caught their sticks and took them away. So they could not do anything and at night they went home. The next day they went back again. He had gone out from the cave, and they tracked him, across the hill, toward the north. They followed him, but could not overtake him. Then went back home. They went back the next day, to where they left the track. They could see his blood stains on the ground, the dirt on the hillside was covered with blood. So they followed him, to the side of the mountain, still to the north. They overtook him at *tohse'uba*.[1] There they killed him. That's why at *tohse'uba* the mountain side is red all over, with the giant's blood. Then they came home, and ever since then the people increased.

Variant 4[2]

Once were living Turkey and his wife. They had one daughter. They used to tell their daughter not to go out in an easterly direction lest an accident or some misfortune happen to her. One day the girl came to a decision and said, "I will go toward the east and see why my father and mother do not want me to go that way." So she went in the direction she was forbidden. As she descended she came to a pumpkin field. She picked the pumpkin flowers. As she was picking, the big giant came to where she was. The giant said to her, "What are you doing?" The girl replied, "I am picking pumpkin flowers." Then Giant said to her, "Come on here! I have some nice ones here in my big jar. Look in!" Then Giant said to the girl, "Go in!" That girl went in. Then Giant took the girl away off to his home in a cave. There the Turkey girl saw dead people, their hands and feet bound with yucca string. The girl was not killed like the others in the cave but merely became the wife of the giant. The girl was treated nicely by her husband. Giant would go out during the day and at nightfall bring in a whole dead deer for the girl to eat. The next day he would go out and bring in dead people for himself to devour. The girl did not like this, Giant eating dead humans, nor did she like being at the center of bloody butchering. She kept asking her husband where he had his life. He said he had no life anywhere, but that he feared God only in making solemn promises, in

---

[1] t͟us'iwbo, Questa (T).
[2] Written by a townsman.

making crosses with his fingers (in making the sign of the cross). The next day he went out. In the evening he brought in a big dead deer. The girl stood at the entry of the cave and made a cross. Then the giant succumbed, bowed to the ground and said to his wife, "Do with me as you please. I am yours." The girl took the big, wide, flat, sharp flint and cut his ears off. Then the giant came to the end of his life. All the people who were sitting with their hands and feet tied she untied, and they expressed their deep gratitude to the girl by saying to her, "Our daughter, because of you and your wise thought we shall once more enjoy our life in this world." Then they scattered to their different homes.

3. The Striped Ones Save him from the Giant

They were living at *patilapahana*[1] (hot springs), Tsiuha'a[2] and his grandmother. He was always going out rabbit hunting. His grandmother said, "My grandson, you may not go to the north." He was out hunting rabbits and he said, "I wonder why it is my grandmother said I was not to go hunting north, past the pine tree. I think I will go." When he went to the pine he found lots of rabbits. He camped there and put around a string of rabbits.[3] He took two rabbits to cook. "*Maku*,[4] grandchild!" he heard, "where?"—"Somebody hunting," he said. "Grandchild, where?"—"*Yaipi,* here, grandfather!"—"Grandchild, where?"—"Here, grandfather!" Came a giant. "Grandchild, you have had good hunting?"— "Yes, grandfather. You may sit down."—"Grandchild, Tsiuha'a, your rabbit is cooking?"—"Yes, grandfather, you may have it." He thought, "This is Giant. If I don't give him everything he asks for, he will swallow me." He gave him the second rabbit. "Grandchild, Tsiuha'a, you may give me the string of rabbits you have here."—"Yes, grandfather, I will give it to you if you dance for it. Giant danced with his arms out and sang:

Yaaipus![5] pus!
Yaaipus! pus!

Giant made a grab at Tsiuha'a, but he had sneaked away. "Well you are mine. I am going to get you." Tsiuha'a got to the *kawiuna*.[6] "*Kawiuna,*

---

[1] p'òł,ilap'ò?'ona, water-hot-water (T).
[2] ciw = eagle + ? (T).
[3] Rabbits are strung by the legs with yucca or deer sinew.
[4] m!aku (T).
[5] No meaning.
[6] Striped things: bumblebees or chipmunks (compare p. 34) or polecats; but as translation was withheld from T. possibly Spirits of some kind are meant. They are called holy, they dance, and, as kachina would elsewhere, they get raiment from the one they kill. See too p. 59.

can you help me? Giant is after me."—"Yes, brother, come in!" They painted him like themselves. "We must hurry, before Giant comes." They started dancing and singing:

Hili   kitaiwan[1]   taiwan
What our people came people came
Mamawa talapapu[2]   talapapu
Don't make yourselves heard heard
Haiya haiya

"Grandchildren, didn't Tsiuha'a come here?" They did not answer. They kept on dancing and singing:

Hili kitaiwan taiwan
Mamawatalapapu talapapu
Haiya haiya

"Listen! I am asking you if Tsiuha'a got here." They stopped. "Well, grandfather, is it this one you are looking for?"—"No,"—"Is it this one?" —"No."—"Is it this one?"—"No. I want you to bring him out. I will eat you all up."—"I don't know which you want. Come in and get him!" —"How can I come in this small place?"—"We can make it larger." Just as he came in they took hold of him and threw him down and trampled him and danced on top of him. They sang:

Kawiunmama
Powahaha powahaha

They trampled him to pieces. "He is not holy or fortunate like us and he is always trying to be." They put him into the fire and burned him into ashes. They called to Wind old woman, "You may come and blow away the ashes!" They said, "Now, Tsiuha'a, your grandmother is swelling from sadness. You go home! Now you can go hunting wherever you want without fear of the giant." When he got home he found his grandmother sitting by the fireplace, swelling with sadness. Then she got well and they lived happily. People say Tsiuha'a lived at Hot springs and he was a good hunter, and Tsiuha'a said, "Those who want to be good hunters, they can come and ask [pray to] me."

Variant[3]

At *wepuavada*[4] (pine-near-water) lived Saiofaa who was a rabbit hunter.

[1] kit'oyw̧on (T).
[2] mamowòt'̧olop'apu, second person plural reflexive negative future; t'olo- hear, p'a make (T).
[3] Written by a townsman.
[4] w̧e-puo-p'òto, pine-near-water-at (T).

He always had a string of rabbits hanging in a bunch. Then the giant came after him, calling him by his name, "Saiofaa, grandchild, grandchild!" —"Who is that? Somebody who must know me is about here." He was sitting on his little shack of pine brush. Then the giant got to his shack. He saw a kind of human that he had not seen before or known. Then he asked him to give him his rabbits. He was afraid. He told the giant he would give him the rabbits. The giant took the rabbits, one by one, and swallowed them. When the giant ate all the rabbits, he said, "Saiofaa, my grandchild, you look fat, too." Then Saiofaa ran out underneath his little shack. The giant chased Saiofaa. At *hiohkualdah*[1] (stone fence) lived Kawiyonah. Saiofaa ran into the house. The giant arrived there. Saiofaa said to the Kawiyonah, "My grandchildren, hide me! A giant is after me." Saiofaa was spotted as Kawiyonah were spotted. They were all spotted jut the same. The giant said, "My grandchildren, is Saiofaa here?" They told the giant he was there. Then they all began to dance. The giant did not listen, he went into the house. All the Kawiyonah said, "Is it I? Is it I?" and so on. They were all spotted just the same, all of them. Saiofaa was there, but the giant did not know him. Then they killed the giant. They danced, kicking him, trampling on him all they could, as in the war dance, singing:

Kawiyoyo Kawiyoyo

Saiofaa was safe. The Kawiyonah took the skin of the giant and measured themselves dresses and leggings, moccasins, gloves (!) and all. Then they hid the giant under water.

4. Magpie and the Corn Mothers[2]

Magpie lived at Cottonwood, also his wife, Yellow Corn woman and her sister, Blue Corn woman. One day Yellow Corn woman went to invite her sister to come to her house and help to grind corn. So they were both grinding corn. Yellow Corn woman stopped grinding corn and went down to the river for water. Magpie was painting his face with red to go for wood. While his wife was gone for water, Blue Corn was grinding, and he caught her with his red painted hand, that Blue Corn woman. Then Blue Corn woman got hold of Magpie with her hands covered with corn flour. She bedaubed Magpie with

[1] h,iwk^(W')ialto, stone-fence-at (T). Shrine? See p. 99.
[2] Compare Picurís, De Huff, 186-190; San Juan, Espinosa, 96-97; Santa Clara, Parsons 4: 118-119; Cochiti, Benedict 1: 88-90, see also 95; Laguna, Boas 2: 177-180, 220; Siama, De Huff, 194-197.

the flour. Also Magpie caught Blue Corn and bedaubed her with red paint, embracing her. So he left a stain on the woman, and the woman left a stain on Magpie. When Yellow Corn woman came back to the house with water, she saw her younger sister with red stain on her clothing[1] and she also saw Magpie with a stain of flour on his body. She looked at both of them, but said nothing to them. She went to her room, and got her best dress (*koa'pana,*[2] wool dress) and wrapped moccasins. She dressed up, and went outside and started eastward. In a little while Magpie told Blue Corn woman to go outside and see where Yellow Corn woman was. The girl came back and said to Magpie, "She is going to the east." Magpie said to Blue Corn woman, "Go after her and call her back!" Her sister went after her, and asked her where she was going. She said she did not want to come back. She sang,

> ainai' howina
> ai'nai howina
> ai'nai howina
> ai'nai howina
> ainai' ho'wina
> ainai' ho'wina
> ah nai hoi hoi
> ah noi hoi hoi
> ainai' howina
> ainai' howina

Then, as they did not seem to come back, Magpie followed them. The two sisters were now on the road, at *kankööba.*[3] They kept going and going and singing,

> ainai' howina
> ainai' howina

They were now up to *łułepa'tsiba*[4] still singing the same song on their way. Yellow Corn was going to *łapewa.*[5] Blue Corn was asking her all the time to come back, but she did not want to come back. They were now at *kwiebiba*[6] (where there are many small springs running downhill). Magpie was coming all the time behind them. They kept on going and

---

1 For give-away by red paint compare Cheyenne, Kroeber 1:181, also for jealous wife, 187.

2 k'₁uop'ana (k'₁uona, sheep + p'ana, dress) (T).

3 k₁onk''ɔobo, buffalo-up. k₁on'ena, buffalo (T). Here, half a mile east from Taos, anciently a buffalo turned to stone.

4 ł₁ułip'òc'ito, old man-spring-at (T). This spring is associated with the white łatsina.

5 ł'opiwạ, tree-back to (T).

6 kw'ialpibo, downhill-toward (T).

singing all the way. They were now at *konłi'pana*[1] (buffalo grass plain).[2] They kept on going. When they approached *toh'chula pa'tsiba*[3] (hummingbird spring), they were still singing the same song.

They approached *łihainaba*[4] (grass hat), still singing the same song. They arrived at *pa'xemųtųta* (fog mesa).[5] They kept on singing the same song. They arrived at *pah'potöna*.[6] Their clothing was torn and ragged. They no longer looked like pretty girls, all tired and worried and sad looking. They kept on going. They arrived at *pahw'eanatuleáa*[7] (lake port.) They kept going. Now Magpie was coming up to them. He was hurrying to catch them. The two girls were nearing the lake, that Big House (*töła'e*).[8] When Magpie was about to catch them, they jumped into the lake.[9] After the water quieted down, a yellow corn ear (*kuyuna*)[10] and a blue corn ear came up on top of the water.[11] Magpie grasped them,[12] and went back home and arrived at Cottonwood and said to himself, "I never will be a human being (*nałetai*)."[13] People say Magpie lives at Cottonwood.

Variant

At the cottonwood Yellow Corn girl and Blue Corn girl were living happily. They were married to Magpie-tail boy. Yellow Corn girl gave birth to a boy. As Yellow Corn girl lay there, Blue Corn girl would play with Magpie-tail boy and she neglected the turkeys of Yellow Corn girl. So Yellow Corn girl said she would go to the Big House (at Blue Lake). She was grieving that Magpie-tail boy was in love with her

[1]　k‚onł'ipǫno, buffalo-grass-plain-at (T).

[2]　Five miles east, the first camp on the annual pilgrimage to Blue Lake (Parsons 10: 99).

[3]　tùculop'òc'ibo, hummingbird-spring-toward (T).

[4]　ł‚ix'įenebo, grass-hat -toward (T).

[5]　p'òx'ęmmųtuto, fog + tu meaning unknown + at (T). "A mountain where fog rises." Possibly Fog House (t'ʼǝnto, house-at). See p. 49.

[6]　"Something like a bullfrog lives here," Pâköałanna (? water horned toad or big water bear), the mythical Big Water man who corresponds to the Horned Water Serpent of other Pueblos (Parsons 10: 99).

[7]　p'òxᵂìa- lake + ? (T). "Within a mile of the Lake."

[8]　t'ʼǝło?i, where the *łatsina* live, beneath Blue Lake. In the Picurís version the girl goes *into the hole* to live with the good spirits.

[9]　Note that in Aztec religion suicides joined the Rain gods (kachina).

[10]　kuy'una, sacred corn (T).

[11]　Note for a similar kachinalike suggestion among Cheyenne, Kroeber 1: 163. Two young men go into a spring and bring back corn and buffalo.

[12]　They were to become his "corn mothers."

[13]　Among Jicarilla Apache Magpie is a patron of hunters (Opler).

sister and that the turkeys were neglected. She fed corn to her little turkeys and said, "I am going to the Mothers and Fathers. I leave you and my child to Blue Corn girl and I am going to the Big House, to the Fathers, never to return."—"No," said the turkeys, "we are going with you." When she was crossing the bridge and the little turkeys were following in a string behind, the people said, "Something is happening. Yellow Corn girl is going with her turkeys to the east." The turkeys were singing:

> selo sel kwanto
> ihibo kwanto[1]

She went on. Then her sister overtook her as she was shelling more corn for the turkeys. She said, "Oh, sister, nurse my little brother, then go wherever you wish!"[2]—"Sister, go back and live with Magpie-tail boy! I am going to the Big House never to return." They started on, and the turkeys sang:

> selo selo kwanto
> ihibo kwanto

She went on to *łiyienneta*[3] (a mountain peak) and again she fed corn to the turkeys. "My sisters and brothers, on this mountain you may roam, I am going to the Big House never to return." Blue Corn girl said, "Sister, if only you would nurse my little brother! He is crying." The turkeys sang:

> selo selo kwanto
> ihibo kwanto

They went on to *paputöna,* and she shelled corn again for the turkeys and begged them to leave her. Blue Corn girl said, "Sister, if only you would nurse my little brother!"—"You feel bad, just as I felt when you were playing with Magpie-tail boy." They started again and the turkeys sang:

> selo selo kwanto
> ihibo kwanto

When they came to the divide to go down to the Lake, Yellow Corn girl shelled her last ear of corn, and asked the turkeys to roam there. "I am going to the Big House never to return," said Yellow Corn girl. Blue Corn girl said, "Sister, if only you would nurse my little brother! He is crying." The turkeys sang:

> selo selo kwanto
> ihibo kwanto

---

[1] No meaning.
[2] Note especially Cochiti, Benedict 1: 88.
[3] Perhaps łix'įeneto, grass-hat-at (see p. 20) or perhaps łiʔįeneto, grass-foot-at (T).

Yellow Corn girl started down to the edge of the Lake. "Sister, nurse my little brother!" said Blue Corn girl. "I am going to the Big House to the Mothers and Fathers," said Yellow Corn girl. Then she went into the Lake. An ear of corn came up in the middle of the Lake and floated towards them. Blue Corn girl put it to little brother's mouth and he sucked on it and this was his mother nourishing him. Blue Corn girl went back and found Magpie-tail boy sitting by the fire with his head bowed. He said, "I am Magpie-tail boy and we were living here happily and now we hand on everything under the water."[1] And Blue Corn girl said, "I am Blue Corn girl and now the people have me [as a source of nourishment]."

5. Magpie Drowns Blue Corn Girl[2]

Magpie and his wife, Blue Corn maiden, lived at the cottonwood. Blue Corn maiden was very playful and jolly. She liked to tease everybody, her ways and manner were full of fun. Magpie had an old humpback bow with which he was practicing and exercising to learn the sound of the bow string tied on the bow.[3] He would beat the bow string with his arrow and study the sound—tew tew! Finally he was prepared. The first day he told his wife that he was going to go out on the hunt. He went and stayed in a hiding place to watch his wife coming out from the house. The first day she went to the east to see and converse with the men she found. Magpie came home in the evening first. Then his wife came in late. Then Magpie got his bow out and held his bow close to his ear, beating his bow with an arrow. And his wife was listening. Every time he beat his bow, he said, "*Hah* (yes), *hugaihu*[4] (and then)," making his wife believe that he talked with his bow, which was telling him of what his wife was doing during the day when she was out on the east side of the house. The second day Magpie started on the hunt, but he stayed again at his hiding place. His wife came out from the house and started to the north side. She did the same thing as the first day, she talked to a man. Magpie came in the evening, got his bow and beat the same as before, striking with the arrow on the string and making the same reply as before—"Yes, and then." The third day Mag-

---

[1] See p. 97. Compare White Mountain Apache term for kachina: "They travel in water" (Goodwin, 27).

[2] Written by a townsman.

[3] ? Musical bow.

[4] hǫ, huk"oyhu (T).

pie started again on the hunt, again he stayed at his hiding place. His wife came out again from the house and started to the west. She did the same thing as before, she talked to a man. Magpie came in the evening, got his bow and beat the same as before, striking with the arrow on the bow, striking the same reply as before—"Yes, and then." The fourth day Magpie started again on the hunt, he stayed at his hiding place. His wife came out again from the house, and started to the south. She did the same thing as before, she talked to a man. Magpie came in the evening, got his bow and beat the same as before, striking with the arrow on the bow. The string gave the same reply as before—"Yes, and then." After seeing all he saw about his wife, he put her under water to end her life.

6. Magpie-tail Youth Revives his Dead Wife

Once there lived Magpie-tail youth (*kwaiakwęȫwiyu*)[1] and Yellow Corn woman. They lived at the cottonwood. The witches (*tsahöna*)[2] lived at *uwaalaka*. Yellow Corn woman was soon to have a baby. Then Yellow Corn woman had her baby, and Magpie-tail told his wife not to go outside, not to go for water; nevertheless she paid no attention to what her husband said. So she went down the river with her jar to get water. Her time (of four days) not being completed (after having her baby), the witches were watching for her to come out. They wanted her to be on their side and be one of their lovers. But Yellow Corn woman refused to be their lover as they wished. So they caused her to die by their witch work. (When she exposed herself to them by going out before her confinement was finished.) The newly born child stayed with his father. So Magpie-tail buried his wife, and they had four nights after death to watch for her departure to the other world (*powaka*).[3] After four days she had to live in the world of the dead. So Magpie-tail took his baby on his arm and followed his wife on the fourth night. Wherever they stopped on the journey, the mother gave her breasts to her baby, but she sat always in the dark, not facing her husband. When she finished nursing her baby, she gave it back to her husband and they went on their journey again. Towards daylight there lay on the roadside a jack rabbit. When day came the woman turned to a jack rabbit. Magpie-tail sat there with his baby on his arm. When the baby cried he gave it some pollen for it to suck all day till night when the mother appeared

[1] kʷ'₁ay₁axʷ₁ę?'əwyu (T).
[2] c₁ohəo?'ona, witch, pl. c'ohəoną (T).
[3] ? - ogạ, at (T).

again human-like. Then she would take her baby in her arms to nurse. Then the mother told her husband, "Now, listen, father, I am going to the dead world. In our journey the first river we come to is a good river, good water that the living drink. When we get there you drink all the water you want, if you are thirsty. The next river will be Ash River, the third will be Soot River, that water is for the dead to drink, the fourth will be Blood River, that is for the dead to wash in. Don't drink from any of those rivers!" So on their journey first they reached the river of good water. There Magpie-tail drank all the water he wanted to drink, he wet his head and his feathers. Day came again. Again Jack rabbit lay alongside the road. Again he fed pollen mash to his baby, and so all day. At night there appeared again a human-like being, then she said, "Give me my baby!" He handed it to her, and she gave the baby her breast. They went on their journey. They came to Ash River. There she drank water, all she wanted, and wet her hair. Day came again. Jack rabbit lay quietly on the roadside all day. Magpie-tail gave his baby corn pollen mash. Night came, she appeared again and asked for her baby. Magpie-tail gave the baby to his wife, and she nursed it. Again they were on their journey, all night. Toward morning they reached Soot river. She washed her face and drank and wet her hair. There lay again Jack rabbit, all day along the road, and Magpie fed his baby as before. Night came, she asked again for her baby, and nursed it. They journeyed on again. Toward daylight they reached Blood River. She bathed in it, and there again lay as jack rabbit on the roadside. He fed his baby the same way. They went on their journey again at night. That night Magpie-tail heard people singing and saw a light on the hillside, indicating that people must be living there. That was the home of the dead. Then he heard some people talking, calling out from the house top, saying to hurry and take their tools, their axes, to cut timber and carry it to the river to build a bridge across the river; some new people were coming. Magpie-tail heard them talking that way, in the night. He heard the men blowing as if tired, as if carrying logs with all their might. Then he thought they must be carrying a big heavy log. Instead of a heavy log they were carrying dry stalks of sunflower. They crossed the bridge. Dead Yellow Corn woman said to her husband, "Now, my father, you are not to be here in this world yet. This is where I am coming. You stay here!" Then as she left him Magpie-tail began to hear the people saying, "Here my sister is coming, here is my daughter coming, hurry up, go on, meet her!" So they went out to meet her and brought her over to their house. At daytime he saw no houses, no lights, only a hill. He saw the footprints on the hillside of rabbits and jack rabbits and other animals. Magpie-tail lay there all day with his baby, sad and lonesome. Night came, the dead began to talk and they went close to where their mother had gone, near the house. The mother of Yellow Corn woman said, "Hurry up, hurry up, take off those old clothes of yours. Here are your clothes. Put them on!" They handed her new clothing to change for what she had on. The dead were preparing to make a dance for her arrival. So they took her to the dance. (There is a dance song here, but it had not been "caught" by the narrator). So they danced all night, and sang. After the dance was over they all went back to their houses. Day came. Magpie-tail stayed all day with his baby, very sad. Only a hill was there. As he sat with his baby an old crow came flying around. Magpie-tail said, "This old crow, why is he flying around here while I am sitting so sad and lonesome?" Crow said, "My grandfather, don't feel sad. You will get your wife back." Magpie-tail said, "I am very thirsty, where can I get water?"—"When night comes you go to where your wife went, to her people, and speak to her through the little hole-like window, ask her to give you water." So he went to the little window and asked his wife for water. So his wife took a long handled gourd cup and passed the water to him through the window. Magpie-tail said to his wife, "No, I don't use that kind of long handled gourd cup to drink. Give it to me in a short one." (He was told by Crow when his wife handed him water to catch her by the middle of the arm and pull her out.) When she handed him water in a short handled gourd cup he caught her by the arm and pulled her out of the window. And there was a jack rabbit. The people inside called out, "*Woh'wą, woh'wą hadą,*[1] there, there already, somebody was watching to take her away from us." Crow had told him he would send him an eagle. The eagle came flying where Magpie-tail was sitting by the jack rabbit. The eagle sat on the jack rabbit and tore the jack rabbit to pieces, into bone and hair and meat. Then he picked up all the pieces he could see on the ground and made a ball of it and tied it up in a corn husk bundle, and gave it to Magpie-tail. Then Magpie-tail went back to his home, with his baby. Eagle told Magpie-tail to go to *iaköbaba*[2] where the grandfathers[3] are. They went there and the eagle flew toward the same place. He notified the guard (*pokwetana*) at that place that Father Magpie-tail was coming. When they arrived there the guard

[1] h'odą, also (T).
[2] įękǫp'òbo, hail-water-toward (T).
[3] The hail or rain spirits.

took them in. When he went inside, the people inside said, "There, there on the right side of the fireplace, on the left side of the fireplace, sit down, our father. What are you doing about here living so peaceably at the cottonwood with your wife, Yellow Corn woman?"—"The witches killed my wife and after four days I went with her where she was going. While there with the dead I asked my wife to hand me out water in a gourd cup. She did hand it to me through a little window, then I caught her by the arm and pulled her out, and she turned to a jack rabbit. Then the eagle came flying over us, around and around. Then he alit on top of the jack rabbit lying there, he tore it to pieces and he picked up everything from the ground and made it into a ball, wrapped it up in a corn husk, gave it to me to bring to you here at your home." They said to him, "Pity our poor father, here we are, we will work for you." So the guard brought out a white Moki (Hopi) blanket (*pöalenamo*)[1] and spread it on the ground and covered the ball with it. People in there began to sing:

> heena na
> ah hena hena
> yaai ya

By and by it began to move while they were singing. Then it began to move more and more and then it came to life. Then the guard uncovered her and she sat up, very tired. Raising her hair from her forehead, she said, "*Huwi!* I slept a little while." Then they told her, "You were not asleep for a short time, you were to be asleep forever." She asked for her baby to nurse. They gave her her baby, she took it in her hands to give it her breast. Then she asked for water to drink, and they gave her water to drink. Then they gave clothing to the woman and to the man. Then the guard went into the east room and got out for Magpie-tail a buffalo robe and a mountain lion hide quiver and a bow and arrows and moccasins. Again he went in the north room, he got out for the woman a white Moki blanket and wrapped moccasins. Then he went in the west room and south room and last the east room again and brought different kinds of fruits, huckleberries, chokeberries, green corn, for them to take home and eat. He told them, "Now you take all this, when you get to your home at the cottonwood husk this green corn and throw it outside of your house, also the fruit peels, for the people to see and for the witches to see. Then go for water to the creek for the witches from *uwaalaka* to see you." When they got home she went for water, and the witches saw her. Then the witches said to themselves,

[1] pəol'enemą (T).

"Did we not take Yellow Corn woman whence she never would return? You see there she is, she got back." Then she went back with the water to her house and remained there enjoying a good time.

Variant

Yellow Corn girl and Blue Corn girl were living. They were very pretty. Then a witch made Blue Corn girl sick, and she died. They buried her close to her house. Then they saw her go out at twilight with a water jar and go and fill it at the river and take it to her grave. Her sister was crying and calling her. The dead girl said, "It is not time for you to come yet." Yellow Corn girl went to her grave to sleep and she could hear her sister just as if she was sweeping in her house or making a fire. On the fourth night she came out with a big load on her back, and she was going to the north. Yellow Corn girl followed her and Blue Corn girl said, "Do not come, sister, you are not to come yet." She had the blankets and shawls they gave her on the fourth night. When it was daytime Yellow Corn girl saw a little rabbit lying under a bush. She slept there in the daytime. At night she heard her sister say to go home, it was not for her to go where she was going. Her sister said, "I will follow you wherever you go." They came to a river of ashes. Blue Corn girl took the water and washed her head and face and hands and she told her sister not to wash and to go home. But she followed and they crossed the river. They came to another river which was very black. Blue Corn girl washed, but she did not let her sister wash or drink. In the daytime there was the little rabbit and Yellow Corn girl slept next to it. That night she went on again and came to a red river. Yellow Corn girl heard some one calling out like the Governor, "A new person is coming! People, go and put out a bridge for her!" While they were sitting by the river lots of people brought a bridge, and they crossed on it. The people were calling, "Build a new estufa, so we can have a dance." So at once they built the estufa and took Blue Corn girl down to dance. Yellow Corn girl was peeping in through the hatch. The people below were saying, "What are we going to name the estufa?"— "Skull (*pit'amulu*)[1]." Some said, "Don't say that, some one is around." So they named it by another name (I forget it). Then they danced and danced. Yellow Corn girl threw down bits of yarn which became large pieces of cloth. By day there were only rabbit holes wherever the houses had been. Yellow Corn girl spoke into one hole, "Sister, give me

[1] p'ˌiṭam'uluṇạ (T).

some water. I am very thirsty." — "Sister, go home, but I will give you water." There was a gourd dipper in the hole and Blue Corn girl reached it up. Yellow Corn girl said, "Stretch up your hand. I can't reach." The rabbit reached up and Yellow Corn girl caught the rabbit and put it into her dress. And she went back, but she did not find the same rivers. She met a man (*łachina*) and she was crying. The *łachina* said to her, "Where have you been?"—"I was following my sister and I caught her and I have her," she said. She asked the *łachina* if he could make her sister live again. "Yes," he said, "if you wish, I will. When you go back to your home, do as I tell you! Put this little rabbit on top of the grave and cover it with a white dance kilt! When it starts to rain you must not go out or peep out, no matter what happens." She went back and did as he told her. It began to rain and she could hear thunder (*nłatsi-tetuna*);[1] and Lightning (*u'pele*)[2] tore the kilt to pieces, and her sister came out. That man felt sorry for her, that is why he helped her.

7. The Corn Girls Follow Red Snake

At the cottonwood were living Magpie-tail boy and Yellow Corn girl and Blue Corn girl. They were living happily with their father. He stayed in the kiva and came to eat with them when they called for him. Young men came to ask for them but they would not accept them. Yellow Corn girl and Blue Corn girl were always making baskets (*puatene*,[3] food baskets) of squawberry (*puahone*)[4] bush. They told their father that the next day they were going to get the young sprouts for their baskets. The next day they went and were gathering shoots when they heard a song:

> he na hena
> he na hena e a a
> liuma liuma
> a la ha lena a
> haiyapi![5]

Elder sister said, "Sister, listen! Somebody is singing a beautiful song." They listened. He sang again:

> he na hena etc.

"Sister, let us catch him and have him sing for us while we are making

---

1 nal͡ˌacit'ꞌəotuna. nạ, place prefix, łaci, thunder, rain or the like in connnection with Spirits, t'ꞌəotuna ? (T).

2 up'ẹlena (T).

3 pˌuot'ꞌẹnạ, pl. - ne (T).

4 puoh'one, balls (T). See pp. 50-51.

5 "Right this way." *Yaipi*, here!

our baskets." They went to another bush and there was a little red snake (*paihâna*).[1] "Sister, here he is! Let us try to catch him." They took off their white embroidered blankets and threw them over him, and he slipped away. He sang again:

he na hena etc.

They threw their blankets again. They approached *hiułiaia*[2] (two and one half miles up the Canyon). He sang again:

He na hena etc.

They approached *suleaia*[3] (bluebird saddle). "Sister, we have come so far. We may get him. Wherever he goes let us follow him!" From there he started to Blue Lake. Their moccasins were worn out. After a long time they approached the Big House. Snake boy dived into the Lake. They sat there on the edge of the Lake. Out came a man from the Lake and asked them why they had come. They said, "We were picking shoots for our baskets and we heard somebody singing and we followed him and every time we tried to catch him he sang and told us to follow him. He went into the Lake." The man said, "You may come in."— "We can not swim." He went in and came out again. He asked them who they were. "Yellow Corn girl and Blue Corn girl." He went back again and came out. Then there came up a ladder and trapdoor and they went in. They said, "Yellow Corn girl and Blue Corn girl, you may sit on the north of the fireplace or on the south of the fireplace, you may sit in the middle." They saw a man passing his hand over his hair, and he was sweating. He was a good looking man. "Yellow Corn girl, Blue Corn girl, you and Magpie-tail boy, your father, are living so happily at the cottonwood, why are you going about here?" They said, "Yes, we are living happily with our father, Magpie-tail boy. We were always weaving baskets. One day we went after squawberry bush twigs and while we were gathering them we heard somebody singing. We listened. We said, 'If only we could take that to our house and have it singing to us while we are making our baskets.' We followed him and came to Blue Lake. Then he dived into the water, and we sat on the edge of the water."—"Well, Yellow Corn girl and Blue Corn girl, don't think very hard! You may take him (Red Snake) home, he is yours." Then the errand man (*chaiane*)[4] went into the east room and brought out moccasins. He went into the north room and brought out

[1] p̓ʼay- red + ʔ (T).
[2] h̨iwł'iaʔoy̨a, stone-old-toward (T).
[3] sùl'eʔoy̨a, bluebird-toward (T).
[4] Keresan for shaman.

manta. He went into the west room and brought out beads. He went into the south room and brought out jerked buffalo meat and fruits. "Now you pack these! Your father is sitting in his chief kiva and he is swelling from sadness to the knees. Now you go with Red Snake and live happily!" Then Red Snake packed on his back all the things that Magpie-tail boy might need in his kiva. They went back to their house and went and called their father. "Father, we came back. Why don't you call the people?" — "Why should I call the people when I am so sad, sitting here with my legs swollen to the knees."—"Well, anyway, call the people!" Red Snake was a good hunter and a good singer. They lived happily and Yellow Corn girl and Blue Corn girl said, "We are Yellow Corn girl and Blue Corn girl and we give ourselves to the people. If the people want to be basket makers, they can go to *tuɫatan*[1] and ask (pray to) us so they can make baskets."

8. Little Bleary-eye Gets a Parrot Skin

Some people were living at the cottonwood, *chiɫa'o*,[2] (little bleary-eye) and his younger brother, *toɫapkatsa* and his wife, Yellow Corn woman. *Pa'na* (Gopher) wanted to be her lover. Then the Gophers (*töɫapa'na*,[3] kiva gopher) made them trouble. Then they called them to *t'öat'at'a* (? kiva). Little Bleary-eye went into the place before the Gophers. When he went in, they said to him, "*Yęhǫ pagato'yoga pagatokwewa*,[4] right here fireplace toward east, fireplace toward south, sit down!" He sat down. "I call you in," said the Town chief (*töhtunena*,[5] house chief), "we are in need of a parrot (*talu'na*), that is what we need for what we are about to do this term (*nohakwiyee'*). We want you to get us this parrot, the whole bird." Then he replied that he would try to get one for them. Then he went back to his house and told his wife, "They, the Gophers, want me to get them a parrot, the whole skin."[6] Then his wife (*anɫiwae*)[7] said, "You go in the morning to grandmother (*ɫitona*)[8]

---

1 The cottonwoods to the east of the pueblo.
2 c'iɫoʔù, eye-big-little one (T), Little Big-eye; but as my narrator always used Little Bleary-eye, I keep to that.
3 t'ˌəɫop'ǫna, kiva (big house) gopher (T). Compare Parsons 10: 96 n. 150.
4 y'ęhu pˌak'əot'əyʔoga pˌak'əot'əkʷiwạ (T). My narrator always translated "fireplace right hand, fireplace left hand," from which, given a little more information, the orientation of the kiva may be inferred.
5 t'ˌəot'ˈunena (T).
6 Compare San Juan, Parsons 4: 39 ff.; Hopi (Shumopovi), Wallis, 22 ff.
7 anɫiwwáʔi (T).
8 ɫˌit'una, mother's mother (T).

Spider woman (*payyona łiu*)!¹ She will tell you where to go." So in the morning little Bleary-eye went to Grandmother Spider at *payyun-pö'aga*,² Spider house. When he got there he went in. "Grandchild, come in!" said Grandmother, "What is in your mind now?" Then said Little Bleary-eye, "Grandmother, the Gophers want me to get them a whole parrot. If I do not get it, they will kill me."—"Yes, my grandson, you can get it." Then Grandmother Spider stood up and went in to the east room, and got out a bundle in which was tied some medicine³ (*wo'lene*)⁴ and gave it to Little Bleary-eye. "Now you go in the morning toward the Big House.⁵ When you get there, you untie this bundle and put the medicine into your mouth and spit it out in the four different directions so the water will flow away for you to go in. Then you will tell them, the people there, what you want." Then he went out and went back home. He got home to the cottonwood. Then his wife said, "How did you make it?"—"Grandmother said to me I can get what they want. I have to go in the morning to the north lake. You make up my lunch to go early in the morning." So at night his wife began to grind meal to make his lunch, all night she worked. So when morning came, he started on toward the Big House with his younger brother. They sang,

> ainai ho'wina
> ai'nai ho'wina
> ainai ho'wina
> ah noi yoi yoi

They are now at *tulkeaba*⁶ (sun trail). Then the younger brother looked back toward home and said to his eldest brother, "It seems to me our mother (i. e. his sister-in-law) is coming." Little Bleary-eye said, "Why do you say that? Nobody is thinking about us. They don't think of us." —"But she is coming." Then they started on and they sang again,

> ainai ho'wina etc.

Then they arrived at the place called *cheakwaaia*.⁷ The younger brother said again, "Our mother is coming, I hear her sing. She is singing,

> ainai ho'wina etc."

---

¹ p'ò?'ọyona łiw (T).
² p'ò?ọyon t'ˡə?ogạ, spider house-at (T).
³ Pollen and squawberry meal.
⁴ wol'ene (T).
⁵ t'ˡəłopiwạ (T).
⁶ t'ùl-, sun + ? + -bo, toward (T).
⁷ cᵢiak^w'o?oyạ < cia- knife, k^w'o- ax + -oyạ, place (T). "*Cheakwa* is a long stone, resounding like a bell."

While they were resting there their mother got there. Their mother said, "Wait and rest a while, and eat and rest a while!" Then they ate their lunch. Then they started on again. Then they came toward the Big House. Then he said, "This is the place we were coming to." He got the bundle given by Grandmother Spider, untied it, he put the medicine in his mouth and spit it out in the four directions so the water would lower for him to go in. Then he told his younger brother, "Now, younger brother, don't go in! You can not go in there. I'll go in myself." About that time, Crow (*ko'ke'na*)[1] came flying above them. Little Bleary-eye said, "Why is this crow flying around above us? I am feeling so sad." Then Crow said, "My elder brother, don't feel sad, I will help you, whatever way I can. I will take care of your younger brother while you go in."—"All right," he said. Then he went near to the water, and took out the bundle of medicine and spat in the four directions for the water to lower. When the water was rising mad, Crow hit the water with his wings. Then Little Bleary-eye hurried to the pit. Then the guard (*poxw'etana*) of the lake said to Little Bleary-eye, "Why is it you are about this place, you living so peaceably with Cottonwood Plumule at the cottonwood?"—"Yes, it is so, but the Gophers are molesting me, that's why I came here to get what they need for this coming term of duty. So my Grandmother Spider told me where to go and get it." Then the guard said, "You will find it here." So he opened the pit (? hatch) for Little Bleary-eye to go in. So he went in and found many people sitting all around. They said to him, "Right here, our father, sit down on the right side of the fireplace or on the left side, sit down! Why do you come around here, living so peaceably at the cotton-wood?"—"Yes, it is so, but the Gophers are molesting me and told me to get a whole parrot for this coming term. That is why I come here." Then they said to him, "Yes, you will find the parrot here." Then the guard was told by the Town chief to go in his room; from there he got out the whole parrot and gave it to Little Bleary-eye. In the north room he went in and got a bowlful of dried meat and again he went in the east room and got a quiver and bow and arrows and some green corn, fruits of all kinds to give to him. Then he told him, "Now you go back home! All this fruit is for your wife and you to eat. When you get home, peel this fruit and throw all the waste outside of your house, so the people (*nałetain*) will see it." This was in the midst of winter. Then he took him outside. And he got to where his little brother was lying sadly. From there they went back home. When they got home, his

[1] k̦oki?'ina (T).

wife spoke with surprise about the green corn and the fruit he brought since it was in the midst of winter. He said this was given to him by the people in the big lake and also the parrot was given to him to present to the Gophers. His wife husked the corn and peeled the fruit and threw the waste outside of the house for the people to see. Then in the morning he was seen by the people who said, "Little Bleary-eye has got back home. We sent him whence he could never return. He is a powerful medicine man. Come and look outside! Look! He has husks of corn and peels of fruit thrown outside his house, in the midst of winter!" They were surprised, they could never do anything with him. Then at nightfall he went to the kiva with his parrot for the kiva Gophers. He gave it to them, and they thanked him. Then he went out. Then the Gophers said, "He is very powerful. We can never do what we want to him. We sent him whence he could not return, but he got the parrot and returned. Men are poor, but some men have very powerful ways of doing. Although they are poor they are lucky, having power (*itoayemu*).[1] We expect to live long through him. The people are living at the cottonwood, and thus we remain."

9. Variant: Rescued by Chipmunk: Metate Bundle: Gopher will Provide a Dress

People were living in the village. Turkey old woman was living at *wąlatönagų*[2] (wind-big-lives-at) with her grandchild, *Chųdou*. The little boy said, "My grandmother, I wish you would make me a wheel to play with." She went to a damp place and dug herself in and rubbed off her feathers and with them made a wheel for her grandchild to play with. "Now, my grandchild, you must not go any further than one roll of your toy wheel." One day he rolled it east and followed it and re-turned home. Next day he went toward the north and rolled the wheel and picked it up and returned. Next day he said, "I am going to play on the west side." Grandmother said, "Don't ever go beyond one roll!" Chųdou rolled the wheel west and picked it up and said, "I wonder why my grandmother does not want me to go beyond one roll?" He rolled it again to *kw'ętelatumtum*[3]. He saw an old man. The old man said, "My grandson, you and your grandmother are living so happy at *wąlatönagų*; what are you doing around here?"—"Yes, grandfather, my grandmother

---

[1] See p. 10. Compare term *natoiyemu* for the winter ceremonies (Parsons 10: 83).

[2] w̜ǫlot'ʼənʔogą (T).

[3] xʷ'ę· tail + ? (T).

and I are living happily. I came out to play and my wheel came here."—
"Yes, grandson, here is your wheel. You should not go farther west. Return to your grandmother!" He gave him the wheel. He went out. "I
wonder why they tell me not to go further westward. I am going to try
it anyhow." So he rolled his wheel and it disappeared. It was a bad
place. The cliff was deep. His hair was blowing. He found himself on a
little ledge. He was crying. He saw a man below. "Father, can you help
me?" The man said he could not help him. Then he saw a little chipmunk (*kuaw⁽iauna*)[1] far below. He hollered. "If there is any way to help
me, I want you to help me."—"All right, brother, be brave!" Chipmunk ran with a spruce seed in his mouth and he buried it under where
the boy lay. Soon the spruce began to grow and the chipmunk was running up and down, up and down, chattering and chattering. Then the
spruce grew up to the boy. "Now, brother, reach to the strong limb
and come down!" Chipmunk kept running up and down on the tree
until it grew shorter and shorter, down to the seed. "Now, brother,"
said Chipmunk, "I came here only to help you down. Now I am going
to where I roam, and you go on your way!"[2]

Then Chụdöu came to a place where there was a white jack rabbit. He
killed it and packed it on his back. As he was going along he heard
somebody saying from a crack in the ground, "Well, Chụdöu, where
are you going? You have something that is very useful to me. You and
your grandmother are living so happy at *wạlatönagụ*. What are you doing
around here?"—"Well, my grandmother told me not to roll my wheel
beyond the first roll and I did and now I am looking for my wheel."
Spider said, "Your wheel is at Metate Bundle[3]. He kills people with
rocks. You give me that rabbit, grandchild, and I will give you something so he will not kill you. He is very wealthy. After you kill him all I
want you to bring me from him is an abalone bowl (*pahötienụ*)[4] and a
parrot tail (*kwẹlatuna*)."[5] She gave him a soft white eagle feather. "My
grandchild, when you come to Metate Bundle, he will be sitting there
with a stone behind him. He will ask you to help him up with it. Then
he will let it go to kill you. When you start to help him, hold this feather
behind him. When he says lift, you lift and this eagle feather will keep the

---

[1] k'ụoxᵂ⁽iwna (T).
[2] Compare Zuni, Benedict 2: II, 70-71.
[3] ‚o?⁽ilena < ⁽ona, metate + ⁽ilena, bundle (T).
[4] p'òx‚ət'⁽iẹnemạ (T).
[5] But parrot is *taluna. Tune* is stick, probably ritual or prayer-stick. Does *kwẹlatuna*
mean tail (feathers) prayer-stick?

stone from going to you, it will go to him." When Chụdöu got down there he saw a man with a rock ready to lift. "Well, grandson, you and your grandmother are living happily at *wạlatönagụ*, what are you doing around here?"—"My grandmother told me not to roll my wheel beyond the first roll and I did and now I am looking for my wheel."—"Since you have come I want you to come into my house; but you must help me up."—"All right, grandfather! I will help you up." He tied the soapweed line a-round his shoulder. Then he held the feather behind and when Metate Bundle let go, the stone fell against him and killed him. Then Chụdöu went into his house and he saw all kinds of powerful people tied up. Then Chụdöu spat out the medicine Grandmother Spider had given him. He said, "Now you go to your homes!"—"We thank you, brother. If you had not come we would have been here forever." He went into the room on the east and brought out a *manta*. This I will take to my grandmother," he said. Then he went to the room on the north side and brought out the shell bowl and the parrot tail. Then he started back, to Grandmother Spider. As he was going along he saw a pretty bird. "I am going to get that bird." He chased him into a hole in the cliff. Chụdöu went in and he saw a man sitting there. He said, "My boy, you chased me. I am very tired." Then he went back and picked up his load. He said, "No matter how pretty a bird I meet I will not chase him." He reached his grandmother Spider. "Grandmother, I killed that Metate Bundle. Nobody on this earth will kill us any more."

When Chụdöu was presenting the bowl and tail, Spider took the *manta* and went into her hole. There she dressed up and began to dance. Chụdöu was so upset he cried and cried and fell asleep. Ponłiuu[1] (Gopher old woman) went underground and made a little hole up to his ear. Gopher said, "Why are you crying? You and your grandmother are living so happily at *wạlatönagụ*." Chụdöu said, "Grandmother Spider told me to bring her the shell bowl and parrot tail feathers from Metate Bundle. I killed him and brought them and a *manta* for my grandmother. Grandmother Spider grabbed the *manta* and went into her hole and I fell asleep crying." Gopher said, "I know what your Grandmother Spider likes. Go and get her a white jack rabbit. Hold it by one ear and grab her!" So Chụdöu went and hunted and got her a rabbit. He took it back. "My grandson, you have just what I need."—"Well, grandmother, come out and get it!" She came out. He held the rabbit in one hand and he grabbed Spider with his other hand. "Grandmother, I gave you what

[1] p'ǫłȋw?ù (T).

you asked and you took the dress I was taking to my grandmother." So she gave him back the dress. Then he dropped the rabbit for her. He started home. He had been away so long his grandmother was sitting there with her legs swollen to her knees from sadness. He said, "Grandmother, I return," and went into the house. "My grandchild, I never expected you to return." She wore the dress when she went to the dances. She said, " I am Turkey. I will roam forever in the mountains. When people want dresses they may go to Gopher and ask for them."

10. *Witch Wife*[1]*: Rescued by Morning Star and Chipmunk*[2]

Magpie was living at the cottonwood, also the two sisters, Yellow Corn and Blue Corn. The witches lived also at *uwaᵃlaka* (the home of all the witches). Their old men were trying to catch a girl to be their lover. The girl was refusing them all the time. So the witches were angry with her. So they put bad medicine into her body, by their power. The girl got sick and died. They buried her. After she was buried, they made four days. The fourth night the witches took her out of her grave, to their kiva (*t'at'ana*).[3] They brought her dead into the kiva. All the witch chiefs (*tsahötunenömu*)[4] were sitting around in there. They told the errand boy (*imtsait'omee*)[5] (who does their work) to go into the room and get the sea shell wheel (*pa'xöta'wana*).[6] So he got the wheel from the room and brought it in. Then they told him to roll it over the dead one, lying in the middle of the floor. He rolled it once from the east side. Then from the north side, then from the west, then from the south side, lastly from the east side. Then the dead body became alive, and human again. Then they pulled out the bad things, arrowheads or spear heads, from different parts of her body. Each of those who had put something in said, "This side I shot," and pulled something out. Another said, "This side I shot," and pulled out something. Another

---

[1] Compare Isleta, Parsons 7: 431-432; Isleta, Lummis, 194 ff.; Picurís, Harrington and Roberts, 297-313; San Juan, Parsons 4: 61-66; Santa Clara, Parsons 4: 66-70; Cochiti, Benedict 1: 90-93; Laguna, Boas 2: 130-132; Siama, San Juan, Sia, Hopi (Second Mesa), De Huff, 175-180; Zuni, Benedict 2: II, 141 ff.

[2] Compare Picurís, Harrington and Roberts, 297-313; Laguna, Boas, 2: 133-140; Zuni Benedict 2: II, 143-144.

[3] Compare töataana (Parsons 10: 74).

[4] c̣ohǝot'ʼunenemạ (T).

[5] imc̣ọyt'óme?i, their-work-he did-the one that (T).

[6] p'òx̣ǝt'ʼawanạ (T).

said, "This side I shot," and pulled out something. Then she screamed and said, "*Huwi! kleapina,* on your account, you pityless ones!" Now the head men said to the errand boy, "Get another wheel and roll it over the girl." He rolled it over from the four sides. Then the girl turned into a deer.

Yellow Corn girl and Blue Corn girl had been invited to come to the meeting of the witches. They prepared the meal to take to the meeting. When night came, they put to sleep their man (*her* man, Yellow Corn's). Magpie lay down to sleep. He lay down covered with a blanket. He was looking through the hole of his blanket. He pretended to sleep, really he was not alseep, he was looking at his wife and his sister to see what they were going to do. So they put up the bundles of meal to take to the meeting. While they were doing that, they went to look at her man, stepping quietly to see if he was asleep. Then she said, "He is asleep now." So they left him and went out from the house and went to the meeting. They went in. Everybody said to them, "Why did you delay so long?" They replied, "He could not sleep. We waited for him to sleep." Magpie left the house and followed them, but he did not dare to go into that kiva, so he hid himself under the hatch screen. When they began to roll the wheel, they could not do as they wished to do. Usually when they rolled the wheel everybody turned into Coyote, Owl, Crow, but this time when they rolled the wheel they could not transform well. So the head man said, "There must be somebody here!" They began to look all around in the dark corners. They did not find him. The errand boy turned the wheel over again, but they did not succeed in doing what they wanted. So the head man said to him, "Go on top under the straw screen." He raised it up and found Magpie there. And he said, "My poor father, why don't you go inside, you are lying here." And he informed the head man inside that Magpie was under the screen, in the hatch. He said to the errand boy, "Go up and bring him in!" He brought him in and sat him down on the right side of the fireplace. Then they went to work to make him sleep. Pretty soon he began to sway as in sleep, he went to sleep.

So the witches took him out and carried him off to a very precipitous rock and laid him there in a hole about as big as he was. They went back and said they had put him in a place whence he could never get out. So they went to work to do as they wished without any one disturbing them. So again the errand boy got the wheel and turned it over the girl and turned her into a deer. The deer was jumping around among the people. They killed the deer. Then everybody took part in skinning the deer. After they took off the skin, they cut the deer in small pieces to cook the meat. When it was cooked, they served the meat all around to the people there. They began to eat. Towards morning, each went to his house.

When the morning star (*töbapaiłana*)[1] came up, it sounded to Magpie like a bell. When Morning Star passed over where Magpie was lying in the rock, he stopped and asked Magpie what he was doing. He told him that the witches had put him there, because he went where they were turning a dead girl back to life, and were going afterward to turn her into a deer, he went there to see and was found up at the entry under the screen, and was taken inside and put to sleep; while he slept, they took him up that high, precipitous rock. Morning Star said to him, "*linowi'łeano ǫntamena*[2] (poor my father), Magpie-tail young man, bear the hardship as best you can while I do something for you. I will call Chipmunk child (*kwoawiöouna*)[3] to do something for you to get you down." Morning Star went off. Magpie was looking down off that high rock, he could not see the ground below, it was so high. There he saw many old bones of human beings and skulls that the witches put in that hole. When they got tired and hungry they fell down, and were killed. Little Chipmunk came to him, and said, "My poor father, bear the hardship for a little while!" Little Chipmunk had a spruce cone in his mouth. He ran down to the ground and buried the cone in the ground. Then he hollered and ran up and down, to make the tree grow up as high as where Magpie was lying. Now the spruce began to sprout up from the ground. Chipmunk kept running up and down, until the tree grew clear up to where Magpie was lying down. "Get up, my father, slowly, and reach your hand to the tree." Then he put his foot over the tree and grabbed it and got on the tree, and went down to the ground. While there the little Chipmunk gave to Magpie a buffalo robe and a quiver of mountain lion skin, a sage (? *tołeana*)[4] bow and four arrows in the quiver, and buckskin leggings and moccasins. He told him to go back to his home. "Your wife, Yellow Corn, is without any concern for you and is having a good time. She is married to Horned Toad (*koałahanaona*)[5] and she keeps him on a cradle of cotton. The same cotton spool string is tied to the cradle and hanging to a beam in the house." So Magpie got home and went

---

[1] (Or tömpaxöłana, Parsons 10: 112.) t̗əbop'öxəł'ona, east star = morning star (T).
[2] ǫntòm'ena (T).
[3] k'̗uox^w̗įwʔùʔ'una (T).
[4] ? Osage. Sage is t'̗'owluną (T).
[5] k'̗uoł̗axenloʔ'ona, lizard (T).

straight down to the foot log of the river in the village. He began to sing,

> he a a hea hea
>
> ya na hea ena eya

Then Yellow Corn and her sister Blue Corn heard it. Blue Corn girl went outside her house and heard the song, and told her sister, "My elder sister, somebody is singing at the bridge at the river just like my elder brother (*npapana*)."[1] Then Yellow Corn said, "My younger sister, let us go down there and see. We will bring him up." As they went out from the house Horned Toad began to cry,

> yahonina yahonina
>
> he e e iana
>
> he e e iana

But they went on down to the river to get Magpie and bring him up to the house. In the morning Magpie told his wife Yellow Corn also Blue Corn, to put on their best dresses and to take along with them Horned Toad. So he took them out from the house. He said to them, "Take a bundle of lunch." So they started out. Then Magpie began to sing,

> ainai' howina
>
> ainai' howina
>
> ai'nai' howina
>
> ai'nai' howina
>
> ainai' ho'wina
>
> ainai' ho'wina
>
> ah noi hoi hoi
>
> ainai' howina
>
> ainai' howina

(Magpie takes them to each place mentioned in "Magpie and the Corn Mothers," and between each stopping place the same song is repeated.)

They went down to the Lake. "Here is where the fathers and the grandfathers are living, and you will remain here forever. You took me only whence I could return; I brought you here whence you will never return." Then he pushed them into the Lake. Yellow corn and blue corn floated on top of the water. He picked them up and carried them under his blanket and went back to his home at the cottonwood. The people still say, "Magpie's home is always at the cottonwood."—"I can not help it, this is my home. Yellow Corn and Blue Corn were always very careless in their thoughts, and Yellow Corn and Blue Corn I have sent under the water of the Lake to the people living there." So Magpie remained there in his home.

[1] ạnp̦op'ona (T).

Variant (Witch Wife)

There was a very pretty girl, and a witch boy came to ask her to marry him. The girl said, "No, I do not want to marry you." He was very [much of a] witch and in a few days that girl got sick and died. And after four days they had to make a feast for her. (On the fourth day they, the dead, take it [the food] along with them.) On the fourth day the witches went to dig her up and take her to the boy's house. The witch chief rolled a wheel over her, and she came to life and said, "Oh, I am so tired!" The people said, "Hurry up, roll the wheel again!" He rolled it. Then she turned to a deer, and they shot her with arrows, and the women who came in had big bowls to cook the meat, after the men cut it up. Early in the morning the women took out the bowls of meat. There was a little girl in a house nearby looking at them. The chief said, "Some one is looking at us." When that little girl heard that, she lay very quiet. Then she peeked again. Early in the morning she told her mother what she saw. When a woman came into their house with meat, she threw it at her and said, "You cannibal (people eater)! I would not eat that, you eat it yourself!"

11. Little Dirt and Deer Girl : Race between Deer Boys and Hawk Boys[1]

The people were living. And Little Filth or Dirt (*xiqu*)[2] was living with his grandmother. He lived in the dirt corner[3] of the house. The people went hunting and brought in their meat. He would go around among the people and beg. The people were talking about it, that Little Dirt never went hunting, but just went around among the people. One day Little Dirt told his grandmother he was going hunting. "My grandchild, you don't know the tracks of rabbit or of deer." That night his grandmother showed him the tracks in sand. Rabbit's track was like this ₁'ₗ. Jack rabbit's track was the same but a little longer. The deer track was of a split hoof. Next morning very early he started north. He was so

---

[1] Compare Isleta, Parsons 7: 386-390; Isleta, Lummis, 12 ff.; Cheyenne, Kroeber 1: 161-162.

For rainmaking in race see also Shumopovi, Wallis, 42; Zuni, Parsons 1: 222; Zuni, Benedict 2: I, 130, II, 75-76.

[2] hiʔ'ięʔù (T).

[3] Actually a small pit near the door.

small and slow he made little progress. He came to *tulkaba* (sun-high).[1]
He went on to *weta* (at the pine).[2] There he camped. Next morning
after he ate he started out to hunt. He saw a little track. "This is what
Grandmother said was a rabbit track." So he followed it and came to
where the little rabbit was lying under sage brush. Little Dirt was very
small but through his power he could pack it. He took it to his camp.
"Now I have something for my grandmother."

His fire was just as fresh as when he had left it. Next morning he
started out again. He found another track. "This must be a jack rabbit.
Grandmother said it was just a little larger." He followed the track to
where the jack rabbit was lying down under brush. He shot it with his
bow and arrow and packed it on his back and started back to his camp.
When he got back to camp, there was a pot and the rabbit was well
cooked. "I wonder who is around here. I got that rabbit to take to my
grandmother and somebody cooked it. Who is doing this?" He sat
down and ate. Then he dressed his jack rabbit and hung it up. "I will
take this to my grandmother." It was Deer girl who did this. Next day
he went hunting again. He found a deer track. "My grandmother said
they stepped single and the hoof was split." (While he was away people
were saying that he could not hunt, he was so small.) He tracked all day
and came to a big buck. He shot it. "I have to take it to the camp," he
said. He tied it up to put on his back. When he came to his camp, the
fire was burning and the jack rabbit was cooked. "I wonder who is
doing this, cooking the rabbit I was going to take to my grandmother!"
—"Never mind, my father!" she said. "I am the one. When you came
you were tired and had to have something to eat. Now you have a deer
to take to your grandmother. Before you go I want you to come with
me. I am your wife. I want you to see the children that have been born
from you. Follow me, because the people are envious of you and will
treat you mean." She took him to the eastward and they came to a patch
of soap weed. She said, "This is the place. Here your children are with
their deer grandparents." She pulled up one of the soap weeds and there
was a trapdoor. "Go in!" she said. When he went in they said, "Our
father, you may be seated in the middle." Out stepped two little deer
and called him father. "These are your children. Soon the people will
ask you where you are getting your deer. You will tell them. They will
come out to hunt and if they don't find us they will kill you. But you are
our father. We shall all be there." They gave him a little fortune and

[1] *t'ùlk'ˌɔobo* (T). A mile from town.
[2] *w'ęto* (T). Five miles from town, one mile from Seco.

some medicine to spit. "They will surround us and every one will get a deer. These two little ones will run to you and you will take them home. When you come home the people will make a bet with you on a long distance race ("round the world race," see p. 46) to run against you and your children. If they beat you, they will kill you. If you beat them, spare none!"

He went back to his camp and took his deer and started home. The people saw him coming from the north. "Come out to see Little Dirt! He is coming with a deer on his back." Others said, "He is no hunter. How can he get a deer?" When he reached his house he called his grandmother, "Come out and help!" He was under the ladder with the deer. She took in the deer. A man came to tell him to go to the kiva. "I have not eaten yet." They were curious people. Another man came and called him to kiva. In kiva they gave him a smoke[1] and then he was to tell. He told them where the deer were. They said if they got no deer they would kill him. Next morning they started out. At *tulkaba* they overtook him and rolled him around in the road and went on to the pine. Here they made a surround. They called out, "Way over there they are coming to you!" The little deer ran up to Little Dirt. They got home late after the others. His grandmother said, "These are my children. They will care for us when we get old." They were very handsome, with parrot tail feathers tied to their ears. Grandmother said, "I don't know how long we shall have these children with us, the people are so envious."

He just started to eat when a messenger came and said, "Little Dirt, you have to go to the kiva."—"I have just started to eat," said Little Dirt. Then came another messenger. "Little Dirt, you have to go to the kiva." He went to the meeting. "Sit down in the middle! Tomorrow morning we are going to have an around the world (long distance) race. If we beat you, we are going to kill you and your children and grandmother. If you beat us, you may kill us. We will start just as the sun rises." He went back to his house. "My grandson, why do you look so sad"?—"Why shouldn't I look sad? The people want us 'to go around the world.'" If they beat me, they are going to destroy us all, and if I beat them, I am to destroy them." (They were a bunch of witches.) Next day he took out his medicine and spat it out at the end of the race track and gave the little fortune to his children. As the sun peeped over the mountain they started west. The others were square shoulder, raw boned men. As they approached *paŧihanenai*, the two men turned to hawks, chickenhawks. They said, "Come on, little deer, we are going!" They

[1] In these circumstances it must be a pipe smoke.

passed them. The Deer boys took out their medicine and made a big
rain. The Hawks' wings got wet. The Deer overtook them. The Hawks
said, "Let the breath talk (i. e., have mercy on us)!" They turned south
and reached the mountain called Coyote Ears House (*tuwʻatʼatöatyta.*)[1]
The Hawks passed them and laughed at them. Deer boy said, "Try hard,
my little brother, for the sake of our father and mother!" He spat out
his medicine and the bushes were loaded with raspberries (*tilhöne*) and
the Hawks came down to eat. They said to the Deer boys, "Stop to eat!"
Deer boys said, "We have already eaten," and went on. The Hawk boys
said, "Let the breath talk!" The Hawk boys overtook them at *wʻilnamba*[2]
(bow-up there). The Deer boys spat their medicine and soap weed was
there in fruit and the Hawk boys stopped to eat. The Deer boys overtook them. "Stop to eat!"—"No, we have eaten." The foot of the little
Deer boy was bleeding. "Try for the sake of our father and mother!"
Now they had to run back as human boys. "Our boys are ahead"! said the
people. Little Dirt and his grandmother said, "Our boys are coming
ahead!" All the people were hollering. The Deer boys reached the race
track ahead and then they and their father started to club all those
against them and when the Hawk boys came up they killed them. They
went to their house and said, "Now, we shall live without fear of the
envious people. Now you are little deer and will live in the mountains
and I am Little Dirt and will live in the corner, and whoever wants to be
a good hunter he will address me. (I will stay here to be asked.)[3]

Variant (Deer Girl)

There was a hunter. He had a gun made of wood, also a bow and arrows
with flint arrowheads. He was called wood gun (*klatawe*)[4]. Once he
went hunting to the south. He passed a Mexican town on his way. When
he saw the town he hid away, he slipped out of the road and into the
woods. He came to a pond of water and made his camp there. Next day
he went into the mountain to hunt. He went over the mountain all day,
but killed no game. He had a little clay cook pot. That day when he
came back he found his camp with fire built and the clay pot on the fire
and meat in it cooking. In the wooden dish was a corn mash (*paouna*),[5]

---

1 t̩uxᵂatʼ̩ołəotʻˈənto, coyote-ears-house-at, two peaks near Taos junction (T).
2 xᵂˈilnạbo, (T).
3 See Parsons 10: 109.
4 ł̩otʻˈowinạ, wood-gun (T).
5 p'òʔùʔˈuna (T).

freshly made and steaming. When he moved the clay pot, the steam also came out. He said, "Who could have been here? I am alone." He looked around his little camp for foootprints; but he could not see any marks. So he sat down by the fire, thinking how it could have been done. He began to eat his supper. Before he ate, he threw out a piece of meat and of corn mash, back of him, into the dark. He said, "You eat, whoever you may be!" Then he began to eat. When he finished eating, he was sitting by his fire, then he went to sleep. In the morning he went again up the mountain, in another direction. He killed a deer, he skinned it and cut it into pieces. He packed it up into its hide, and carried it down to his hunting camp (*chŏ'tun'ta*).[1] When he arrived there with the deer, the meal was cooked again, the clay pot was boiling, and the corn mash made. He laid his deer there, he looked and wondered what kind of meat it was, as he had none the first day. He took a piece out of the pot and looked at it. He found it was rabbit meat. He said, "What living thing can be around here to do my cooking?" He unpacked his meat and hung it on a pole. Then he said, "Tomorrow I am going to watch, I won't go away." He built a little brush place, and made a little lookout where he could see who would come to his camp. "If he comes, I am going to shoot him," he said. Nothing came. He saw nothing. Night came and he cooked his own meal, roasting the deer meat in the coals, and he made his corn meal mush. He threw the pieces of meat and mush out as before and said, "Here take this, eat it, whoever you may be. Why did you not come today when I was looking for you?" He sat there 'til late at night. He slept again. Next day, he went out again. He did not kill anything. When he came back, there again was the clay pot boiling, he looked at his meat, and half was gone. He looked at the pot and there was the deer meat, boiling. Then he said "Somebody must be around here, he pities me and does my cooking." He ate his supper. But he did not like having his meat cooked in this way. He watched the next day again, in his brush place. Nothing came. Then he said to himself, "I guess I will move my camp somewhere else. If I stay here, I guess he will finish cooking my meat." So he packed up his game and went away from there. He went north. He reached another mountain. He made camp there. He slept there, it snowed that night. Next morning he went out hunting. As he was going along he saw the track of a rabbit. He followed the track and came to where the rabbit was lying. He shot at him and killed him. He tied him to his belt. Then he came again to another track, the track was larger. He followed a good

[1] c̣ət'ʼənto, hunt-house-at (T).

way around. He came to where the animal was lying, it was a jack rabbit. He shot at him and killed him. Now he had two, a rabbit and a jack rabbit. Then he tied them together and carried them on his back. He got to his camp. He unpacked them and laid them in the bush. He said, "Now I am having good luck, I killed two." He cooked his supper and sat by his fire. Later he went to sleep. Next morning early he got up and cooked his breakfast and went to hunt again. He found a bigger track. He said, "I guess this is elk or maybe deer." Then he followed it, up the mountain. He did not overtake it. So he left it and went back to his camp. When he came near his camp he saw the smoke away up from his camp. He reached camp. First he looked where his two animals were hanging, one was gone. Then on the fire the pot was boiling, he looked and there was the rabbit meat cooking, and there was the corn mush cooking, and there was the corn mush steaming in the wooden dish. "Here is the same trick as before! Somebody cooked my meat. I wanted to have the meat to take home. Who can it be, watching me wherever I go, and cooking my meal?" He ate and threw back in the dark some small pieces. "Eat this, you must not steal my meat," he said. "I want to take it home." He ate, then he slept. Again the next morning he went out to hunt. As he went he found the same track he had left. So he followed. He saw the deer in a pond of water, drinking. He pointed with his wooden gun. When he was about to shoot, the deer exclaimed, "My father, don't kill me! I am the one helping you to make your meal because I pity you, you are a man alone, with no wife. That is why I cook for you, wherever you camp. I am a woman." So he said, "Come out from there then." Then she came out. The deer showed herself a woman. So he took her to his camp. When they got there, she cooked the meal, and they ate. "I am the one who cooked your meal, I pity you without a wife. I cook so you don't have to cook when you come back at night and feel tired. I will go to your house and I will be your wife and we will live together." Next day the man packed up his meat and they went back to where he lived.

Variant (*Race between Antelopes and Hawks*)

Some time ago people lived at the Mouth of Red Willows. At that time a little band of witches lived at *owa'laka* (practice place for witchcraft.) The good people never agreed to do things together because the witches were bad people. Whatever the good people did the bad people would destroy. They did not like each other. So these bad people told the good people that they would make a race, betting their lives. If the good people won, they would kill all the witches, if the witches won, they would kill all the good people.[1] So the good people (*itoikuyuina*)[2] went to work and began to train two boys for a round the world (*kwihölima*) race (*kwiawina*).[3] When the good people were ready with their boys, they told the witch people that they were ready to make their race around the world. So both parties set the day for the race. When the set day came, before sunrise they were at the starting place, ready to start. Then at sunrise the two boys of the witches came to the place, looking very fearful, their flesh was poor and thin. The boys of the good people were looking strong and in good health. So they started at the starting point in the east to run to the west. When they came about to the point of the big river (*pohłana*),[4] the witch boys passed the boys of the good people by turning to hawks (*tohkena*),[5] flying swiftly. So the good boys turned to antelopes. They were well trained for the race, they had each his little bundle of medicines. So they untied their bundles of medicine, and put the medicine in their mouth and spat it in the four directions, praying for rain. Very soon it began to cloud up and lightning began and soon big rain. So those hawks had to look for shelter in the rocks. So the two young antelopes passed them while the heavy rain was falling. They came to a point of mountain where they were going to go around five times. The young antelopes were making the last of their five rounds, the two witch boys could not yet be seen. The antelopes made their way back to the starting place. When they were approaching the starting point they saw the two witch boys way far behind. So the antelopes got back to the starting point first and they won the race. And the people were waiting to see which boys came first. The witches were saying, "Our boys are coming first!" The good people were saying, "No, it is our boys, we have beaten you." When the Antelope boys got there first the good people began to club the witch people and kill them with their war clubs. So some of them ran into their pit, the good people followed them. So they shut up the hole, they threw in dirt and rocks. About that time the two witch racers came. They killed them. The good people won the race. But somewhere they left a little hole where they could see through. If they had not left this, we would not have had any more witches. That's the end.

[1] Compare Hano, Parsons 4: 276.
[2] it'oyk''uyuʔina, the people that are good (T).
[3] ʔ-xəlima, round, kᵂiaw'ine, race (T).
[4] p'ół'ona, water-big (T).
[5] t'okena (T).

Variant[1]

There lived people and other different peoples. There were an old man and an old woman and they had one child, Fihuena. All the boys of good standing wanted to court her and marry her, but she always refused them. There was a boy. He had no father nor mother. His name was *paiselelailulai* (Poor Old Blanket). One day the girl was sitting on the top of the house. Poor Old Blanket came where the girl was sitting. She saw him and told him to come up and stay with her. Never before had she noticed any boy as she did this Poor Old Blanket. They stayed together all day. Late in the day Poor Old Blanket said, "I am going home." The girl said, "No, you must not go! Stay with me at my house and sleep with me!" The girl told her mother at nightfall to fix her bed upstairs. They both went into the upper room. All night long they laughed and talked aloud. Her father and mother could not sleep all night and said, "Why is our child awake now and talking? She must have somebody with her." In the morning the girl said, "Mother and Father, call the attention of the people to it," meaning that they had a son-in-law. Her mother said to her, "No, you are too young to call the people's attention to it. You did not let us sleep all night." Then the girl told the boy to vomit. The boy vomited all the waste stuff that he had eaten, whatever he had found, like old rags and rotten hides and other things. They cleaned him up and soon he became a goodlooking boy. After a while the boys who had failed in courting the girl became jealous of Poor Old Blanket. The girl found this out and she did not let him go outside the house. She kept him well dressed and clean. The boys decided to call on the old grandmother who lived by herself and ask her how they could persuade Poor Old Blanket to come out and talk and agree to a race. The old woman said, "Yes, my grandson, I can help you," and she gave a bundle of medicine to one of the boys. He went to the house where Poor Old Blanket was. He untied the bundle and spat to the four directions to get him out. Poor Old Blanket came out. The boy told him that they wanted to make a race around to a big mountain standing at a distance from the place, and bet their wives. If they beat Poor Old Blanket, they would take his wife, and if he beat them, he would take the wives of the two racers. This was their firm decision. The morning came. The people gathered at the starting point. The opposing party were a kind of witch people. They started the race at a distance from the starting point. The racers of the

[1] Written by narrator of preceding version.

witch party were seen to be hawks, swift flyers. Poor Old Blanket was seen far behind. The wife of Poor Old Blanket also had her magic power to overcome the witch party, so she called for an angry strong shower to pour from above so those two racers of the witch party had to hide in a rock crevice. Poor Old Blanket proceeded on his race. He went around the mountain five times and started back to the starting point, yet the two racers could not yet be seen. So Poor Old Blanket got first to the starting point. A long time afterward the racers of the witch party got in to the starting place. So Poor Old Blanket won the race and took the two wives of the two racers of the witch party, and he remained with three wives.

12. Turquoise Boy Races the Deer Boys

Turquoise boy (*chalmụyuöwiouna*)[1] was living with his grandmother at the Edge-of-the-grass. He was a good hunter. His grandmother said, "You are going farther and farther away. You may not go beyond to the east." One day he went over the mountain and he met a bunch of deer. They said, "Turquoise boy, what are you doing here, you who live happily with your grandmother at the Edge-of-the-grass?"—"Yes, I am living happily with my grandmother at the Edge-of-the-grass." Deer said, "What pretty turquoise you have! Let us run a race around the world!" (The people of the Great House were challenging him.) "This is what my grandmother was afraid of. Now I must tell her what the Deer boy said to me." When he reached the house he said, "Grandmother, you told me not to go beyond to the east. I did go and I met the Deer boys and they said they liked my turquoise and my clothes and they challenged me to a race around the world, for the clothing of the people in the Great House."—"This is what I feared, my grandson. Well, now, you must go and see your grandmother Gopher. She has power and may help you." He went to see his grandmother Gopher. She knew their course. "Grandmother Gopher, I have come to ask for help. My grandmother told me not to go beyond to the east and I went and met the Deer brothers and they liked my turquoise and challenged me to a race around the world."—"Yes, grandson, I will help you, and now I have to work on the road." They were to meet at the divide (saddle) down to Blue Lake. They had a pile of *mantas*, etc. His grandmother took a bowl of turquoise. Grandmother Gopher gave him some medicine. They started. The Deer boys were ahead. Turquoise boy spit his medicine.

[1] c̣ọlmụyu?ᵊwyu?'una (T).

Gopher had made so many holes, Deer could not pass. He went on ahead to Coyote Ears House; they passed him there and turned south. He said,"*Kwialalumu*,[1] make yourselves strong!" They caught up at *tuitaiba*[2] (mountain of white earth). He spat again and there were berry bushes. "Eat with us!"—"Make yourself strong!" They overtook him again. He spat and there was more fruit. They stopped to eat. He came to *maw'aluna*[3] or Taos Peak. When he came to *pa'xemututa* (Fog House), fog could be seen by people. Some people said, "The Deer boys are ahead." Others said, "No, Turquoise boy is ahead." The little Deer boy came limping, his hoof was cracked. Then the people gave Turquoise boy the *mantas*, the wrapped leggings, etc. Grandmother gave her turquoise to all, "so you may help the world! That the world may live longer!" That is the reason why a hunter today always overtakes the deer. They put the things on their backs, and Turquoise boy and his grandmother lived happily. Turquoise boy said, "All who want to be good hunters, they may come to the Edge-of-the-grass to ask me."

13. The Envious Hunter[4]

People were living. There were two boys, good friends to each other. They always went out hunting together. One was very rich. "This time we will go to hunt at *piltöna*[5] (summer house)," they said. So they went there hunting. They went out in the morning. Just at sunrise, one boy killed a big deer with big horns. By night he had his deer in camp. His friend came and saw he had killed a big deer. "I will give you half of this deer," he said. But his friend was envious. And when they sat down to eat, that witch boy showed off his belt. His friend said, "What a pretty belt you have, let me see it!"—"You may have it if you go through it when I throw it in a ring," he said. The boy said, "All right."—"I will count one, two, three! and the third time you must go in," he said. Before he counted three, he started to run. "No, do not run until I count three," he said to his friend. At the third count he went into the ring and he turned to a coyote. He said, "Now, my friend, you may go around the ash piles and eat rags!" He ran away with tears running down

---

[1] ma̧-kᵂ‚iaw‚al ʔ‚ammá (T).
[2] t̓uy- ? - bo, white-earth- ?-at (T); white earth-people-at.
[3] m‚oxᵂolun̜a (T).
[4] Compare Isleta, Parsons 7: 432-437; Isleta, Lummis, 35 ff.; Hopi, Second Mesa, De Huff, 141-148.
[5] pìlt̓‚əna (T).

his face. The witch boy put the deer on his horse and went home. The
coyote would go to the summer house of his uncle (*tǫłu*)[1] where they
raised pumpkins and melons. His uncle told his dogs to get him. When
they ran up to him they stopped barking because they knew it was a
person. His uncle went to him and saw he was thin and his eyes haggard.
"Poor thing, maybe you are a person and your eyes worn from crying."
And the little coyote nodded his head. His uncle caught him and carried
him down to the *po'toia*[2] (water people) estufa and he called all the
people to come in and see the coyote. The people said, "Maybe the
witches turned you into a coyote," and he nodded his head. So they
rolled a knife wheel over him and they put him in the middle, and there
stood the poor boy who had not come back to his mother from hunting.
They asked him what had happened to him. He told what his friend had
done to him. They said, "Now make him into what will never become a
person again. Take this with you when he comes to ask you to go hunting
with him again." Then they gave him a turquoise wheel (*tsölmyyut'awan*).[3]
He went to his mother's house. His friend learned he had come back and
he went to see him. He said to him, "Tomorrow, let us go hunting again.
Where have you been so long?"—"Oh, I was just hunting," he said. "All
right, we will go tomorrow to the same place." His mother did not want
him to go, but he went. When they got there, they sat down to eat. He
showed his turquoise wheel, he had it hanging by his side in front. His
friend said, "What a pretty wheel you have!"—"You can have it, if you go
through it." He jumped up to go through the wheel. His friend said, "You
must not go through until I count three times." He was so anxious, at
one he ran. "Wait!" He counted one! two! and he ran. "Wait!" The
third time he counted he ran through, and a great big snake came out.
He said to his friend, "Now you may go around where it is hot, and you
will frighten people and nobody will like you. You did something to me
from which I could be turned back to a person, but I have done something to you from which nobody will help you to turn back into a person."
Tears ran down from the snake and he ran away. The boy went home.

14. The Jealous Girls

The people were living. Yellow Corn young woman (*iachulikwem*) and
Magpie-tail boy and Blue Corn young woman (*iacholikwem*). Squawberry

---

[1] t'u̧łu, vocative of t,u̧łu'una (T).
[2] p'ȯt'oynema̧ (T).
[3]   c,ọlm,u̧yut''awan(a̧) (T).

Flower girl (*pöahöpapkwilena*)[1] lived with her mother, White Corn girl (*iapatökwilena*).[2] Tididipobianu[3] was a great hunter. Early before dawn he would go to the mountains and in the morning he would bring back a deer. Yellow Corn girl and Blue Corn girl liked him, also Squawberry Flower girl. The Corn girls said they would have a contest. The Corn girls were to grind corn and Squawberry Flower girl was to grind squawberries and whoever ground the finest was to marry Tididipobianu. He went to the Corn girls' house. Here were the baskets of meal, a basket of Blue Corn girl, a basket of Yellow Corn girl, and a basket of Squawberry Flower girl. He tasted Yellow Corn girl's meal; it was coarse. He tasted Blue Corn girl's meal; it was coarse. He tasted Squawberry Flower girl's meal; it was fine, also it was sour, it made his mouth water. He said, "You are my wife!"

The Corn girls became very jealous. They asked Tididipobianu and his wife to their house to sing for them while they ground corn. They said, "We are glad you have come. We have some turkeys. We will get one to have something to eat after we have ground the corn." They sent Tididipobianu inside the coop to get the turkey and while he was inside they put their wheel (ring) at the opening. When he came out through it he turned into a coyote. "Now you will not live with Squawberry Flower girl any more. We did this because you did not marry us." The tears were running down his face. They said to Squawberry Flower girl, "Now your husband is a coyote." She cried and as she went home Coyote followed her. She was afraid of him. When she got home she told her parents. Coyote came around; they beat him off with a stick. Coyote went to the house of *chalmuyululi*,[4] Turquoise old man. He was so tame Turquoise old man said, "Perhaps this is Tididipobianu." He asked him if he was Tididipobianu. Coyote nodded his head, tears rolling down his face. Turquoise old man took out his turquoise covered wheel. He told him to go through the wheel. He went through once and part of his skin fell off. He went through again and all the rest fell off him. Turquoise old man gave him medicine to make him vomit all the dirty bones he had eaten. "Now, my boy, I will give you turquoise arm bands and a flute." Tididipobianu went back and at night he blew his flute at

---

[1]   ?-pòb-k^wil'ena, ? flower-girl (T). See Parsons 10: 106. Squawberry (*peaklóawana*) is "medicine." Baskets are made from squaw bush, as by Ute and Navaho.

[2]   ìap'òt'ˌəkʷil'ena, corn-white-girl (T).

[3]   Tininipobienu is Olivella Flower boy in Tewa, and is a Tewa tale hero name. The narrator learned this tale from a man who used to visit San Juan. Compare San Juan, Parsons 4: 29-36; Parsons 5: 289-300; Isleta, Lummis, 54 ff.; Hopi, Voth, 105-109.

[4]   c¡ǫlmˌuyuⱡuⱡi (T).

the bridge. Blue Corn girl said to Yellow Corn girl, "That Tididipobianu is playing his flute." Yellow Corn girl said, "No, he is out eating old bones."—"No, that is he." So they took their water jars along in order to talk to him. They set down their jars. "Oh, are you here?"—"Yes, I am here."—"Oh, what pretty armlets!"—"Would you like to have them?"—"Yes."—"You have to put your arms in them before I give them to you." They put in their arms and they turned into a snake with two heads. "You did the easy thing to me, I am going to do worse to you. Now you will drag yourself in the hot sun and the people will throw rocks on you." The gourds in their water jars turned to rattles.

Tididipobianu went to his house and there sat his wife and her father and mother swollen from sadness. Now they lived happily. And they said people must not be jealous and treat one another like that. They left that word for all the people.

Variant

There was living a boy. The girls liked him very much, he was a good hunter. They went to ask him to marry them. He asked them, "When did you grind your meal?" They said, "When you were starting out, I started to grind; when you were returning, I finished it." He would not marry them. White Corn girl came to him. He asked, "When did you grind your meal?" She said, "When you were returning, I started to grind and I made a hot *łiana* (corn meal drink) for you when you arrived."—"You are the girl I want," he said. . . When she went to get water, Blue Corn girl and Yellow Corn girl came with their turquoise jar rest. They told her to go through it. She became a coyote. She went as a coyote to her own house, her tears were falling. She lay by the side of the ladder, and when her husband came he saw her and knew some one had turned his wife to a coyote. He picked her up and took her somewhere to be turned to a person again. And Blue Corn girl and Yellow Corn girl they turned into snakes.

15. Grass Flower Boy Courts the Corn Girls[1]

At Corn-lying lived *bałipabioyoh*[2] (grass flower boy), and Blue Corn girl and Yellow Corn girl lived at the cottonwood. Grass Flower boy would come courting to the river near the home of the two girls and

---

[1] Written by a townsman.
[2] p'òłˌipòbʔˈəwyu (T); ? water-grass.

would try different ways to make them become his wives. Every time he came dressed in his best clothes to please the girls who did not like him. Meanwhile Grass Flower boy met Skunk (boy) (*koichoteoyoh*)[1] and talked with him and told him that he was trying to win Blue and Yellow Corn girls to become his wives, but was not successful. He asked Skunk if he knew how he could make them his wives. Skunk said to him, "Yes, there is a way. You can succeed by getting what they need and like—a turqouise ring and a white shell ring for them to use on their heads to carry their water jars. I will bring them to you," said Skunk. He brought them to him. Then he went to the river and waited for the girls to come. They came and he told them that he had something nice they would like to have for their use. He showed them the rings. Then the younger sister said to the older sister, "He has something that we need badly." They both said, "We will accept them." The boy said to them, "Go over there! I will roll them to you. If you go through while they are rolling, they will be yours, and you will be my wives." They liked the offer. So he rolled them. They went through and both of them turned into two-headed snakes. Afterward, they went to an old man working in the corn-field and rolled themselves up under his buffalo robe. When the old man came where his buffalo robe was he found the two-headed snakes and thought, "This must be some happening. I will see to their transformation and take them to the ceremonial house." There he rolled a white shell bead wheel. They went through it and came out again as Blue Corn girl and Yellow Corn girl. They became Black Cane old man's[2] wives, and remained living at the cottonwood.

16. Sun Begets Twins: Variant (Witch Wife)

Nawłe'taine, the people, were living. The people were living happy and well off. Yellow Corn girl had twin boys. They were not the children of Magpie-tail boy. Yellow Corn girl had been lying out in the sun and they were the Sun's boys. Their mother told them not to hunt eastward, only westward. One day they said, "Why does our mother not want us to go eastward?" As they went eastward a fine looking man approached and said, "I am your father," and he gave them a little fortune. Through it they became good hunters.[3]

---

[1] k̗uyl'uluna is skunk (T). See p. 98.
[2] At Isleta the War chief is so called. See p. 87.
[3] Compare Tewa, Parsons 4: 100; Sia, Stevenson 1: 43; Cochiti, Dumarest, 217-218. Zuni, Benedict 2: II, 16, 43, 46; Zuni, Cushing, 132, 429.

They went south and got a red-tailed hawk (*wę'paimuna*),[1] a little one from the nest. They fed him good meat and he grew up with them. One day their mother was so busy preparing for the meeting she was going to that she neglected Hawk. He was hungry. He complained to the boys, "Brothers, our father just threw me some spoiled hard meat. I would not eat it. I will tell you about our parents, they are not good people. They are witch people."

Their aunt was sick; she died, and they buried her that same day. Their mother always put the boys to sleep early. Red-tailed Hawk told his brothers he would flap his wings and wake them up and they were to call their four uncles. This day when the boys came home with a deer their parents did not pay much attention to them. Their mother sat there with her hair washed. "My children you have been out in the mountain all day, you are tired, better go to sleep!" The boys lay down to sleep. Their parents left the house to go to their kiva at Sunflower stalk place. (It had a hatch made of wire-weeds, *hualane*.)[2] Red-tailed Hawk flapped his wings and the boys called their uncles. Red-tailed Hawk told them, "Our parents have gone to their kiva; they are going to exhume our aunt and turn her into a deer. All of you go! I will give you some medicine and as you go inside spit it east, north, west, south, to keep the dogs quiet." They hid themselves under the hatch of the kiva of the witch people. They had a wheel and when each went through it he became eagle, owl, coyote, hawk. Then they went out. When they came back they went through the wheel again and became human. They brought back with them meat, buckskin and other things. They brought the dead body and laid her down in the middle. They un-wrapped her and took off all her clothes, leaving her naked. One said, "This is the place I shot her." Another said, "This is the place." Each one sucked from the place he shot her. One sucked porcupine quills from her heart and that brought her to life. She sat up and said, "How tired I was! I slept long!" They bathed her and dressed her and just as they were to send her through the wheel to turn her into a deer (for them to eat), the boys and two uncles went into the kiva to club to death all there, all but their parents. Two uncles stayed outside to kill those who tried to escape. The boys said to their parents, "Father and mother, this is the way you have been treating us. When we were supporting you and get-ting the game clean from the mountain we never thought you were doing such things; and we hope that from now on, as we have killed all

[1] x^{w}ˌępʻˌay-?, tail-red-? (T).
[2] h'uolonạ (T).

these bad people, we shall live together clean. All the people know
what you have been doing, and we are ashamed of you. Now we are
going to meet our father Sun." As they got ready to go they sang:

> hi hi a a a ha a
> hihi awa
> tǫyukya
> > they are crying
> kakakumki[1]
> > to care for mother
> tamkakumki
> > to care for father
> maiłatęyi[2]
> > lazy withstand

As they sat each on a wing of Hawk all the people came out to see them.
Their mother said, "My husband, you better go out to see what is
happening. I can hear their voices far off." The boys had told their uncles
to blow corn pollen to give them strength to reach the sun. Whatever
their mother offered, eagle or turkey feathers, fell back to the ground.
They went up and up. Their parents returned to their room and sat
sadly by the fire. The boys reached their father who was happy to see
them. He said, "I am not a man to stay in one place; I am travelling
night and day. I will place you the elder to my left and you the younger to
my right."[3] Hawk did not belong there; they had to feed him and let
him return to earth to be happy in the woods as he had been before.
Their parents died of sad swelling. (They were so sad they swelled from
the feet up.)

Variant (Sun Begets Twins)

People were living at the Canyon of the Red Willows. There was a girl
also living there, she lived alone. Young men were very desirous to be
her lovers, but she always refused them. She went everywhere alone,
without the company of any one. She would grind corn and she sang her
own song. The boys wanted to come in to sing for her; but she always
denied them. Then one day she was grinding corn all day, at noon she
stopped grinding, she sat at a little window where the sun shone in. She
played with the sunshine. While playing she wanted to sleep. The sun

---

[1] ka- mother, -mki, for (T).
[2] m'ayła-, lazy + ? (T).
[3] Isleta, the Sun's sons are red stars next the Sun (Parsons 7: 342); Tewa, the sons
become, one the winter sun, the other the summer sun (Parsons 4: 101-2).

was striking her hard on her body. She said, "How good and loving is the heat of the sun." She had her corn meal on her grinding stone; but it seemed to her she could not go back to finish grinding. She said, "I will go on staying here. How good I feel playing in the sunshine. My father Sun (*ntomena tulena*),[1] how good and kind you are to me! Is there any way I can go up to your home?" Then somebody whispered behind her, saying, "You better not say that. The Sun is apt to make you sick. By and by you will have a baby by him." So she removed from the sunshine, but she always wanted to go back. Finally in a short time she got full and she had twins (*kuiyuna*),[2] boy and girl. Those are the ones who live in the Sun house, in the west, in Sun House Mountain. Sun took them. (The rest of this story the story teller said he did not know.)[3]

17. Testing for the Baby's Father[4]

Magpie-tail boy was living with his daughters, Blue Corn girl and Yellow Corn girl, and the people (*toinema*) (i. e. of Taos) were living. And people asked them to marry, but they would not take them. Blue Corn girl was the elder. She got a baby without anybody knowing her. The people said to look for the father of the little boy who was growing very fast. So the people called her to find out the father of the child. They called Magpie-tail boy, too, with his two daughters and they asked him who was the father of the child. Magpie-tail boy said he did not know how she got the baby. They sat all around and they told Blue Corn girl to put the child in the middle to see which man he would go to. The boy paid no attention to the men, he just played in the middle. Just when the sun came up he ran to the place the sun shone on. When he ran they all said, "He is the son of our father the Sun." The little boy began to sing and it began to rain. While he was singing, he was dressed up nicely in buckskin. The rain filled up the house and the men said, "Please, our son, make the rain stop." But he would not listen. And they stood up because the house was full of water. He kept on singing and he began to climb up the ladder, and the house was full of water and drowned those people who had been mean to his mother. And from those who survived come the people who are living now.

[1] antǫm'ena t'ùl'ena (T).
[2] Boy twins are referred to as *tolu'na,* sun baby.
[3] Compare Tewa, Parsons 4: 99.
[4] Compare San Juan, Parsons 4: 102 ff.; San Ildefonso, Espinosa, 114; Cochiti, Benedict 1: 58-59; Lipan Apache, Opler 2: 187-188; Pawnee, Dorsey 2: 307-308.

Variant[1]

A long time ago there lived some Apache at *piileh* (sunshine hillside) and Bear also lived a distance from *piileh*. There were two Apache girls, beautiful girls. As usual, the young men wanted to be their lovers, but all the young men were unsuccessful suitors. At one time people discovered a bear foot mark on the road. The bear was from *ebbaba*[2] (Wild cherry creek). This bear had the magic power of changing from a bear to human when approaching an Indian's house. He would change to human at night and go courting the two girls. Unexpectedly the girls bore bear babies. When the people heard of the newborn babies they all became jealous and decided to find the father of the twin bears. The Apache chief notified his people to call a gathering of several different kinds of wild animals, deer, elk, rabbits, bears, coyote. All these wild people came to the call, in excitement. The twin bear babies were brought in. The babies at once went in search of their father. They jumped up on Deer's lap, they jumped to Elk, they jumped to Rabbit, they jumped to Coyote. Fifthly they jumped to Bear and they stayed on Bear's lap. The babies had found their father. Bear was recognized as the father of the two Apache girls' babies.

The Apache and Bear began to discuss holding a race to a mountain which stood towards the setting sun—Coyote Ear Peak. They were to go around it five times and back to the starting point. Two boys, antelopes, were to be the runners for the Apache, and the baby bears for Bear. The stake was to exterminate the loser. The ensuing morning before sunrise they started the race. The baby bears looked husky and heavy at the start. The antelope boys looked swift. They went to the mothers of the baby bears who had their "luck," power to win the race. They saw them coming back. Bear old man said, "My sons are coming ahead, approaching closer and closer." The bear boys were coming ahead, they got first to the starting point. So the bear boys won the race and remained together with their mothers to live in peace.

18. Spider Man Impregnates Blue Corn Girl

Tołakaptsana[3] lived at the cottonwood and Blue Corn was his daughter. Everybody wished Blue Corn to be in love with them and everybody

---

[1] Written by a townsman.
[2] ə̀b'ep'ò, wildberry water (T).
[3] See p. 30.

courted her; but she did not want to marry any one. She refused everybody. Spider man was also living about there. Spider man made up his mind to try for her. Spider man was angry that she refused everybody. Spider said to her, "I will see if you can be my wife." He watched her all the time. One day Blue Corn girl went to the river for water. She had a long handled gourd, she was filling her jar with that cup. Then Spider man (*paöyatsöanana*)[1] was by the river watching her, so he dropped a little white ball[2] into the river, to float along on the water to where Blue Corn girl was filling her jar. She did not notice the white ball and took the water and with it the white ball. She went back to the house with the water. In a short time Blue Corn girl had a baby boy. Her mother knew she never had a man. "Why should my daughter have a baby?" Then Tołakaptsana went on top of the house like the crier, and sang a song for calling all to find out who the baby's father was. [The song was forgotten but the words were: *töibata* (east) *to'ta* (north) *toinawa* (west) *toikwita* (south), *wiwa töibata*[3] (again east), peoples of different nations, come to my house!] Then very quickly they gathered. Tołakaptsana said to them, "My daughter has a baby. You people know my daughter did not want to have any man, but now she has a baby. I wanted to find out, that is why I have called you." They were all sitting in Tołakaptsana's room. As the baby grew very fast he was crawling about now. The boy began to crawl up to the lap of everybody. He took a look and then dropped down to the ground, and went to the next man, and the next, all around where they were sitting, looking for his father. Then he came to Spider man, he jumped on his lap, there he lay on the lap of Spider man. So he found his father. Then the other boys and men went out laughing and mocking at the girl, "So many handsome young men were courting you so long, and were refused, and now this queer looking man is your husband." Spider lived at Spider house. He took his wife there and there they lived.

19. Echo Boy

There were a man and a woman who had no children. The man would go every day and get wood on his back. Every day in the mountain he heard some one singing and playing the drum. On the fourth day where he chopped the wood was a hole. In it was a little boy dressed in white deerskin and nice moccasins with mockingbird feathers in his hair. The

---

[1] p'ò?¡ǫyos'ɔonena (T).
[2] The egg he carries behind his body.
[3] t'ɘyboto, t'ɘwto, t'ɘynạwạ, t'ɘykʷit'o, wiwa t'ɘyboto (T).

man said to him, "What a pretty boy you are, and you are living in this wood. I will take you to live with us." The little boy said the same thing, "What a pretty boy you are, and you are living in this wood. I will take you to live with us." He wore his blanket belted in and he put the little boy in his blanket, while all the time the little boy kept up singing and dancing. He went home without wood. His wife said, "Why did you not bring wood"?—"Because I found a little boy." And the little boy repeated, "Because I found a little boy." Whatever they said, he repeated, and he was dancing and singing. The woman said, "It is night time. Let me put away your clothes because you might soil them." The little boy said, "It is night time. Let me put away your clothes because you might soil them." The woman laid down a buffalo hide for him to sleep on. "Now you go to bed!" The little boy said, "Now you go to bed!" All night the little boy danced and sang, and they could not sleep. In the morning the woman said, "We can not do anything with him." The little boy repeated, "We can not do anything with him." The woman said, "You better take him back where you found him." The little boy repeated, "You better take him back where you found him." So the man put him in his blanket where he kept up dancing. The man took him where he found him, and there the little boy told him he was not a little boy, he was *kaiuuna*.[1] That was why he was dancing and singing. He said to him if he needed clothing to come and ask him and to tell the people to come to that place[2] to ask him for whatever clothing they needed.

20. *Yellow Corn Woman and Blue Corn Woman Jilt Shell Flower Youth*

People were living (*itai'tööna*)[3] at the cottonwood. Yellow Corn woman and Blue Corn woman went for water. Arriving at the river, they met *kuichutöwia*[4] (Black Shirt boy) and he wanted to be their lover. He asked them to be his wives. Before him they had another young man named *hąnłapöwia*,[5] Big-Shell Flower boy. When Big-Shell Flower boy discovered their promise to Black Shirt boy, Big-Shell Flower boy worked his great power (*napienma*) and turned the two girls into rattlesnakes (*pętsuna*).[6] He rolled a turquoise wheel over them, and turned them into snakes. That's the end of that.

[1] ʔ - ùʔ'una, ʔ - little one (T). A spirit, see p. 16-17. Compare Tewa, *kaye*.
[2] At the foot of Taos Peak.
[3] it'ˌoyt'ˈəʔąnạ (T).
[4] ʔ- cùd-ʔ'əwyu, ʔ- shirt-boy (T). The tale name for black beetle (*pumena*).
[5] hˌǫłopòbʔ'əwyu, shell-big-flower-boy (T).
[6] p'ęcunạ (T).

21. The Corn Girls Give their Milk to Fly Old Man :
Morning Star Kills the Redheads

Yellow Corn girl and Blue Corn girl were living. They were very pretty and the boys from Taos came to ask them to marry and brought them moccasins and belts, but the girls would not take them. That Water man (*pakölaana*)[1] came to ask them to marry him. They would not marry him. He went and told the "Mother"[2] and they talked together about what they would do to punish those girls. Then the "Mother" told the girls to go and look for seven red-headed men (*pipaiyenemo*,[3] head red[4]) and if they did not find them not to return to the pueblo.[5] They baked their bread for lunch and they started. They were crying. When they were away seven days they found no water to drink, the rivers were dried up and where there were springs was a little wormy water. They sucked it up with their mouth as babies suck. And they were sitting down crying day and night. Then Fly old man (*pu̧tu̧ti*)[6] came and asked them for milk. He said he would help them if they would give him milk. They squeezed their nipples and a little milk came out. Fly old man said, "Now I will go to Elder brother, to Morning (East) Star, to ask him to help you." He went to Morning Star and asked him to help the girls to kill the seven redheads. Morning Star said, "Yes, I am sorry for them. If you do not tell anybody in the world, I will help them." And Fly said, "Yes, I will not tell, because they gave me milk, and I will give my life for them." Morning Star said, "We will do this work at midnight so nobody will know about it. You tell Yellow Corn girl and Blue Corn girl to be up at midnight to look at the star coming down to the earth.[7] And they must go where the star comes down and he will kill the seven

1   p'ȯ- ? -łoʔ'ona, water- ?-big one (T).
2   Town chief (?) or perhaps chief of the Black Eyes.
3   p'̩ip'̩ay'enemą, head-red ones (T).
4   In Spanish, *gente cabeza colorado*, (Espinosa, 127). Inferably this was an early term for Spaniards or enemies (compare Isleta, Parsons 7: 203), as it was in Mexico. Aztecs represented enemies with red hair. Pueblos put red hair on Navaho kachina masks. Compare Kiowa, Parsons 6: 78 ff. See pp. 84-85.
5   Reminiscent of the Tewa (Hano) girl, Pohaha, who was sent to war for misbehaving (Parsons 4: 191).
6   p'̩ul'uli (T).
7   This may refer to a belief that East Star comes down at midnight just as it is believed at Isleta that the Sun comes down at midday. Compare the Isletan ceremony for bringing down the stars. At Isleta and Taos the stars are pointedly associated with war (Parsons 7: 342; Parsons 10: 108).

and they will get their heads." So the girls were up all night, watching and waiting. They did not want even the birds to know because they might tell on the star for helping them. All the birds, the insects, and Water had been told not to help them. When the star came down they ran to see what happened. There they found the seven red-headed men dead. They took off their heads. They got a long pole to put them on the top and carry them home. When they turned back, the water was flowing and the birds were singing. When they got to *po'tsiuaka*[1] they made a fire, and the "Mother" went on top of the house and called out to the people to go out and meet the girls. "Now we are going to have that big dance (*nötahöa'wa'e*),"[2] he said. Then the people went to meet them. They had the pole with the seven heads. Their "Mother" and the people went to the girls' house and told them from now on not to be unkind and that no matter how poor a man was who came to ask them to marry him they should marry him.

22. Escape up the Tree[3]

The Yellow House people[4] were travelling. They came to a lake. They stopped there. To reach the deep water they put down a buffalo head to step on. The chief's wife was a goodlooking woman (*łiukupimęena*).[5] She picked up her water basket and went for water. When she reached the lake she looked at the head and said, "My father, in the past what a goodlooking man you were! I would like to have seen you when you were alive. What a pity you are being trampled in this mud!" As she finished speaking up sprang a big white buffalo. He said, "I am the man you speak of. I am White Buffalo chief. I want to take you with me. Sit on my head between my horns!" She left her water basket right there. The sun was going down, and his wife did not come. The chief said, "Something has happened to my wife. Better I go and see." When he got to the lake he saw the basket lying there. He looked around and he saw his wife's track and the track of a big buffalo. The track was toward the

[1] p'ò- water + c¡iw- ? + ?oga, at (T). It is "an insect which is noisy, greasy, and black, appearing in June; Spanish, *cicale*." At *po'tsiuaka*, kaolin is collected.

[2] nąt¡ohɔowá?i, we dance-big-that have (T).

[3] San Juan, Parsons 4: 116-118; Zuni, Parsons 1: 235-240; Kiowa, Parsons 6: 76-78; Crow, Lowie, 204-205, 213; Cheyenne, Kroeber 1: 182-183; Wichita, Dorsey 1: 18; comparative, Parsons 3, including parallels from Northern Shoshone, Gros Ventres, Arapaho, Kutenai, Siberia.

[4] "Perhaps xiwana, Apache." x'iwana (T).

[5] łiwk'u- ?-mę?'ena, woman-good- ?-the one who (T).

east. He said, "The buffalo head that was here took away my wife." He went back to his camp and for many days he was making arrows. When he had enough arrows he told his people he was going to find his wife. He started and came to the house of Spider old woman. He almost stepped on her house. She said, "Sho! sho! sho! my grandchild, don't step on me! Grandchild, you are Apache chief living happily, what are you doing around here?"—"Grandmother, I am looking for my wife. Buffalo chief took her away."—"Yes, grandchild, he is a powerful person (*t'aipiasii*).[1]"—"Grandmother, can you help me?"—"Yes, I will give you medicine and you go to Gopher old woman." He started on, and on the plain he came to Gopher's house. Said Gopher old woman, "What are you doing around here? You are chief of the Apache, living happily. Why are you around here"?—"Yes, grandmother, I was living happily when my wife went to get water. Buffalo stole her. I am going after her. I would like to ask you for help." Gopher said, "My grandson, your wife has as husband a powerful man. He is White Buffalo chief. She is their female-in-law (*söayeina*)[2]. When they go to sleep she is in the middle and they are lying close around her. Her dress is trimmed with elk teeth and it makes such a noise that it will be difficult to get her out. You go to the edge of where they lie, and I will do the rest." The Buffalo had her dancing and they sang:

> ya he a he
> ya he iya he
> ya he e ya
> he ya hina he
> hina ye ne
> he mah ne

When Apache chief got near the buffalo he spat out his medicine, and all the buffalo went to sleep. Gopher old woman made a hole to the ear of the girl and said, "I have come for you. Your husband is waiting outside the herd." The girl said, "My husband is a powerful man. My dress is made of elk teeth and it makes such a noise it will wake up my husband." Gopher told her to gather her dress up under her arms. Then Gopher went ahead and they worked their way through the buffalo. There her husband was waiting. He said, "I have come for you. You are my wife and I want to take you back."—"Yes, we have to hasten to a safe place, because the man who took me is a powerful man. He is White Buffalo chief." The plain was large. They came to three cottonwood trees.

[1] t'ˌoyp'iasiʔi, person-mean-that (T).
[2] s'əoyiʔ'ina (T).

When they came there they could feel the earth trembling. White Buffalo awoke and said, "Get up, Buffalo! Some one took my wife!" They followed the track toward the cottonwood trees. Apache chief said to the cottonwood, "Brother, the buffalo are coming after us, I want you to hide me." The tree said, "Go to your next brother! I am old and soft." He went to the next tree. "Brother, the buffalo are coming after us, I want you to hide me!" The tree said, "Go to your next brother." He went to the third tree, a young tree with one branch. "Apache chief, you can come up and I will help you." After they were up she said she wanted to urinate. He folded up his buffalo hide and told her to urinate on it. It leaked through. The buffalo were passing, the dust was rising and the earth was trembling. In the rear were a shabby old buffalo and a little buffalo. As they came under the tree the little buffalo said, "Grandfather, I can smell the water of our daughter-in-law." Then they looked up and saw them in the tree. The old buffalo said, "Grandchild, you are fast. Run on and tell them, and each will tell the next one." Then they all turned back. Each one in turn butted the tree, and Apache chief began to shoot them. Then White Buffalo chief butted the tree. The cottonwood tree was nearly down. Crow was calling above them, kaw kaw kaw! Apache chief could not kill White Buffalo chief. Apache chief said to Crow, "Why are you calling out when I am in so bad a way?"—"I came to tell you to shoot him in the anus. That is where his life is." Then he shot him in the anus and killed him. They came down from the tree and by a little fire he started to butcher the buffalo. The tears came down her cheek. "Are you crying because I am butchering White Buffalo?"—"No, I am crying from the smoke." He kept on butchering. "You are crying!"—"No, it is just the smoke." He looked again at her. "You are crying! After all our trouble you still want this man! Now you die with him! He got his bow and arrow and shot her. He said, "I am Apache chief, chief of a roaming tribe. I will roam over these plains watching the earth, and if any woman leave her husband what I have done may be done to her."

Variant

There the Yellow House people were living. There was a spring and it was mushy around it. A buffalo head lay there for them to step on. A girl went for water and she stepped on the head. She said, "How beautiful you must have been when you were living! How much country you must have travelled! And here now you are being trampled on!" Just as she was picking up her water bag, up jumped a fine big buffalo. "I want to carry you home," he said. "Sit on my head, it is soft." So she sat on his head. When he reached his herd they put her in the middle, with the buffalo all around. They gave her a beautifu dress of elk teeth. They had her dancing every night[1] and they would sing:

> he hi hi ya he ya
> he ya hai ne ne
> hine he ne ne ye

When her father went to look for her he saw her water bag and no buffalo head. He got all his braves and tracked the buffalo. They had to pass by the buffalo to get to her. He chewed some medicine and spat it over them to keep them quiet. He said, "My daughter, I have come for you."—"Well, father, how can I go? My dress makes so much noise." She held up her dress and they passed out of the herd and went to their horses and reached their home.[2]

23. Variant: Rolling Skull :[3] Magic Flight[4]

Wiba[5] (once) there lived a band of Apache at *naötsulbaba*[6] (Yellow Leaf creek). Two young girls went for water at the spring with jars (*toa'muluna*) (basketry, with greens inside) on their backs. When they got to the spring there was an old buffalo skull. Elder sister (*t'otona*)[7] said to younger sister (*pai'yuuna*),[8] "This buffalo skull when he was alive I guess he was a nice young man. If he came to life now I would marry him," said elder sister. Then younger sister said, "Don't say that! You always say what you ought not to say, anyway." As they filled their jars of water and started away from the spring some one spoke out from the spring and said, "Yes, here I am. This is the way I look. Now I will marry you, as you said." And the buffalo got the girl up on his back and started away. And the younger sister started for the camp with the two jars of water.

---

[1] Here the narrator would have a little girl get up and dance.
[2] The narrator was aware that he had forgotten the latter part of the tale.
[3] Compare Zuni, Benedict 2: I, 55, 171-174; Kiowa, Parsons 6: 71-74; Cheyenne, Kroeber 1: 184-185; Pawnee, Dorsey 2: 116-118; widespread distribution among other Plains Indians.
[4] Combined with Rolling Skull in the Kiowa tale also. Compare Zuni, Boas 1: 83. Distribution worldwide.
[5] w'ibo (T).
[6] nạʔɔc'ulp'òbo (place)-leaf-yellow-water-at (T).
[7] t̩ut'una (T).
[8] p'̩ayuʔ'una (T).

When she got to the camp, she was asked where her sister was. Then she said that when they got to the spring an old buffalo skull was lying there and then her elder sister said, "'If this was alive and a nice young man, I would marry him.' I asked her why she said that and she replied, '*Hoiho* (anyway).' So we got the water and started back, when some one spoke and said, 'Here I am, this is the way I look. Now, as you said, I will marry you.' So he took her up on his neck behind his horns and carried her away. They went east. And I came." Then the Apache chief (*xiwałauwana*)[1] went outside and hollered out to his people that his daughter was taken away by a buffalo. He said, "You women do not think carefully before you speak. So all you young men make ready your bows and arrows, we will go in search of my daughter." So in about four days the young men started out in search of the girl. And the chief himself went, in the direction of the east. On getting to a certain place, he sat down; tired and weary, he lay down to sleep. Then in his dream somebody touched him from underground and said to him, "*Anukaiye*[2] (my son), what are you doing here?" He answered and said, "The buffalo took my daughter away from our camp when she went for water, and I am looking for her." Gopher said, "You will find your daughter. She is not very far from here. She is married to the buffalo chief. She always goes with the band who guard her very closely. At noonday they all lie around, and she is in the centre with her husband. Her dress is a buckskin with small bells. Whenever she moves, they sound. Then all the buffalo wake up. So it will be very hard for you. But I will give you something, some medicine for you to spat out in the four directions so they can go sound asleep. When the buffalos' eyes are open they are asleep, when they have their eyes shut they are awake. Then you can go there and go right through the centre to get where your daughter is and tell her to lift up her dress very quietly, up to the waist and then take her out from the centre, stepping in the spaces between the buffalo, until you get away from them." He went and got his daughter out and they started for some cottonwood trees. One little buffalo woke up, he did not see his female-in-law and he called to them. "My female-in-law is not here!" said the little buffalo. "She is gone." Then they all woke up and got up and started to chase. To the first cottonwood tree the Apache chief reached he said, "My father, take me up on you for the buffalo are chasing me because I took my daughter away from them." The cottonwood tree said to the man, "I am not strong enough, go to the

---

[1] x͓iwał͓owaʔ'ana (T).

[2] ą̇nʔùk'͓'oyi (T).

next." He went to the next big cottonwood tree. He said to the cotton-wood tree, "My father, take me up!"—"Yes, I will take you up." So they went up, on the top. When they were sitting up there, they saw the dust from the buffalo running. Pretty soon the buffalo approached. The buffalo chief was coming ahead of the others and the buffalo got under the tree where they were sitting very quietly on top. They were hooking the tree, trying to break it down, but the tree was too big and strong. They all passed on. Way behind were coming the little buffalo (*tsoalena,*[1] meaning yellowish, as is the yearling) and his grandmother. So they got to the tree and stopped and rested under it. Then the girl said, "I am nearly bursting, I want to make water."—"Wait, stop a while! The old woman buffalo and the little buffalo are under the tree."—"But I am nearly bursting." So before the old woman buffalo and the little buffalo went away she made water, and it dropped on the back of the little buffalo, and the little buffalo exclaimed, "Some thing has fallen on my back." Then he started backward a little past the tree. He looked up, putting his hand up before his eyes, and saw his sister-in-law way on top of the tree. Then he told his grandmother, "Grandmother, there is my sister-in-law way up."—"What is the matter with you," said the old woman, "your sister-in-law is not about here."—"Anyway, that is she up there." Then the old woman started back away from the cottonwood tree, looking up to the tree, raising her hand to her forehead. She saw them sitting up on the top of the tree. She said to the little buffalo, "Go and run and overtake the buffalos, your elder brothers!" So he ran as hard as he could run to catch his brothers. He caught up with them and said to them, "My elder brothers, my sister-in-law is way over there on the cottonwood tree." So they came back. When they got to the cotton-wood tree, as they came they hooked the tree. Then the Apache shot at the buffalo chief with his bow and arrow. He killed him. As the buffalo chief fell dead all the other buffalos went away. They got down from the tree. Then the girl sat down against her man, turning her back to her father and crying. Her father said to her, "Why do you cry?" The man skinned the buffalo. While he was skinning him the girl kept on crying. Then the Apache turned to his girl, shot with his bow and arrow and killed her. He laid her by the side of the dead buffalo and left them there lying dead. He took only the loin of the meat and went back to his camp, to his people.

He had been a long time away. He had two children, one girl and one boy. When he got back to the camp he told his little son and daughter

[1]   c'ɂolena (T).

that he had killed their mother and a buffalo, built a fire and set the buffalo head and the woman's head on the fire to cook—"Way up there. So in the morning you can go and eat the meat." In the morning the little boy and his sister went to look for the place. They saw the fire burning, and the smoke. When they reached there, there were two heads. They were hungry and tired. They sat down close to the fire and reached their hands over to the fire. One of the heads whispered to them, "sh—h!" But they paid no attention, as they were hungry. They got the meat. All the time they were reaching out, the whisper came to them, "sh—h!" They ate until they had enough. Then they started back home. And the skull of their mother followed them. "My children" (*anumuwaina*),[1] the skull said, "You can not get away from me, you are my children." They got to their camp. They told their father, when they got to the place and reached for the meat some one whispered to them, "sh—h!" Their father said, "Yes, that was your mother, I killed her because she cried when I killed the buffalo." Then the little boy and his sister went out to play in the field. Then the Apache chief told the people to pack up and start away, somewhere else. So everybody packed up and started away. When the little boy and his sister came back to camp they found nobody, no fire, nothing to eat, only one old dog was lying on the ashes. The old dog said to the boy and his sister, "My grandchildren, I waited for you, they kicked me and wanted me to get out from here, but I did not mind them. 'Til you came back I lay here." So he got up, it was late in the evening. The children had no way to get fire. But the old dog told them, "Never mind, I have the fire." He got up. He had the fire in the centre of his paw. So they picked up sticks and built a fire. By his luck (*hǫka*)[2] as medicine man (*towa'yega*) he obtained some food for the two children to eat. So they stayed there that night. The dog was very old, he could not walk.

So they started out along the tracks of their people. Along the road they sat down very tired and sad. Then Gopher old woman came out to them and said, "My grandchildren, do not worry and be sad. Your father is married to another woman and they are starving; but you will be better off than they. Do not pity them, never think of them or their starvation! Here is this bundle for you and luck for you to make your living. So you can use it praying for your daily bread." She gave him an awl, a brush, and a looking-glass to protect them. She said to them, "When they are after you, first you throw this awl, next the brush,

[1] aṇamʔùwáʔiṇa (T).
[2] hǫ- + ? (T). Probably power (see pp. 70, 150) which is often translated as luck.

lastly the looking-glass." They thanked the old woman and went on. As they went on they saw smoke from fire. They went over to it, thinking it was their people. They found at the camp fire a very old woman, grey-headed and ugly looking. The old woman said, "My grandchildren, you are welcome, come to the camp!" So they stayed there. At nightfall, as they were tired and hungry, they went to sleep. Then the old woman sat by the fire and as the little boy was looking through a hole in his blanket he saw the old woman raise up her dress. She was scratching her leg. Soon her leg swelled up big. Then she got up and walked to where the little girl lay down asleep. But the boy was not asleep. So when the old woman came up to them the boy threw off his blanket and said to the old woman, "My grandmother, do not kill us! We will bring you water and wood and live with you." Then the old woman said, "Get up, then!" So the boy got up. When the day came, the old woman said to the boy, "Bring me water!" He got the water bag and went to the river and got water and gave it to the old woman. The old woman was very angry because the boy brought some nice, good, cold water. The old woman said to the boy, "This is not the kind of water I use. This is not good. Go out and get me good water! I do not drink that." Then the boy went out crying and sorrowful. The old woman called the boy back. "Go and get me wood!" The boy brought her some nice sticks of wood. The old woman said, "*Etawö!*[1] I do not use that kind of wood." So the boy went out again, very sad and crying. He sat down in the middle of the field crying. Crow came flying around above him. Crow said to him, "My grandchild, do not be sorry, do not cry! Your grandmother is not human; she is a dead woman, once she was a big witch, so she does not like the good water we drink nor the wood we burn. I will tell you what kind of water she likes to drink and what kind of wood she likes to burn. She likes the old waste water of the pond that has been there for years and years mixed with bullfrog dung, that is the kind of water she drinks. And the wood she uses for her fire is dry sunflower stalk, that is what she burns." Then the boy said, "Thank you, my grandfather!" Crow flew away. He went back to the old woman. His younger sister was still there. Then, informed by Crow, he got his water bag and went for water, to an old pond of waste water. He filled up his bag and brought the water to his grandmother, and said, "Grandmother, I have brought you water." Grandmother said, "Let me see what kind of water! This is the kind of water I drink, my good grandchild." She was very pleased. Then the next day the boy went for wood. He got dry sunflower stalks. When he

[1] "Given something you do not like, you say *etawö!*" See p. 71.

got back he said, "Grandmother, I have brought you wood." The grand-mother was pleased. "This is the kind of wood I use." Then the boy said, "Grandmother, my younger sister wants to make water."—"Let her make water right there where she is."—"No, grandmother, if she does, it will become a very big lake."—"Go outside then, not far from the door." Then the little girl made a dump outside the door. She made the dump talk (i.e. grunting as when a child has a movement), and they ran away. The old woman said, "Why do you stay so long? Hurry up!" Then she went to the door and put out her hand to grab the girl, but nobody was there in the doorway. So she started out to chase the children. She was exclaiming, "Oh *pasałana*![1] you can not get away from me. You are mine." When she was about to overtake the children, the children knew it. The boy had his younger sister on his back. When they felt that the old woman was approaching them, the boy placed the awl in the trail, the sharp point up. When the old woman saw that, she thought it was the boy. Then she grabbed at the awl. Then her hand caught on the awl. Then she pulled out her hand and it was bloody, she thrust out her other hand and that was fastened to the awl, and her feet were caught on the awl and were all bloody. Meanwhile the children went on. The old woman exclaimed, "Such small children, yet you know what to do!" Then she got out of her trouble and ran all bloody in the direction of the children. When the boy and girl felt the old woman approaching them, they threw the brush in the trail. Then all kinds of bushes sprang up, shaggy and thorny, so she could not pass through them. But she tried to go through. Her dress was all torn, her body scratched. She was in the midst of the bushes, her face was badly scratched that delayed her a long time. So the boy and his younger sister were quite a distance ahead. Then the old woman got out of her trouble and exclaimed, "Oh *pasałana*! You children are so little and yet you know the tricks! You are mine. You can not get away from me." So she ran. Again the boy and his younger sister felt the old woman overtaking them. Then he threw the looking-glass on the trail. It appeared an immense plain of ice, so slippery that she could not pass over it. As she ran, she ran onto it. She fell down on the ice. She got up and fell again. She could hardly walk a step. As she got up, she fell down again. She was trying to walk, but it was im-possible. Before she got half way across the ice, her flesh was torn, her head was broken, her limbs were cut into small pieces. That was the last of her. She died again then, a second time. Then the children escaped, they knew she would not come after them again. Then the boy

[1] p̣asał'ana, "a bad word" (T). "Scolding word." Possibly, ghost big.

and his younger sister came near to where their people were living. The boy had been given by the old woman power (*hǫka*) to be a great hunter. (This was his fourth gift.) So when they came near his people he did not want to join his people. His people were almost starving, no game to kill. On the side of the boy was big game, buffalo. So he had plenty of meat, for himself and his younger sister. His people heard about it, that the two children, once their children, were living near them, very happy, with plenty to eat. Then they knew them as their children. But the boy denied them. He did not want them to come to where they lived, nor to go where they lived. So they lived there happily. People used to say that the Apache used to live at Yellow Leaf Creek. People who want to live a happy life should ask for fortune (*ahǫ'ma*)[1] to be given to them by us.

24. Rolling Skull: Their Half Brother Kills the Coyote Children

A long time ago the Apache lived at Sun House Mountain (*tultönpianaka*).[2] An Apache man went to hunt buffalo with his wife out in the plain. They found bunches of buffalo. He killed one buffalo and his wife came where he killed the buffalo. His wife sat nearby while he was skinning the buffalo. He turned around and looked at his wife, she was crying. He said to her, "Why do you cry?" The woman said nothing. So he went on skinning the buffalo. He finished skinning, he cut it apart, he cut the legs and the shoulders. He looked at his wife again, she was still crying. The man got angry, he took his bow and arrows and killed his wife. He cut off her head. He built a fire and put the head to roast. Then he packed the buffalo meat on his horse and went back home, leaving the head of his wife roasting on the fire. He got home with the meat. Then he told his children that he had killed a buffalo and left the head roasting on the fire, way out in the plain, on the river. And he said to his children, "In the morning you and your younger sister will go over there on the plain by the river to eat the meat." So the next morning about breakfast time the boy and his younger sister went out in the direction their father told them. They saw the fire still burning, they reached the place. There was the head on the fire roasting. As they were hungry he set his

---

[1] ah'ǫmạ, you are lucky: ạ, second singular prefix, h'ǫ- stem be lucky, -mạ, resultative suffix (T). Finding a thing, perhaps a purse, away from town, or, if visiting, being pitied by one's hosts and given presents, such experience is *ahǫ'ma*. Compare term for medicine bundle, p. 83. n 1.

[2] t'ùlt'ʲɔnp'ʲianʔogạ, sun-house-mountain-at (T.) in the range where Sun travels north to south, and back.

younger sister close by and they began to go near to eat the meat. As they stretched their hands to the meat, a whisper came sh—! They paid no attention, the elder brother said, "Who is talking there? We are going to eat anyway, we are hungry." They reached again for pieces of meat and the whisper again came sh—! The roasting skull said, "My children, do not eat me! I am your mother. Your father killed me and roasted me." They stopped and he put his younger sister on his back and started back toward home, crying. Then the skull followed her children. "You are my children, you can not get far away from me. I must get you." So the boy kept running with his younger sister on his back. They came to the river, a very deep river, and wide. It looked to him as if they could not cross. They went along the bank, and on the edge of the bank lay Pâköɫeana. He asked him if he could take them across the river. Pâköɫeana said, "Yes, my grandchildren, come on, ride on my head, by my horn." So they rode on his head and he took them across the river. Then he said, "Now, my grandchildren, your mother is coming after you, chasing you. While you are going far ahead she will come to me to take her across, but I will make time and delay her." So he jumped into the water and crossed to where he had been. He lay there. After a while the skull got there where he was lying and Skull said, "You yellow round eye, come on and take me across the river before my children get very far!" Pâköɫeana said to Skull, "Come on, look over my head for lice." She looked for lice in his head. When she was looking, spreading his hair, she found a great big bullfrog—that was Pâköɫeana's louse. Then Skull said, "Oh you dirty (*ötawa*)! This is not lice. I do not eat them." [Much laughter by the narrator.] Then she picked one off, lay it on the stone and hit it with a small stone to crack as if she was biting with her teeth. Then Pâköɫeana said to her, "*Ötötötötötötö!*" and scratching, "here is where I itch." Then she looked again and found another bullfrog and cracked it on the stone. Then Skull got cross and said to Pâköɫeana, "Hurry up, you yellow round eye! My children are going too far ahead of me. I want to catch them. Hurry up! Put me across the river!"—"Then come on and sit down on my horn."—"But your horn is too sharp."— "Then come on and sit down on my head!"—"No, you have too many lice on your head."—"Then come sit on my back!" So she sat on his back. Then he jumped in the river, swimming. About the middle of the river he sank down into the water, and threw Skull into the water. And then Pâköɫeanə got out and watched her. Skull never got out of the river, but went under the water and disappeared. That ended her chase of the children.

Then the boy and his younger sister as they were going along the road came to the hole of a gopher. As they sat there, Gopher old woman came out and asked them where they came from? They told her that their father told them that he killed a buffalo and put the head to roast on the fire and for them to go the next morning to eat that meat way out in the plain by the river. "So we went there and saw the fire burning and we were hungry and tried to eat the meat off the skull, then the skull whispered, 'Sh——! my children, I am your mother, don't eat me!' So I put my younger sister on my back and we ran away and Skull, my mother, was chasing us." Then the old woman said, "My children, your mother will not catch you. Pâkółeana sank her into the big river you crossed. Now when you get back home you will find your father married to Coyote woman. He has three children. Here, take this bow, quiver and arrows. Your elder sister is treated very meanly by Coyote woman, your stepmother (*kökana maseena*).[1] Your sister is in a sad way. She is carrying the three babies in a bag on her back all day. Whenever the babies cry, old Coyote woman chases your elder sister with a burning piece of charcoal. When you come near to the camp you will see them, they are moving somewhere else. Your elder sister is walking on foot all the way with the babies on her back, behind the band." So they went, they overtook them as they were going on. He saw his sister walking behind the others. Then he got out one arrow from his quiver, he shot just a little ahead of where his sister was walking. The arrow fell right in front of her, sticking in the ground. She picked up the arrow, and ran to overtake her father and stepmother. She told her father, "I was coming and this arrow dropped in front of me and stuck in the ground. I picked it up. It is my brother's arrow." The father said, "No, it can not be your brother's arrow. Your brother will never come back."—"Anyway, this is my brother's arrow." Then the father got angry and chased her back to where her brother was coming. The coyote babies were asleep on her back. And her brother came to her and said to her, "What are you carrying on your back?"—"My father's babies, the coyotes. My father is married to Coyote woman." The boy said, "Let me see them!" Then she opened the bag. There were three little coyotes. He picked them out of the bag, one by one. He hit the head of the first on a rock. Then he hit the second the same way. Then the third the same way. He killed the three of them. Then the girl said, "My elder brother, why do you kill them? Now my stepmother (*nkamaseena*)[2] will

[1] ką-k,a-mąs'iena, your-mother-"step" (T).
[2] ąnk,amąs'iena (T).

kill me."—"No, you come to me! I will kill her. I will shoot her. Now you go and take them over to them!"—"But I am afraid." The boy was dripping blood. She went to her stepmother. "Why aren't the babies crying?" asked the stepmother. The girl said, "They are asleep." She took the bag off her back. Stepmother said, "Let me see them!" She opened the bag and found the babies all crushed and bloody. Then Coyote woman took a piece of burning charcoal and ran after the girl, and she ran away toward her elder brother. Then he saw Coyote woman coming after his younger sister. He shot Coyote woman and killed her. Then their father was very angry. The boy got out his bundle of medicine (*waltseina, walena*, medicine, *tseina*, bundle)[1]; then he untied the bundle, took the medicine in his mouth and spat it out in the direction his father was coming. That was to bore a hole clear through down (*kuinata*,[2] underneath). So he fell in there and never came back. That cut off all the trouble they expected to have from their father.

Now their father was way down in the hole. Then Gopher old woman was going about nearby and heard whispering and singing in that hole. So she went close to listen.

ea ea ea eaaa

ea ea ea eaaa

Then he spat and said, "*Tötötötötötö!* My grandmother (*antitowaiye*),[3] Gopher woman, get me out! I fell in this hole. Can you get me out?"—"Yes, I will try to. I will go and get my rope of rawhide." Then she went to get her rope, a long one. She came back to the hole and said to the man, "I will throw this down to you and you get hold at the end." Then Gopher old woman straddled the hole, holding the rawhide string. She said to the man, "My grandson (*anmakuwai*),[4] do not look up to me, because if you look, the string will cut and give way. Then I can not get you out." So Gopher old woman pulled the first pull and then the man forgot what he was told by Grandmother Gopher, he looked up. Then the string cut and gave way. Down he fell again. Grandmother Gopher had only one time to do that, she was not allowed to do it twice. So she did not try again, and the man remained there forever. And the boy with his younger sisters (*anpaiyuna*)[5] went back to their old home, to Sun House Mountain. The people say that the

[1] wol- medicine + not identified (T).
[2] k'ᵢuyn'ᵻat'o (T).
[3] anᷱtituwáʔi (T).
[4] anmᵢakuwáʔi (T).
[5] anp'ᵢayunᶏ (T).

Apache lived at Sun House Mountain. There they remained and no one troubled them and they lived there forever.

Variant

The Apache were living. The chief was always going out hunting. His wife had a friend who was a snake and would turn into a man. She would pound meat very fine and take it to the tree where the snake (*pętsuuna*)[1] lived. The war chief wanted to know what his wife did when he was away. He watched and saw his wife go to a tree and sit down with meat in her lap and the snake came and crawled down her neck into her lap and ate the meat. Because her husband was looking on, the snake did not turn to a man. Then the war chief shot his wife and the snake with his arrow and killed them. He took off his wife's head and put it on top of a tree and he put her ribs on the fire and left them there and went home. He told his little daughter and son he had killed a buffalo and to go over to that tree and eat the ribs. The children went over there and found the ribs well cooked, and they looked so good they tried to eat them right away. As they stretched out their hands to the fire, some one called sh! They stopped and listened and looked around. They reached out again and they heard sh! They looked around and they saw their mother's head in the tree, and the head said, "Do not eat me, my children!" and they ran away to their tent. The Head ran after them, rolling, rolling.

The chief called out to the people to move to another place. After they moved away the chief married Coyote woman. When the children ran back to the tent they did not find their father, only the tracks of the horses and of the tent poles. They ran after them and they came to a river and they did not know how to cross that river and they saw a beaver (*poyana*)[2] and they asked him to take them across. Beaver said, "First you must look for bugs in my head and you must eat those you find." The little girl looked for bugs and found frogs, and she bit on the beads around her brother's wrist to make Beaver think she was cracking the bugs, and the frogs she threw in the river. "Now I can not find any more," she said to Beaver. And Beaver carried them across the river. The Head came and said to Beaver, "Hurry, take me over, my children are over." Beaver did not listen. He said, "First, you have to look for bugs in my head." The Head said, "How can I look for bugs in your head,

[1] pįecuʔ'una (T).
[2] p'öy'ona (T).

I have no hands," she said. Beaver said, "With your mouth." So she looked and found frogs. The Head said, "Nasty thing! You have frogs in your head. I won't eat them." And she dropped the frogs in the water. Beaver got cross and said, "You get on my back!" The Head jumped on his back. He carried the Head into the middle of the river and sank down into the water. The water carried the Head away and the worms ate it.

The children got to the place where the Apache were living and they found their father living with Coyote woman. The chief did not want his son to live with him and every day he sent him out to hunt, and his daughter he kept to carry the little coyotes in a sack on her back. One day when he told his son to go hunting he told the people to move to another place. When the boy came back he did not find the people and he followed the tracks and he found a very old woman they had left behind, she was so old. He asked her where they were going and she said that his father did not want him and so had told the people to move and they were still going on. She said his sister was very miserable carrying the little coyotes and she cried every day and her eyes were full of rheum. "Do not follow any more! Let us stay here! But you must follow your sister. She is way behind. The coyotes are very heavy and she wears old moccasins. Coyote woman hits her on the head for not hurrying and keeping the little coyotes hungry." He followed his sister and when he was near her, he shot an arrow in front of her. Then he overtook the Apache. The chief told the people to dig a hole and put that boy into it. So they put the boy into it and they moved on. The old woman (she was a medicine woman) came and heard some one singing and she looked and there was the boy standing and singing in the hole. She gathered up all the pieces of cloth the people had left and she made a rope and dropped it down to him and she straddled the hole and told the boy not to look up. Then she took him out and told the boy his sister was very sad from carrying the coyotes and not to follow the people but to live with her and to get his sister. He followed the people and overtook his sister who was tired and crying. He shot his arrow in front of her. She picked it up. "This is my brother's arrow," she said. "Stop, sister!" said her brother. He said, "Sister, what have you in your bag?"— "They are my father's children," she said. "Let me look at them. How pretty they are!" Then he took them out one by one and hit their heads on a stone and killed them. His sister cried because her father would kill her, she said. He told her not to be afraid and he put all the dead coyotes back into the sack. And he told his sister to throw the sack to her mother. And just when they were raising their tents she got there. Coyote woman ran out, "You lazy thing, you! Why do you let my children go hungry!" The boy behind her shot her with his arrow. His sister threw the little coyotes at Coyote woman and ran to her brother. He shot all around with his arrows. He was singing with his sister and from his song the fire started to burn. And all the Apaches were burned. Only where the boy and girl stood it did not burn. As they stood there a coyote came up close with his ears on fire and the coyote said, "Why are you singing while all the people are burning and the world is ending?" He shot that coyote with his arrow. Then they went back to the old lady and stayed with her. And all the Apaches were burned but two, and from them come all the Apache today.

25. Suitor Tests :[1] Hiding the Animals Away : Escape up the Tree[2]

They were moving camp, some Apache. One old woman was slow, and she was left behind. She heard some one crying, like a baby. She went out to the place where they throw things away [refuse heap] and she found a baby. She kept him and began to call him Na'sagi. He had very thick, bushy hair and a big belly. He asked his grandmother to make him a bow and arrows. After a while they came to where the other people were. The chief said whoever could shoot the eagle could marry his daughter. So Na'sagi took his very round little bow to shoot the eagle. He was a dirty little boy, his eyes were small, and he had a big belly; the people made fun of him. But he shot the eagle. Then the chief said he had to shoot a fox. So he went and shot the fox. And he married the chief's daughter, and they called him a chief.

Then the people were very poor because Na'sagi hid all the animals away, the buffalo and the deer, underground, in a place like a kiva. Then he went and opened that place, took away the stone, and all the people had a great deal of meat.[3]

The wife of Na'sagi was washing with the other women in the river. There was a buffalo skull there for them to step on. She picked up the

---

[1] Compare San Juan, Parsons 4: 123-125; Kiowa, Parsons 6: 49 ff.; Cheyenne, Kroeber 1: 170-172; Pawnee, Dorsey 2: 239-244; Crow and comparative, Lowie, 46-47.

[2] All this complex tale was heard, according to the narrator, a middle-aged man, from his maternal grandmother who was an excellent story-teller and would tell the family stories at night. It should be noted that the narrator once went acourting among the Kiowa.

[3] Compare Zuni, Cushing, 121; Kiowa, Parsons 6: 53; Lipan Apache, Opler 2: 132-134 Compare the feat of the Cheyenne culture hero, Motseyouf (Dorsey 3: 46).

skull and said, "You poor thing! Once you were flesh and now they step on you." Then the skull became a big, live buffalo, and carried her away. So Na'sagi went to look for his wife. He met that little animal that burrows. "The only way I can help you," said that little animal, "is to dig a hole underground to the buffalo, and you follow behind." So he dug a hole to that big buffalo's ear. There in that buffalo's house they were all dancing, all the buffalo boys and girls.[1] Then Na'sagi got his wife and they started back. They travelled all that night and at sunrise the buffalo found out that she was gone and they went after her. There was a big cloud of dust. Na'sagi and his wife came to a tree, a big tree. "Brother, can you help me?" asked Na'sagi. "No, I can not, but my brother ahead, perhaps he can." So they went on and came to another tree. "Brother, can you help me?" asked Na'sagi. "No, but there is my brother ahead, perhaps he can." They came to another tree. "Brother, can you help me?" Now the cloud of dust was getting bigger. "No, but my little brother ahead, he can help you." So they went on and they found a little tree and they climbed up. Now all the buffalo were coming past. And the woman wanted to do something [urinate,] and Na'sagi told her to wait, for the buffalo would smell her. But she could not stand it. And there was a little buffalo passing and he smelled her. "I smell our sister," he said to the buffalo next to him, and each passed the word on, and they all came back to hook the tree. Then Na'sagi shot the buffalo chief and killed him, and all the buffalo went away. And Na'sagi and his wife came down from the tree and went home and found their people there very sad about them.

Variant (*Hiding the Animals Away*)

There was an old Apache woman living with her grandchild, Bushy Hair or Snotty Nose. She was a medicine woman (*tuwaiana*). They were starving, and the old woman told the chief (*łauwaana*)[2] that her grandchild was going to bring some buffalo, to get ready. Some of the men laughed, "Snotty Nose won't bring anything," they said. Others made ready their bows and arrows. The next day he was to bring this buffalo. The chief said to the old woman, "If he brings the buffalo, he may marry my daughter." The chief told the men to go out hunting deer or buffalo. Any one who found them he would give his daughter. The little boy went out; next morning at sunup he brought the buffalo. The chief had

---

[1] Here there was a song and the girls and boys listening to the story would get up and dance to it.

[2] ł,owaʔ'ana (T).

two daughters. The elder girl said she would marry him, no matter what he looked like. The younger one said she would not marry him. When he came back with buffalo, looking very pretty, the younger wanted to take him. But he married the elder one, and they had plenty of meat. Since then we have had deer.

26. Magical Impregnation: Suitor Tests

Olden time the *tŏchulitaine* (house yellow people)[1] were travelling, and a little girl went astray. She made herself a brush house and grew up alone. When she was grown up she had a boy and she claimed that the child was the child of the Sun.

The boy began to play around and his mother had to make a bow and arrow for him. Hs would go out and get rabbits and squirrels for his mother. As he grew older he wanted a stronger bow, so he made one with eagle feathers which were very beautiful. His mother told him if he went hunting and saw an eagle on top of a tree and shot at it, he was not to pick up the arrows. One day he went deer hunting and he saw an eagle on top of a tree and he began to shoot at it. He got the eagle and started home. Then he looked back and saw the arrows on the ground. He said, "I have no father to make me arrows. I better not waste them." So he began to pick them up. As soon as he began to pick up the arrows, although it was a quiet day, the wind began to blow. His mother noticed the wind and she began to think that her boy was doing what she told him not to do. A big storm blew up. His mother opened the flap of her tent for him to come in, and just as he was about to enter the wind picked him up and carried him away. It broke her heart to see him fly away as she was looking at him.

The boy fell in a beautiful meadow. The Yellow House people were travelling and in this meadow they had camped. They had begun to cut grass for their ponies. There was a very old woman who came to cut the grass and she saw the boy lying there. "Why are you lying here?" she asked. "Get up! I want to cut the grass." He said, "Grandmother, I am lying down here so the people won't cut the grass and it will be left for you to cut. I will cut it for you."—"All right, grandson. Where are you from?" He said, "I was living with my mother and she told me not to pick up the arrows I shot. But I picked up the arrows and started home and my mother opened the flap, but the wind picked me up and here I

---

[1] t'ˌəc'ˌulet'ˈoynemạ (T). Compare the Yellow Earth people (*namchurtainin*) [nˌamc'ˌur-t'ˈayṇin (T)] of Isletan narrative (Parsons 7: 386).

fell."—"Well, then you can be my grandchild."—"Yes, grandmother, I will live with you and support you." He was a fine looking boy. She took him to her tent, and he fed the horses. She looked at him and said, "If I keep you here, you are so goodlooking it won't be long before some one will take you away." He said, "Grandmother, you can change my looks." So with her power she changed the looks of the boy and made him very ugly. She named the boy Nasigi and they lived happily together.

One day the chief announced that a white eagle was on a tree near camp and any one who got that eagle could marry his daughter. Nasigi said, "Well, grandmother, I want to go and shoot the eagle, if you will let me."—"My grandchild, you have no good bow and arrow like the others."—"Still I will go," said Nasigi. Next day the chief made the announcement again. The old woman painted his face and he went over. All the young men started shooting at the eagle. They said, "Now let Nasigi shoot!" Old man Coyote was there. He knew Nasigi had power. He said he would shoot at the same time Nasigi shot. Nasigi brought down the eagle, and Coyote ran quickly and picked it up. The people told Coyote it was Nasigi who had shot the eagle. But Coyote took the eagle to the chief's camp, and the elder daughter of the chief—he had two daughters—took the eagle and said to Coyote, "That is what my father promised, and now I belong to you." So all the people went home and Nasigi also went home. Grandmother said, "What luck did you have, grandson?"—"Coyote stood alongside of me, and he shot when I shot. They told him not to shoot, but he shot too and ran very fast ahead and took the eagle. You better go and get it."—"Grandson, they are mean people, but I will go." So she went to the chief's camp, and Coyote was there. She asked for the eagle. Coyote said, "I shot the eagle, your grandson's eyes were bad." But she kept on asking for the eagle. Then Coyote threw the eagle into the fire. The feathers were burned. She snatched the eagle from the fire and took it home. "Never mind, my grandson," she said. She made some medicine and spat it over her grandson and he became a fine looking boy again, and she spat over the eagle, and the eagle feathers were as good as ever. So Nasigi took the eagle and went to the chief's camp, and the younger girl came out and said, "That is what my father promised, and now I belong to you." Nasigi stayed a while with the girl. Then he went home to his grandmother. "Then she spread her medicine east, north, west, and south, and that kept the buffalo away from the people, and they were starving.

So one day the chief announced that if a yellow fox were to come whoever got that yellow fox was to marry one of his daughters. The old woman told her grandson about it. "Well, grandmother, I am going to get the fox." These people made a trap with a loop of sinew to catch foxes. Everybody was making such a trap. Nasigi told his grandmother to make him one. "Yes, my grandson, I will make one for you." Coyote came along and put his trap next to Nasigi's trap because Coyote knew that boy had power. The people told him not to put his trap next to Nasigi's trap, but still he put it there. They baited traps with buffalo meat, but Nasigi had a deer bone without any meat on it in his trap. He and his grandmother were poor. Along came the yellow fox. People said, "He is coming to mine!"—"No, he is close to mine!"—"No, he is going to Nasigi's trap." Coyote said, "No, he is going to mine." He went to Nasigi's trap and got looped. Coyote ran to Nasigi's trap and got out the fox and ran with it to the chief's camp. All the time the people were calling out that the fox was trapped in Nasigi's trap. When Coyote arrived the elder girl came out. "This is what our father promised, and you got the fox, and I am yours." Nasigi told his grandmother to go and get the fox. She said, "That Coyote is so mean he will throw it into the fire." When she arrived at the chief's camp she said, "I came for the yellow fox my grandson trapped." Coyote said, "Your grandson can not see well. The fox was caught in my trap." Then he threw the yellow fox into the fire. She snatched it out, but the hair was burned. She went home crying. That night she spat her medicine over the yellow fox and over Nasigi, and they both became fine looking. Nasigi took the yellow fox to the chief's tent and the younger girl came out and took the yellow fox. Then it was announced that the younger girl was to marry Nasigi and the older girl to marry Coyote.

After the marriage Nasigi told the chief that he would bring the buffalo to a certain place. All the people made a place for him to drive the buffalo. Early in the morning he started his song. (I know this song, but we may not write it.) They saw the dust made by the buffalo, and the people went out and killed all the buffalo they wanted. Away behind, Nasigi was driving an old buffalo, a dirty old buffalo covered with the droppings from Magpie. They said, "Our father Nasigi, why are you driving that old buffalo? Why do you kill a buffalo like that while we kill the best of the herd?" Nasigi said, "Well, I know what to do." The older girl packed a buffalo stomach with blood and put it on her back. Nasigi told his wife to go and cut it open. The blood came down on her and she went back ashamed. A crow was flying above her, he was her sweetheart. . . (?) she never came back.[1]

[1] This incident is confused. The narrator skipped something, deliberately, I think.

One day Nasigi told his father-in-law that now that he had saved the tribe it was time for him to go and see his grandmother. So he started. His grandmother saw the dust flying in the plain and she said, "That is my boy coming!" Then they were happy living together.

Now you got the tail!

27. Magic Flight: Buffalo Medicine Bundle

The Yellow House people were travelling. They had a pet dog and as they were moving the dog ate some beads. The beads came out with his droppings. There were three children, two little girls and their younger brother. Elder sister said, "We better pick up the beads." While they were stringing the beads the people went on. The children followed. Elder sister saw a smoke. She said, "My little sister, somebody is living there. We better go there." As they aproached, an ugly old woman came out to meet them. She took the three children into her house. In order to kill them the witch woman (*chahöałiu*)[1] told the girl to put her brother and little sister to bed. But the girl lay with her brother at her back. She peeked through the hole in her buffalo pelt. The old woman went and killed the younger girl. One day the old woman told the elder sister to bring some wood. She brought it. "That is not the kind of wood I burn," said the old woman. She was going to eat the little girl. She sent her down to the spring. The girl carried her little brother on her back. When the girl brought the water the old witch woman said, "I do not drink that kind of water." The little girl went back to the spring. Frog came out and said, "Witch old woman uses sunflower stalk for firewood and drinks putrid water. I will help you." Frog gave the little girl a hair broom, a mirror, and an awl. "Witch old woman will follow you and you must cast away the broom and she will get into a tangle. When she overtakes you again, cast away the awl. Now start off!" The girl started. Witch old woman called, "Make haste! My pot is burning up!" Frog answered, "Grandmother, my water bag is torn and I am mending it." After a while, Witch old woman said, "Are you coming with that water? I will club you to death."—"Grandmother, I am coming." By that time the children were far away. Witch old woman went down to the spring and saw Frog. "Long-legged, pop-eyed! You fooled me!" She started after the children. The girl cast away the broom. Witch old woman got

---

[1] c₁ohəołiw ʔù (-little) (the -ʔù diminutive is used with many proper names, even when there is no direct idea of smallness (T). When used with woman it appears to mean indirectly old, small therefore old.

tangled up. After she untangled herself she said, "They are mine! I am going to get them!" She followed them. The girl cast away the awl. Witch old woman got stuck in the thorns and became bloody. She followed them. "You are mine! I am going to get you!" The girl cast away the mirror which turned to ice. Witch old woman kept falling down. She followed them. "You are mine! I am going to get you where-ever you go." The children met a crane at the river. "Will you help us across?"—"Yes," said Crane, "but you have to pick the bugs from my hair." Little brother had an elk tooth. He chewed on that to imitate the chewing of lice. Crane took the children over the river. The old witch came and asked him to carry her over. "Yes, but you have to eat the bugs in my head."—"You nasty thing! I do not eat lice." So Crane took her and in the middle of the river he doubled up his legs and dropped her into the water. She grabbed at a branch and got out and started after them. The children met a big bear. "Brother Bear, will you help us? Witch old woman is after us with a club to kill us and to eat us."—"Yes, now go on to Brother Buffalo!" Witch old woman came up and she killed the bear. Buffalo said, "You go on to Brother Mountain Lion while I talk to her." Witch old woman came and with one swing of her stone axe she killed the buffalo. The little girl said to the lion, "Brother Lion, can you protect us?"—"Yes, you go on to Brother Elk, while I entertain her." Witch old woman came up to Lion and said, "I killed Bear and Buffalo and I can kill you just as easily!" She swung her stone axe and killed Lion. The little girl said, "Brother Elk, can you protect us?"—"Yes, go on to Brother Deer!" Witch old woman came to Elk. She said, "I killed Bear, Buffalo, and Lion, and I can kill you just as easily!" She swung the axe and killed Elk. The little girl said to Deer, "Brother Deer, can you protect us?"—"Yes, go to Brother Antelope!" Witch old woman came to Deer. She said, "I killed Bear, Buffalo, Lion, and Elk, and I can kill you just as easily." She swung the axe and killed Deer. The little girl said to Ante-lope, "Brother Antelope, can you protect us?"—"Yes, go on to Brother Wolf!" Witch old woman came to Antelope. She said, "I killed Bear, Buffalo, Lion, Elk, and Deer, and I can kill you just as easily." She swung the axe and killed Antelope. The little girl said to Wolf, "Brother Wolf, can you protect us?"—"Yes, go on to Brother Coyote!" Witch old woman came to Wolf. She said, "I killed Bear, Buffalo, Lion, Elk, Deer, Antelope, and I can kill you just as easily." She swung the axe and killed Wolf. The little girl said to Coyote, "Brother Coyote, can you protect us?"—"Yes, go to little baby Buffalo. He will protect you."—"Now, little sister, you stand behind me!" The little girl cried, "How can this little buffalo protect us when she killed the biggest of the buffalo, Bear, Lion, Elk, Deer, Antelope, Wolf, and Coyote!" Little Buffalo was throwing up the dirt. Witch old woman came up and said, "Little Buffalo, you are smart, but I can kill you as I killed Big Buffalo, Bear, Lion, Elk, Deer, Antelope, Wolf, and Coyote." Little Buffalo tossed her up. The third time he tossed her so high, to the sun, that she did not come down.

Little Buffalo gave the girl a little fortune[1] to tell the future by. "Go on to where your people are! Your grandfather is waiting for you." (That was their dog.) They came in sight of the tents; the people were moving. The dog lay in the fireplace. People were whipping him to make him leave. The children came to their parents who said, "No, we never had children like you." The old dog was lying there to save the fire. The people started off. The old dog got up and said, "My children, now you have the fire for yourselves." One day the girl said, "Our little brother Buffalo gave us this fortune. I am going to use it." The little boy would go hunting. They were living well. The people who had left could get no game; the children were hiding the game from them by means of their little fortune. The father of the children said, "We better go to the camp we left. We better return to those children who have some power and are keeping the game from us." Then he saw that they were his children. They were living well, they had plenty to eat, plenty of jerked meat. When the boy went out he saw the dog coming ahead. Said the boy, "Well, sister, I want you to get our best meat for our grandfather (the old dog). The chief came and said, "Our children, we have come to you."—"Yes, we had no parents like you." The old dog took the meat. They told their parents not to desert their children again. After that they had plenty of game, because of the fortune Buffalo gave them.

28. The Apache Youth Takes a Redhead Scalp

There lived a band of Apache at Sun House Mountain. The man and woman had one boy. The mother loved her boy so dearly she did not want him to go out far from home. She kept him home all the time. The old man spent his time making bows and arrows. He had one fine Osage bow (*kwilpaimona*). He loved that bow. He kept it in a lionskin quiver, very carefully. As the boy grew up the father said to him, "My son, many of the young men are always going to war, far from home, and you do not

[1] Spanish, *virtud;* Tanoan, *pöahanuna,* tied up in bundle, i. e. medicine bundle.

go as the young men go. I am making so many nice bows and feathered arrows, yet you do not go to war. When you go to war and bring the scalp of a Redhead then I will do a mocking dance (*łotuwaiya*) until I get tired." The boy was very quiet, so when his father said that, he did not answer. But the boy kept in mind what his father said. Then one day he went in to where his father kept his Osage bow. He got the bow and quiver and arrows and went away quietly, without telling his mother or father. Then the old man, when he did not see his boy all day, said to his wife, "Where is my boy? I do not see him around." His wife said, "Don't you remember you were telling your son all the time that while other young men went to war he did not go. And if he brought the scalp of a Redhead you would dance the mocking dance until you got tired. That is why, I guess, he has gone to war." Then the old man went to see where he kept his best bow and quiver, and the bow and quiver were gone. Then he said to his wife, "I guess he went to war."

On his way the boy came to Gopher old woman. "My grandson, where are you going?" He replied, "I am going to fight the Redheads."— "My grandson, there is a big river for you to cross. I will give you this bundle of medicine. When you come to the river, spit this medicine into the water!" The boy came to the river and untied the bundle and spat the medicine. So the water lowered. Then he saw Paköałaana. There he lay with his round yellow eyes. The boy said to him, "My father, can you not take me across the river?"—"Yes," said Big Water-man, and he took the boy across. Just beyond the river he found the Redheads. Then he killed one, and took off his scalp and went back to the river. Big Waterman was there, he took him back across. Then he went on and came to Gopher old woman. He said to her, "My grandmother, I had good luck, I killed a Redhead and I am taking his scalp home." Then Gopher old woman took hold of the scalp and spat on it and pissed on it and lay with it and danced.[1] After she got through, the boy went on. He got home to his father and mother. He reached the house, quietly, and was not seen by his father or mother. He had the scalp and the scalp-lock on a stick. He stuck it in the ground in front of the house. And he lay down to sleep. Then towards morning his mother woke up and said to her husband, "It seems to me that my son has arrived home." The father said, "No, he will never come back, he went to a place where he can never return." "Anyway, I think my son is back." Saying that, she looked out of the door. The first thing she saw was the scalp-lock in front of the house. "Here you see the scalp. I tell you my son is back, and

[1] All this the old women actually did when a scalp was brought in (Parsons 10: 22).

has brought a Redhead scalp." The old man went outside and saw the scalp. He began to yell and war whoop and jump around and around the scalp. Then he called out to his people to come to the dance, that his boy had brought a Redhead scalp. So everybody came, they danced all day, until he [the old man] got very tired and fell down. So they finished the dance.

29. Man Eyes[1]

There was a man going along looking for the Redheaded men. He came to Spider old woman and she asked him where he was going. And he said he was looking for the Redheads. She said, "My grandchild, I don't think you will get those Redheaded men because they have an eagle tied up on top of their house, and that is the one who takes care of them and nobody can get them. But I will help you to get one." She took out a bunch of medicines (little bags). She said when he was near there he must take out the medicine, put it in his mouth and spit over himself so he would change and they would think he was a woman. He went on and as he came close to their village the eagle hopped around, and they untied him and he flew to where the person was and then he flew back and they tied him again. Then they found that man dressed as a woman. They wanted to kill her; but one of them liked her and said, "I will take her for my wife." So they lived together. Then the Redheaded men went to war and they left that man and his wife. "It is not a woman; but a man," some said. They called her *söayi*[2] *söantsixö'*[3], female-in-law man eye. She asked her husband to let her look for bugs in his head. He put his head in her lap and then he went to sleep. Then she cut off his head and ran away with it. She came to where lived Spider old woman under a cover of cow dung. She opened that and went in. The eagle was hopping up and down, and the Redheads came in and saw that their son was dead. "Now we believe that he was a man, and we ought to have killed him right away," they all said. The eagle flew up and followed the man, the Redheads followed the eagle. They went to where the man had gone in, but they could see nothing, so they returned crying for their son.

---

[1] Compare Taos, Espinosa, 127-128; Kiowa, Parsons 6: 78-80; Crow, Lowie, 141-143.
[2] s'əoyi (voc.) (T).
[3] s,əonc,ix'ə, man-pupil of eye (c'i- eye + x'ə - grain) (T).

30. Nighthawk's Cradle

I'amöletiu,[1] *Iamö'letuti,* White Corn[2] old woman, White Corn old man, lived at *koatu'liaka*[3] (sheep jump down). They had three boys and one girl. At night the girl wanted to go outside to make water, and the mother said to the boys, "You take care of your sister, one go out ahead, and one behind." As boys are, they paid no attention. The girl said, "I will go out, I want to make water badly." She went out on top of the house. There Nighthawk was watching for her. As she came out Nighthawk picked her up and took her to his house on the rocky cliff. Then the mother went out and did not find her daughter. She said, "I told you to go out with your sister. You naughty, naughty boys, lazy boys, you do not mind me! Nighthawk has taken my daughter." Then the next day the boys got down their bows and arrows and went out to look for their sister. One of them came to a steep cliff. There he found his sister. He went into the cliff side, and his sister said, "Elder Brother, why do you come here? Nighthawk is very fierce, he will kill you. You better go back and tell our father and mother they have a grandchild." So the boy went back and told his mother and father that he found his sister married to Nighthawk with a child already. So next day White Corn old woman was preparing swaddling clothes and White Corn old man was making bow and arrows for his grandchild, and a cradle. (Men make cradles.) So the next day they went to see their grandchild and took those things. When they got to the place they went in, and the daughter told them to sit down, and the grandmother gave the clothes to her daughter, and the grandfather gave the cradle and the bows and arrows for the boy to use when he was a man. Nighthawk was out hunting. Toward night Nighthawk came with a big buck on his back. He said, "Smell of people!"—"It is nobody but my father and my mother, they have come to see their grandson." Nighthawk saw the cradle hanging from the ceiling and there was his boy lying in the cradle his grandfather made. He was not satisfied with that cradle. "That is not what I use. What I use for a cradle is an old, dried up, discarded shield. That is the kind of cradle I use for my babies." So he took it down and put up his own kind of cradle.

---

[1] ìamą̂ˌelìwʔù, cornstring-woman, from ìamą̂ˈena, string of corn across room (T).

[2] It is a large, round, short ear. See p. 137.

[3] k'ˌuotˈuliʔogą, sheep-jump-at; tˈuli uncertain, perhaps tˈulą, to fall (T).

31. Bat and Magpie Twit Each Other

Tsiliana[1] (Bat) lived at *tołaĺia'baka*,[2] Cottonwood Crack, and Magpie lived at *tołaĺiabpahö'ta*,[3] Cottonwood Windfall. Magpie was trying to fall in love with Yellow Corn. Every day he went flying across the east side of Yellow Corn's house. Then Bat saw Magpie man almost every morning flying across to stay with Yellow Corn. Bat sang[4] mockingly, "Man going this side (i.e. to the east) hiding and creeping in the cotton-wood trees." So he came back toward the sound and said, "Somebody must be speaking to me." Then he returned to the east. Bat said again, "Man going this side hiding and creeping in the cottonwood trees." Magpie returned to look for the sound four times. The fourth time he found Bat. Magpie man was angry and said to Bat, "My legs are not like yours, fastened with membrane, I have not your neck or head." Then Bat felt badly and cried tsh tsh tsh! Then Bat called all the people living about to his house, and many came at his call. He made a complaint to the people. "When I was on the top of my house I saw Magpie man along the east side of Yellow Corn girl's house hiding and creeping under the cottonwood trees and I said to him, 'Man going this side hiding and creeping in the cottonwood trees.' He said to me that my legs were fastened by a small membrane and my arms and head were not like his." Then all the people in the house said, "That is the way you are made." Then they all scattered from the house. Bat cried, "Tsh tsh tsh! Anyway, people say I am Bat and I am living in Cottonwood Crack."

32. Snake Wife

Töiponełułi[5] was living alone at *paŏyahöaka*.[6] He had no woman. Snake woman was living on the hillside. Then Snake woman went to Black Cane old man. He always looked fat and well, while the people living nearby looked very poor and unnourished. Black Cane old man always wore fine clothing. Two of those poor people saw Black Cane old man and

---

[1] c'ͺiliyoʔ'ona (T).

[2] tͺułoł'iabʔoga, cottonwood-crack-at ('T).

[3] tͺułołͺiabp'öh'əoto, cottonwood-crack-ravine-at (T).

[4] The song proper was forgotten.

[5] ? - p'ͺunеł'ułi, ? - black-old man, first element refers to something connected with wood (T). My informant was also secretive, translating "Black Trunk old man," but see p. 92 for cane, *teitöna*, and *tawehfoneyłułi*, written by townsman and translated Black Cane old man (p. 137) so I am translating Black Cane old man. See p. 53.

[6] p'òʔ'ͺoyo- spider + hu- ? + -ʔoga, at (T): "Spider height, but it does not mean that"!

thought they would watch and follow him to his house and see what he had and what he was eating. Also they saw Snake woman going every evening to Black Cane old man's house. As they watched the house, two persons began to talk inside. They looked in and they saw Snake woman turned to a human woman. She was a nice woman and well-dressed. The man also was well-dressed. They were laughing at each other, teasing and loving each other. These two they saw, then they went back to their house and they said to the people, "We used to think Black Cane old man was living alone. He has a woman there at his house, a snake that turns human. They had plenty of buffalo meat to eat. That's why that man is fat and always wears good clothes. The snake has the power to get clothing for him and for herself." Then the old men of the village sent word for him to come to their house. They sent boys to call him. So he went down to the village. When he entered the house, the men said to him, "We invite you to make a dance, the best dance we have, and the best dance you have. You must use your best clothes and we will wear ours. We will see who beats in the dance." He said he would come, the next night. He went back to his house. When he came back, the woman was there. He told her that those poor people were making a dance and wanted him to join, with his own kind of dance. She said to her man, "Yes, you will beat them. They want me, they want to get me. That is why they are acting so. But we will go," said the woman. So next night she came to her man and they went to the dance, in their finest clothes. Those poor people looked very poor; for earrings they had pumpkin rind, and for beads, pumpkin rind, and instead of turtle shell leg rattle, they had pumpkin rind. And they danced, those poor people. They finished dancing. Then Black Cane old man and his wife took their turn to dance. They stood up to dance, in abalone shell earrings, and fine shell beads. The woman had a black cloth dress and a Hopi woven belt,[1] and fine boots. The people were surprised to see them so well-dressed. They beat in the dance. Then Black Cane old man became chief (*t'unena*) of those people. They went back to their house and in a short time the Snake woman had babies.

33. Horned Toad Goes Deer Hunting

Horned Toad[2] was going hunting. He lived at *kantöaba*[3] (rabbit village).

---

[1] Such as the women wear when they dance.

[2] Koała'helaana (k''uona, sheep, ła-+ ?, fæces. T), Horned toad is so called because he looks it.

[3] k''ǫt̯ǝobo, rabbit-village-at (T).

He was preparing to hunt deer in the morning. He had a song. At day-break he got up and dressed and sang,

> aikimkim aikimkim
> kwanaai sulkwaiaa′ pẹna[1] (deer)
> tewiw'ilkohumumum[2]
> I am fixing bow
> tewiw'ilkohumumum
> I am fixing bow

Now he is fixing the arrows and he sings,

> aikimkim aikim kim
> kwanaai sulkwaiaa′ pẹna
> tewiłuakohumhum[3]
> I am fixing arrow
> tewiłuakohumhum
> I am fixing arrow

He is dressing and sings,[4]

> awiho′lehum
> I am putting on (i.e., shoes)

Now he sings again,

> awitsömahum[5]
> I am going to hunt

Now he is on the road to *kankaba*.[6] He sings,

> awitsömahum
> I am going to hunt

Now he is at *tȯłapatemau′* (cottonwood shade). He sings,

> awitsömahum
> I am going to hunt

He reaches the crossing of the creek (*o′paba*, child water).[7] He crosses. Now he is climbing up the hill [*wẹłelba*, pine scattered (at)]. He sings,

> tewie′muho′ama[8]
> I see the track

---

[1] p'ẹna (T).
[2] tiwix^wilk'uhumụmụm (T).
[3] tiwiłuok'uhumụmụm (T).
[4] In all the following verses the form is the same except for the essential line, which is always repeated.
[5] owic'əmẹ́hum (T).
[6] k'ongabo, buffalo-when-at (T). See p. 120.
[7] ùp'ȯbo, child-water-at (T).
[8] tiwi?ìmẹ̀ụhu (T).

He sings again,

tewimuhom[1]
I see it (the deer)

He sings again,

tewitaw'um[2]
I shot it

Again he sings,

tewihow'um[3]
I kill it

Again,

tewipahw'ilew'um[4]
I am skinning it

Again,

tewiilpaw'um[5]
I am wrapping it in a bundle

Again,

tewie'lew'um
I am rolling it up on my back

Now he goes back home,

tewehoihum[6]
I am carrying it
awimew'um[7]
I am going (along)
awimuyaw'um[8]
they are looking at me
anłitona[9]
my grandmother
awimuyaw'um
is looking at me
awiwanw'um[10]
I am arriving

[1] tiwimụ̈hum (T).
[2] tiwit'ʼawhum (T).
[3] tiwih'uhum (T).
[4] tiwip'ŏxᵂilihum (T).
[5] tiwiʔʼilpahum (T).
[6] tiwih'oyhum (T).
[7] owiméhum (T).
[8] ạwimụ̈yahum (T).
[9] Meaning "my wife".
[10] awiw'onhum (T).

His wife came to meet him. She wanted to take the deer on her back; but Horned Toad said to her, "No, it is too heavy for you, you can not carry it." The woman said,"*Hunka*, anyway," and she went under the bundle to take it off her man. But the man went on with it, it was too heavy for her. He carried it to *tölapa'na* (Gopher kiva) to cook during the night, to eat for breakfast in the morning. Everybody was invited to come there for breakfast. They thanked him for bringing it in. "We will pray for you to have luck (*kanasuahqwaa*)[1] to kill more in the future."

Variant[2]

Dry-plain Toad (*ohlahelaanah*) lived in the plain with his grandmother. The Indians of the plain used to hunt and kill game in abundance. So Dry-plain Toad had a great desire to go and hunt, too. He told Grandmother Toad to make him arrows. Toad old woman made arrows for her grandson, out of sticks which she used for stirring parched corn meal. When he was ready to go out hunting, his grandmother fixed him up. She wound round his legs some old rags, and she gave him lunch, a kind of corn pudding. Before he went, his grandmother told him what the tracks of the deer looked like. His grandmother made the footprints of the deer thus [making marks]. So he went forth. Arriving at the foot of the mountain, he saw tracks such as his grandmother had described. He followed them and at a short distance he saw the deer standing. He shot at it. He killed it and brought it home. On arriving he called to his grandmother to call it to the attention of the people. His grandmother said, "My grandson, never mind, you are too little. '*Ianoweh* (thanks)!'" People were looking on while he was dragging the deer on the road. On arriving home he took the deer into their house.

34. Bear Digs for Medicine

Bear old man (*köałułi*)[3] was living in the burnt timber.[4] People (*nałetain*) were living at the Mouth of the Red Willows. Bear was coming down

---

1 ka̧na̧suh,o̧wá ?á, you will have luck. ho̧- luck (ka̧na̧suwá ?á, definite future, second person singular, you will have it certainly. T).
2 Written by townsman.
3 k,ǝoł'ułi (T).
4 Literally, *kłatöba, kla,* wood, *töba,* steep. ło - wood, ? + -bo, in (T).

to dig medicine at the place called *klaa'ata*.[1] He got his cane (*teitöna*) and came down. He sang,

> hina nina i a
> hina nina i a
> hina nina i a
> ya he i ha
> a he ina a

He was now half way from his home to the village. He paused there and said to himself, "People are seeing me. I must dance harder." Then he began to sing again,

> hina nina i a
> hina nina i a
> hina nina i a
> ya he i ha
> a he ina a

Then he got to *klaa'ata*. Then he spit with his medicine in four directions. Then with his cane he dug (sunwise movement) and he sang (song repeated). Then he dug, then he chewed and dabbed on his body and legs. Then he put the medicine on his back. Then he started back home. Then the people said, "Lazy Bear old man came again to dig his medicine." Then he went back singing again, (song repeated). He went half way and he stopped and he said, "People are looking at me. I must dance harder." He sang, (song repeated). Then he got to his home and said, "People call me *köatuti klatöba witöama*,[2] Bear old man lives in steep woods. The village people ask[3] good luck (*nohmawena*) of me for themselves and here I remain at my home at *klatöba*."

35. Bear Claws![4]

The fire of *wuchibikwienah*,[5] cedar bird, went out. He sat on top of a high rock to watch and see where he could spy fire smoke coming out. He saw smoke coming out of Bear's home, *kelandah*,[6] Bear's cookhouse, so he went down there to ask for fire. When he got there, he went in. "Here, sit down, *yoima'u'*, which was Bear language for Cedar bird. Then

---

[1] ło-, wood + ? - to, at (T).
[2] wit⁽ˡ⁾ᵊmạ (T).
[3] inameleho, they ask (in prayer). inạm'ẹlehu (T).
[4] Written by a townsman.
[5] h,ục,ibik'ina < hụ- cedar + c,ibik'ina, small bird (T).
[6] k,ᵊoł'ọlto, bear-cook-at (T). See p. 138.

Cedar bird said, "My fire died out, so as I saw smoke coming out of your house, I came down to get fire." Bear said, "Take it!" He reached his hand to the fireplace for fire. He had tied around his wrist a string of bear claws. Bear said, "What have you got there on your wrist?" He said, "*Po'pɥyɥmɑtselene*,[1] water fly nail." As he stepped out the door he called out, "*Keamachelenah*,[2] bear nail!" He ran away with the fire in his hand to his home. Bear chased him. Cedar bird's home was on a high cliff. He flew up there. Bear never got him.

36. The River Waters are Released

Pa·săkana[3] was living at the river. The river went dry. Then he went jumping, calling *pa·săkă! pa·săkă!* trying to scratch out the water with his bill. Then he went to other rivers looking for water. The first day he could find no water. Then he came back to the river. Then he went in another direction. All day he could find no water. He came back again. The third day he went in another direction, again he failed to find water. The fourth day he went again and again came back without finding water. The fifth day he started out again. He flew straight up in the air; but as he was not used to flying that way he found the wind very strong for him. He came back to the river, and started out again, where he thought he could find water. He came to a place in the river and saw a point with ice on it. He sat there. He went over the ice, picking with his bill, and saying *săka, săka, pa·săkă!* He jumped along, picking all the time. Then he saw under the ice a little water running. He said, "Here! here! I get water." So he sat there and began to peck at the ice, saying, *săka, săka, pa·săkă!* It was hard for him. He was boring with his bill and saying *săka, săka, pa·săkă!* He pecked nearly all day. Late in the day he bored through the ice, and water began to come out from the little hole he bored, flowing very swiftly. Then all the rivers where he had found it dry all began to flow in flood. Rocks and pieces of wood were rolling (in the water). So he had discovered the water which kept the rivers flowing. And he was very happy.

---

[1] p'ȯp̣ɥyumɑc'elena (T).

[2] k̦ɔomɑc'elena (T).

[3] ă = a in at. A bird named for its call. Perhaps p'ȯc'akana, wild goose (T). "'He is counting the rocks in the river,' we say, as he goes hopping along."

37. Lizard Song

We are living at Rocky Mouth Canyon (*pahkwehoawe*). Lizards (*natöyana*) are going down to get a drink of water.

> Over at Rocky Mouth Canyon in the hill (*pahkwe'a ho'ta*)
> They are going down in a string,

Lizards remain living over the hill at Rocky Mouth Canyon, people always used to say.

38. Fish Dances and Sings for Water

Pöuna[1] (fish) lived at *paut'a*.[2] During the summer the creek went pretty dry. Fish did not have enough water where he lived. Then he thought to himself that he would jump and dance because the water was so low and dry. Then he started to dance and sing,

> a he a a
> a he a a
> a a a he a
> he a a a
> a a a a

Pretty soon, a big flood of water came down in the creek. Fish remained living in the creek at *paut'a*.

39. The Turkeys Gather Piñon

One time the turkeys lived at *w'ilpianmo*[3] (bow mountain). They were going to pick piñon (*pion*) at *tąnd'miuaiya*[4] [*tąana*, dogwood]. They sang,

> biu biu tạ tạ
> biu biu tạ tạ

Some places they ran, some places they walked. They crossed the river on the east side of the village. They still sang,

> biu biu tạ tạ
> biu biu tạ tạ

---

[1] pə̀ʔ'əna (T).
[2] p'owto (T). A place in Taos River about 500 yards east of the pueblo.
[3] xʷ‚ilp"ianmo, bow-mountain-at (T).
[4] t'ọ̀ʔ'one, "snakewood": tọ- ʔ -ʔoyạ, at (T).

They were at *pęa'taka*[1] (deer jaw). They went along the side of the hill, singing,

biu biu tạ tạ
biu biu tạ tạ

They got to *tạna'miuaiya* and picked up the piñon nuts, scratching away. They filled up their bags (you know they have in front a little bag of their own) and they went back home. They got home and there they lived always.

Variant[2]

A turkey family lived on a wooded hill. They had fun in the evening in making a bonfire (*wakigo*) and in playing *massapânika* (hiding hoop). They would run around about the hills across the ridges. They would run down to the river bottom for water for their jar made of pine bark or a piñon shell. They would run back up in a squad, pushing and pulling, so as to spill their water and run down again to fill their jar, then up hill again. At last, late in the evening, they got on top of their hill home, tired out. In the evening the Turkey boys would bother the females in nuisance funny acts to keep them awake. The next day the boys persuaded the females to go to pick piñon nuts, across the river on the hillside called Bow Mountain. They went singing,

byu byu tan tan

They reached the place and filled up their bags and started back home. When they got home, they gave their people a little here and a little there. They said, "We are the Turkey people living on Wooded Hillside and we remain there to live forever. We are turkeys."

40. Spirit Rats Give Battle to Eagle and Hawk[3]

Two young boys, *chiowialawenaoyo*[4] [Eagle boy ? chief] and *tahkewialawenaoyo*[5] [Hawk boy ? chief] lived with their grandmother in the center of the foot race track. The two boys were hunters of all living animals, big and small. They were great hunters. They used to trap with flat round rocks small game like rats and others that can be trapped with those round flat

---

[1] p͜ẹʔòdʔogạ, deer-jaw-at (T).
[2] Written by the narrator of the preceding version.
[3] Written by a townsman.
[4] c͜iwwᵢialᵢowaʔˈəwyu, eagle-?-chief-boy (T).
[5] t͜okewᵢialᵢowaʔˈəwyu, hawk-?-chief-boy (T).

rocks. They would go to see their traps every morning, wherever they had their traps set. As many (rats) as they found in their traps they would take to their grandmother. All these dead rats had to be fed with corn meal, but the grandmother never did her duty by the dead rats, she never fed them. Then all those dead rats talked mad. The next morning the two boys went to see their traps. They found them all covered with blood, and there was a stain on the rock from which a bloody trail led. Then the boys said, "We are sorry. It never happened to us this way before." Then from there they followed the bloody trail. They reached the mountain called Lion Mountain, the rats' death home. There was a door under ground where the dead rats went in. Then they listened at the hole. They heard talking. They said, "Do you see those soft feathers, white feathers blowing out from the rats' hole underground?" They lay down to listen. The dead rats were talking, mentioning the boys by name. "*Chiowiaławenaoyo* and *tahkewiaławenaoyo*, you both, now we are going to kill you for not feeding us meal when you kill us." Now the dead rats came out of the ground door, prepared with war paint, war clubs, and shields. The two boys were Eagle and Hawk. As the dead rats came out from underground they at once began to throw their war clubs at the birds, injuring their feathers to keep them from being able to fly and to make them tire soon. The two birds flew to a rock called White Rock. They sat there tired and blowing from the fatigue. As the dead rats approached to where the two birds were they again flew toward their grandmother's at their home in the center of the foot race track, and told their grandmother that the dead rats they had been killing were complaining of not being fed on corn meal as they should be fed; that is why they were trying to kill them. They told their grandmother not to do it again that way, but always to feed them before she ate them.

41. Bear and Red Ant Play at Breaking Arm

Spider woman was living with her grandchild *łichichiu* (little trash carrying).[1] He was playing outside. His grandmother told him not to play on the east side. One day he said to himself, "I wonder why my grandmother told me not to play on the east side." So he went there and out came a big bear. Bear said, "What are you doing?"—"I am playing." —"Let us play a game!" said Bear. "Let us play at breaking arm. If you break my arm, I will give you anything I have in my house. If I break

---

[1] Tale name for red ant, *imakinia* (ˀįemˌ̧ekiʔˈina, ant; ˀįemˌ̧ekipˈˌacˈˈiena, red ant < ˀįemˌ̧ekiʔˈina + pˈˌacˈˈiene, lightning (T).

your arm, I will eat you up."—"All right, grandfather."—"All right, grandson. We will meet here tomorrow morning." He went home and told his grandmother, "I went where you told me not to play and when I was playing a big bear came."—"That is just why I told you not to play there. What did he say?"—"He said we were to play at breaking arms." —"Now I will give you some medicine. When you go there put your arm under the sand and you say you will be the first to break arm. You spit the medicine which is your little fortune. Spit east, north, west, south, and east again!" When he got there Bear old man came and said, "Who will be the first?"—"You be the first!"—"No, you be the first!" So he covered his arm with sand. Big Bear was to drop a rock on his arm. Red Ant drew out his arm. Big Bear dropped the rock. He said, "I think it is broken."—"No, grandfather, it is not broken." Bear said, "All right, now it is my turn." Red Ant picked up a rock. "You can't break my arm with that rock. Get a bigger one!"—"No." He put the rock on top of his head and dropped it. "Your arm is broken, grandfather."— "No, it is not broken." Bear showed his arm, the bone stuck out. "Yes, it is broken," said Bear. "Now you come to my house. A man's word is worth more than anything else." They got to his house. "Come in, Red Ant! Sit down in the middle!" Red Ant sat down. Bear went in to the east side and came out with dried buffalo meat. He went in to the north side and came out with fresh elk and deer. He went in to the west side and came out with fruit. He went in to the south side and came out with good clothes for Red Ant and for his grandmother. "Red Ant, you are a better man than I. Take all these things and may you and your grand-mother live well, and when you die under the water (*paɫupanai*)[1], hand it down (*inamahoiwe*)[2], to the people."

42. Snow Breaks Red Ant's Foot[3]

Red Ant (*iamakifanenah*) lived in the field. One warm winter day he came out from his little mound. He was lying quiet, sunning himself. As he was lying down on the side of his house, a snowflake fell on his foot. His foot was broken. So he decided to go up in the sky to scold the snow and be doctored for his foot. When he reached up there he said

---

[1] p'ò- water + ? + ?oy, in, among (T).

[2] inạmàh'oy (T).

[3] Written by townsman. Probably a fragment of the cumulative tale "Who is the Strongest?", see Zuni, Benedict 2: II, 225.

to Snow, "Why do you fall to hurt me?" Snow said, "It is not my fault. Wind blows me and I roll away and fall on you."

43. Rabbit Pretends Toothache

Little Rabbit was living in the sagebrush (*tauluta*)[1] north of the village beyond the cottonwood tree called *kwępöita*.[2] One day he was sitting outside of his house. Coyote old man was hunting. Rabbit thought if he ran Coyote would chase him or if he went into his hole Coyote would dig him out. So he thought, "I will pretend I have a toothache." Coyote had not seen him yet, but Rabbit began to sing:

chinina[3]

chinina

Coyote listened. "Oh, what a pretty song! I have no hunting song. I must learn that one." He followed the sound and found Little Rabbit sitting there. "My grandchild, you are singing a pretty song. I would like to learn it for a hunting song."—"My grandfather, I am not singing. I am crying."—"Why are you crying?"—"I have a bad toothache, that is why I am crying." Coyote thought, "I will get a remedy for him and then eat him up."—"My grandchild," he said, "wait here and I will get medicine for you." When Coyote went up the hill, Rabbit went to the house of *łipia'u*,[4] Little Grass-root, Skunk. "My brother," he said, "Coyote came to my house and I was afraid he would eat me up and I made out I had a toothache. He went to get medicine. Now I want you to help me."—"Come in then, brother!" Rabbit went in to Skunk's house. Coyote came back with a load of medicine on his back. "Grandchild," he said, "help me into your house! I have a big load of medicine." Nobody answered. "Well, I will get you anyhow!" Coyote followed the track of Rabbit to Skunk's house. "Skunk, did Little Rabbit come here?"—"Yes." —"I want him."—"Come in!" said Skunk. "I can't come in. Your house is too small."—"I will make it bigger for you." Coyote went in and grabbed Little Rabbit and as he came out Skunk let loose his fluid on him. He fell down dead. Skunk said to Little Rabbit, "Go home, my brother, and live peaceful. Coyote always interferes with other people. From now on he will be of no use to anyone. His body will rot and scatter into the air."

---

[1] t'ɔwluto, sagebrush-at (T).

[2] kwᵢɛp'əyto, Mexican-nose-at (?) (T).

[3] No meaning.

[4] łᵢip'ia?ù, grass-root-little (T), a tale name. Skunk eats grass roots.

Variant 1

Rabbit lived at stone fence, *yu'kwelta*,[1] and *łipia'u* (little grass root) was around there. Little Rabbit had a toothache. He was lying down and crying. Then Coyote came up to him and said, "What are you doing, my grandson?"—"I am lying down here because I have a toothche." Coyote said to him, "My grandson, I am going to get you medicine. You lie there awhile!" So he went on. Then Little Rabbit got up and went to Skunk's hole and went in. Coyote came back with the medicine on his back. He went to where the rabbit had been lying down and said, "My grandson, help me, pull me up the ladder, I have the medicine root on my back," but there was no answer. Then he said, "I guess he went to Skunk house." So he went there and asked, "Skunk, did Rabbit come here?"— "No," said somebody. "Yes, he came here, I saw his tracks."—"Come in then and get him!" And he tried to go in, but the hole was too narrow for him. Then Skunk widened the hole for him to go in. As he was half way in, he said. "Hand Rabbit over to me, I can't go in any further." So he handed Rabbit over to him, half way on the ladder. Then Skunk shot at him in the eye with his wind and threw him down and he (Coyote) died. Rabbit skinned him and stretched out the hide. He measured with his hand to make gloves to keep his hands warm. And he measured for a scarf to keep him from getting cold. Then he said, "I did not have any toothache and I made him believe it because I was afraid he would bite me." Rabbit went back to where he was at *yu'kwelta* and there he lived. And Coyote was cast away as waste.

Variant 2

Rabbit had a toothache. Coyote was out hunting. Coyote found Rabbit crying. He asked him what he was doing? "Grandfather, I have a toothache, I am sitting here."—"I am going to get you medicine, so you will get well." When Coyote went to get medicine, Rabbit ran to Skunk. "Grandfather, let me in, I ran away from Coyote. He is going to catch me and kill me."—"Yes. Come in!" Coyote went with the medicine, but did not find Rabbit. "This rabbit is a liar. I am going to catch him, track him to where he went into a hole . . . Skunk! Did Rabbit come in here? I got his medicine."—"No, he did not come here."—"Skunk, I am asking you, did Rabbit come in here? If you don't tell me I am going

[1] h iwk^w'ialto, stone-fence-at (T).

to kill you, too."—"Yes, come in!" So Coyote went in and Skunk shot at him and killed him.

44. *The Disobedient Little Rabbits*[1]

The little rabbits lived at *hi'upaxöa'kö*[2] (stone cleft) with their mother. She would go out to get yucca flowers (*puałsikupabene.*)[3] So she said, "I am going to get yucca flowers, so you must not go down eastward." After she was gone, the children said, "I wonder why our mother does not let us go down that way. We will go and see," they said. They went down. While they were playing, Coyote came along. Coyote said to them, "Where is your mother?" The little rabbits said, "*W'apube, w'apube.*"[4] Coyote said again, "I am asking you where is your mother?"—"*W'apube, w'apube!*"—"Tell me where your mother is before I eat you up," said Coyote. "*W'apube, w'apube!*" Then he gathered them up and swallowed them. Coyote went along, very full. He walked a little way and lay down and went to sleep. The mother rabbit came home and called to her children, "Children, pull me up!" No one came out. She threw down her flowers and went down to the east side and there she saw the tracks of her children and of Coyote. She followed the tracks of Coyote and found him. She got a sharp stone and said, "This way I'll cut him! This way I'll cut him!" She cut open his stomach and the little rabbits came out, shaking off the blood. Their mother said to them, "This is what I was afraid of for you, and you did not listen." Then they went back to their home.

45. *Jack Rabbit Chief*[5]

There was a jack rabbit chief. Then where they lived a big snowfall came which was impassable. Then Jack rabbit called out from the house top, "Do not get up! Let the snow make a crust!" The chief said to the rest, "Now you be ready to get up, and walk all over about the snow to leave your footprints all over the snow. Now be ready!" They left their tracks on the snow. The chief said, "Now the hunters will not find us."

---

[1] This story was always told by my narrator's little girl "when they put the tail to her." If her turn came again, again she would tell the story, to everybody's amusement.
[2] h̦iwp'ȯhəoʔoga, stone-cleft-at (= arroyo, ravine) (T).
[3] p'̦uol-ʔ -pȯb'ene: p'̦uol'enemạ, yucca, pȯb'enemạ (pl. pȯb'ene) flower (T).
[4] Childish pronunciation of Yucca flower place.
[5] Written by a townsman.

46. Turkey Maiden Betrays Coyote

Turkey girl (*p'ianlilukwilena*)[1] was living at *węuta'*[2] (little pine). From there she went to Bow Mountain to cook thorn fruit (*klępööna*).[3] Coyote came to this girl and said, "*Yao,* greetings, grandchild, what are you doing?" Then the Turkey maiden said to Coyote, "I am cooking thorn fruit. Come, grandfather, do the same!" So Coyote began to pick thorn fruit with his hand, but his hand hurt him from the sharp thorns. The Turkey maiden had her two sticks by which she pulled the thorn fruit. She said to Coyote, "Here, grandfather, take these sticks and do as I do!" When they got done picking thorn fruit, it was about sunset and the Turkey maiden told Coyote, "Come, grandfather, go with me! It's late now, I can not go alone. Go with me to Little Pine!" So they went. When they got there they saw a light as if in the house. So they went there. Then the mother of the Turkey maiden said, "Come in, daughter (*peu'*)[4] and my son (*anuwai*)[5]." Then the maiden said, "Why don't you call out to the people?" The mother said she was not going to tell the people. "You are too young. You are tired. Go up to the second story house (*töinaya*) and lie down to rest." So they went up to the second story house. Turkey maiden was mean, she carried Coyote way up into the branches of the pine tree. She sat out on a branch and told Coyote to lie down on one of the branches. She lay down, too, watching Coyote go to sleep. Coyote went to sleep. Coyote had his leg over the Turkey maiden. Then she quietly put her head on another branch and flew away. Toward daybreak the Turkey maiden flew away and left Coyote up in the pine tree. When Coyote woke up he was lying on the branch of the pine tree. He looked down and saw he was way up high and could not get down. Turkey maiden and her mother sat on another tree watching Coyote to see how he would get down. He was holding fast to a branch, he said, "*Wiou! Wiou!*" (This was Coyote language). Then he thought to himself, "Nevertheless I have enjoyed my good time with that nice young Turkey maiden." Then the Turkey maiden and her mother sat on the tree, watching and laughing, making fun of Coyote. Then Coyote said, "*Wiou! Wiou!*" as if to jump, but he was afraid to jump. "The second time

[1]   p'ˌianlˌilukᵂil'ena (T).
[2]   w'ęʔùto, pine-little-at (T).
[3]   łˌęp'ˌəoʔ'ona (łˈęnewą, cactus) (T).
[4]   p'ïw (T).
[5]   ąnʔùwáʔi (T).

I will jump. *Wiou!*" but he hesitated to jump. "Now this will be the last time, the third time," he said. "*Wiou!*" He jumped down to the ground and broke his legs and arms. Then the Turkey maiden and her mother laughed at him. "Coyote always wants to do as he likes but he never succeeds. Nobody will make use of him." He lay there and nobody made use of him. His body was scattered around, dead. That was the end of him. Turkey maiden and her mother lived on at Pine Tree.

47. The Ducks Trick Coyote

The Ducks (*pahpena*)[1] lived at the creek *iaköbaka*[2]. They were going to slide on the ice. As they slid they sang,

> *apeała*[3] *inła halbomo*[4]
> big chest big foot slide fast
> *kaya awenu yao*
> he knows how (to slide) this way
> *apeała inła halbomo*
> *kaya awenu yao*

Coyote was out in the fields hunting something to kill to eat. He heard the song. "My grandchildren ducks are sliding on the ice." Then he followed the sound of the song. He arrived there and told the ducks, "My grandchildren, I will join you in sliding." The ducks said, "All right, grandfather, come and join us!" And he went on the ice. He slid once and he went along the ice with his long claws and scratched the ice. The ducks stood and looked at him and laughed at him. Coyote always tries to do something without knowing how. He, too, had his song:

> Big chest, big foot slide fast, etc.

(He sang deep, like a bass drum.) He said, "Ready, my grandchildren, shall I slide?"—"Yes, grandfather, slide on!" Then the ducks slid. As they slid along they cut a hole in the ice and told Coyote to slide. Then he slid, then he came to the hole in the ice and down he went into the hole into the water. He went under the ice, and they heard him still singing,

> Big chest, big foot slide fast, etc.

He never came back, he drowned. The ducks said, "Grandfather Coyote is always wanting to join in the game and wants to scare us, when he

---

[1] p'òp'ianạ (T).
[2] ¡ia- willow + kəb? + ?ogạ, at (T).
[3] ạp'iało, his-chest-big (T).
[4] ¡ẹnło, foot-big; perhaps háwamạ, fast (T).

does not know how. We are doing it because we know how, and what to do. It is our game."

48. Spotted Bird Transplants[1]

Once there lived a little spotted bird at the center of the foot race track. Spotted bird had made a plantation of pumpkin and corn. He was hoeing by singing thus:

> owasitika
> making pumpkin grow
> inasitika
> hurrying corn to grow
> umsitika
> to bear corn soon

About that time Coyote heard the song. He followed the sound of the singing and came to the place of Spotted bird. Coyote said, "*Henawa, maku.*" (Greetings, grandchild.) The bird replied, "Come, grandfather!" Coyote said, "What are you doing?" The bird replied, "I am hoeing my pumpkin and corn." Then Coyote went back to his home to get his family to help Spotted bird work his patch of corn and pumpkin. Spotted bird had wisdom and power to remove his plantation, so he took everything up into the air to a heavenly home. The next day Coyote came with his family to the place where he had seen the plantation of Spotted bird, but he failed to find it. Coyote jumped around the place, saying, "Here it was! Here it was!"

49. The Reeds Dance for Coyote[2]

Coyote lived at Sun house (*tultö'naka*). As he went about hunting every day he came to a village. He was invited to come in and have dinner. The people in the house served the meal. They had deer meat and buffalo meat, and besides, sweet pudding (*łalu'na,* sprouted wheat flour). So they all sat down to eat dinner. Coyote always liked meat, but when he tasted the pudding he liked it most and paid no more attention to the meat. When they finished eating they gave him buffalo meat and deer meat and pudding. But the sweet pudding he wanted most to take to his wife and children. So he went back home. On his way back from the village he passed some *pụune*[3] (tall, white plants like willows), and the day was windy and the weeds were blowing and making a big noise.

---

[1] Written by a townsman.
[2] Compare Lipan Apache, Opler 2: 181.
[3] pụ?'une (T).

When he got back home he said to his wife and children he was invited by *wąłiu*[1], Wind woman, to a dance. He gave the meat and pudding to his wife and children. "The people gave me a good dinner," he said, "and this is what they gave me." His wife and children found the pudding sweet. Coyote old woman said, "I know how to make this, too, and I will make one." So she packed it to take to Wind woman. So they started from their house, the old man and the old woman and the children. On their way they went singing the songs they were going to dance for Wind woman.

> yani yani yan e wa
> yani wa
> yani eyani eyani wa

So they went on and crossed the plain. They were about half way to the Indian village. They stopped and sang,

> yani yani yan e wa etc.

Coyote said to his wife and children, "Wind old woman is looking at us, you must dance harder and harder."

> yani yani yan e wa etc.

They got to the place where the reeds were blowing. Then he said to his wife and children, "Here it was." Then they saw nobody there. Then they jumped and sang,

> yani yani yan e wa etc.

They danced, but they saw nobody. He said again, "Here it was, my wife and children." They danced so hard they got tired; but nobody came out. So they started on to the village with their pudding. Coyote old woman said, "I will take this pudding to the Indian village." So they went singing again,

> yani yani yan e wa etc.

Coyote said, "Now the people are seeing us. Dance hard, my children!" And he went ahead dancing and singing. The old woman had the pudding on her back. She was very tired. She shifted the bundle and exclaimed "*Huwi!*" Still they went on dancing.

> yani yani yan e wa etc.

Coyote said, "My children, don't get tired! Dance as hard as you can! The Indians see us." They were near the village. The people said, "Grandfather Coyote (*tałułi tsunę*), here he comes again." So everybody went on top of their houses, and the Coyotes danced still harder. They arrived and went into the house. Everybody went in to see them. Coyote old woman laid her pack down on the floor and spread it out and told

[1] w'ǫłiw (T).

the people that was the meal for them to eat. But the people appeared not to like it and would not eat. They said, "*Itawe!*"[1] So nobody ate it and everybody went out from the house. Coyote old woman went back to her house, very sad, as they would not eat her pudding. Then they went back to Sun house.

50. Coyote Races Buffalo and Mountain Sheep

The buffalo lived at *taibaba*,[2] people (Indian) creek. The mountain sheep (*piankwana*)[3] lived at White Mountain (*pianbatö′ba*)[4]. The two groups of animals talked of making a race. They would bet eagles. They decided they would go to *pianpamuluna*[5], Water Jar Mountain, and go around it five times and back to the starting place. So they set the day following for the race. The day came and they got ready at the starting place. Mountain Sheep had two eagles sitting on his horns, and as Buffalo always liked to have eagle tail feathers, he wanted to win. They were about to start. Coyote was nearby and came to them and said that he could not run fast, but he would join in the race. So they started, Buffalo and Mountain Sheep and Coyote behind them. They ran and disappeared from sight. They reached Mountain Water Jar. They went around it five times, and went back to the starting place. When they were nearing the starting place Coyote, who had not run hard at the first, now ran as fast as he could. He passed Mountain Sheep with the two eagles on his horns. He passed him swiftly and grabbed the eagles. So Coyote won the race. Mountain Sheep and Buffalo were beaten by Coyote. So Coyote took the eagles and went back to his house and brought the eagles to his wife and children and told them he ran a race with Mountain Sheep and Buffalo and won, and got the eagles. He said that he would make another race with Buffalo and Mountain Sheep. "I will bet one of my sons, Mountain Sheep will bet one of his girls, and Buffalo will bet one of his girls." Then Coyote pulled out eagle tail feathers and eagle down and put the tail feathers in his hair and in his wife's hair and in his boy's hair, and the down over the bodies of them all. He had five sons, four stood at the starting place and one was to run the race. Coyote old man

[1] Exclamation of distaste.
[2] t'¡oyp'òbo, people-water-toward (T).
[3] p'¡iank'¡uona (T).
[4] p'¡ianp'òt''əbo, mountain-white-at (T). White Mountain is at Fort Garland, north of Taos (or in San Luis Valley, Colorado [T]). It figures in the Emergence lore, Parsons 10: 112, 113.
[5] p'¡ianp'òm'uluną (T). West of Taos Junction (T).

knew they would be afraid of him, so he took some bark and tied the bark alongside his leg (as a splint), pretending his leg was broken. Coyote said to Mountain Sheep and Buffalo, "I will go in the race against you both. You see I can not run, my leg is broken." He showed the leg to them. But they were afraid because he had won and they said, "No!" Then his son entered in the race. If he won, he was to take the girls, if Mountain Sheep and Buffalo won, they were to take two of his boys. As they were starting Coyote did not stand still but kept moving back and forward limping. He said, "You see I am a lame man, I can not run."—"No, you can not run." Coyote told his wife, "I will go behind my son. If he sees me he will run fast, if he does not see me, he will not run." Then he started, running with a limp. Buffalo and Mountain Sheep were way ahead of Coyote boy. Coyote old man went behind his boy. When the boy saw his father coming at a limp he ran faster. Then they went five times around White Mountain and back to the starting place. Buffalo and Mountain Sheep were ahead all the time. Coyote and his son came way behind. As they came near the starting place Coyote ran hard and passed his son and Buffalo and Mountain Sheep. As he was running so hard, the leg became untied and the bark was dragging behind. He passed them and beat them. He called out, "*masench'ilotowina*[1], men holler." So he won the race. Then Buffalo had to give away his girl, and Mountain Sheep, his girl. Coyote old woman was standing there covered with down and the Coyote sons were going ahead dancing and Coyote old man and his wife were behind, herding Buffalo and Mountain Sheep, and singing,

> he'ya he'ya
> he'ya he'ya' a a
> he'ya he'ya' a a

They got to where they lived. And now Coyote had the Mountain Sheep and the Buffalo.

51. Coyote Paints with Firebrands[2]

Piapole'na, Red-headed Woodpecker[3], was living in the tree, and Coyote was going about as he always does, seeing what he could do and what

---

[1] mạs,əonc̣ilutụʔinạ, reflexive prefix + men + cry out + speak + those who, those who are men speak and cry out (T).

[2] Compare Isleta, Lummis, 49 ff.

[3] Breast dull red. In English the narrator called the bird, carpenter bird, translating from the term for it in Spanish.

tricks he could play. When he came to the tree where Woodpecker lived he heard the young ones in the tree hole. He looked up where the little birds were crying. After a little while their mother came and brought them feed. Coyote was still looking up, wanting to get up there. He saw the mother with speckled breast and red at the ears and red at the eyes. Then the little ones came out and sat on the edges of the hole. They were speckled with red at ears and eyes. It looked very pretty to Coyote. He said to himself, "How can I get up there? I want to see them. I would like to be just like them. I want to paint myself that way when I get back for my wife to see me." Then he said, "My friend, could you bring your little ones here where I am, so I could see them and yourself, what kind of painting you have on your body and face, so I could paint myself when I go back and my wife could see how pretty I am, like you?" Then the mother bird raised her wings. "Here!" (She was red under the wings.) Then the little ones all stretched their wings and showed the red. He went back where he lived. When he reached there, he told his wife and children that he found some friends painted red under their armpits. "I like the painting of these friends. Tomorrow I am going to take you for a trip, and we will paint as I saw them to show them we have the same painting as they." The children said, "Father, how can we paint?" Coyote said, "I will show you." Then he took some pieces of burning wood from the fireplace. He tied them under the armpits of his children and of their mother. "Now we will go to my new friends, far off there in those cottonwood trees." So they went. When they got there, there were Woodpecker and his little ones. "Come in, come in, Friend Coyote, sit down!" Coyote was painted with white dabs over his body (his own kind of painting). While they were sitting there, his sons kept raising their arms. Woodpecker looked at them and laughed at them. The youngest said, "Father (*tamq*)[1], the firebrands have gone out." The other two nudged him to shut up so they wouldn't think it was burning wood. The little boy said again, "Father, the firebrands have gone out." Coyote looked angrily at his little boy. Woodpecker said, "Coyote always wants to be painted like other people. This is our own way. Coyote can never do it. He is always Coyote, with his own color, and we have our own color." And they flew away from the cottonwood tree and left the Coyote children there with the firebrands under their armpits.

---

[1] tǫ̀mạ (T).

52. How the Deer Got their Spots[1]

The deer (*pęnöma*)[2] lived at the hill *pęhaiba* (deer yawn). Coyote lived at *paḷihainena* with his wife and children. Coyote always went out hunting in the daytime. One day he went hunting toward where the sun rises, to the east. He arrived on his rounds at *pęhaiba*. While around there he saw the little deer playing about. They were newly born and spotted white. Coyote liked the way the deer were marked. So he made his rounds about, and toward night he got back home. While he was talking at night with his wife and children he said to them, "I went across the plain to the east this morning and I came to a hill where the deer live and saw the little ones painted yellow with white spots. They invited me to come in. I went in and asked them how they got spotted so nicely. The older one answered, 'Our mother shut us up in a room and closed all the holes and the door and set corncobs on fire in the fireplace and filled the room with smoke. That's the way we got our spots.' That's what they told me, and I came home. When I left, their mother invited me to come and take you over there." So Coyote woman was getting the lunch ready all night to go the next morning to the deer's home. So early in the morning they started on their way to the deer's home. As they went they sang,

　　　　yane yane wa a
　　　　yane yane wa a
　　　　yaneh' yaneh
　　　　ya neh e wah

They went dancing all the way. Then Coyote old man said, "Don't appear as if you were tired, dance hard! *Naḷetaien* are looking at us." They sang,

　　　　yane yane wa a etc.

They are now at *taupaga*[3] (piñon creek). They crossed, still singing and dancing. They are now at *pahhulba*[4] (poison ivy). They are still singing,

　　　　yane yane wa a etc.

They get to *pakwiuba*. They are still singing,

　　　　yane yane wa a etc.

[1] Compare Isleta, Lummis, 179 ff.; San Juan, Parsons 4: 155-157; San Juan, San Ildefonso, Espinosa, 97, 113; Cochiti, Benedict 1: 160-162; Sia, Stevenson 1: 153-154; Laguna, Parsons 8: 137; Shumopovi, Wallis, 44-46; also Second Mesa, De Huff, 25-29; Jicarilla Apache, Opler 1: 285-286; Lipan Apache, Opler 2: 141-142.

[2] p'ęnemą (pl.) (T).

[3] t'ʼowp'ò ʔogą, piñon-water-at (T).

[4] p'òx'əlbo, poison-ivy-at (T).

Now they were near *pęhaiba*. They reached *pęhaiba*. Deer woman had prepared a meal for them to eat. She took them into the house and served the meal. They ate. While they were eating the Coyote little ones *(tsuneuna)*[1] were watching the little deer so nicely spotted. Then the Coyote boys said to their father, whispering, "*T'et'a'*[2], father, when we go back home, you paint us like that, so we will be spotted like the little deer." Then Coyote old man poked his children with his elbow to make them shut up lest the others heard them. So they finished eating. After they finished eating they said to Deer woman, "Now we have been your company today, we will go back home. We live very far." So Deer woman said, "Hạ, yes, you come back again in the morning!" So they left and went home. Then the children reminded their father and mother that they wanted to be painted with white spots like the young deer. So Coyote woman prepared the corncobs and took her children to a room and shut all the openings and set fire to the corncobs and went out and shut the door. The three children stayed in the room, where smoke got so thick, after a time the Coyote children began to cough and sneeze. They grabbed each other and fell down with the saliva running out from their mouths. They were suffering. They called for their mother; "Klao[3] (Mother)! Klao! open the door! We are dying." But she did not hear. Then a long while after, she came to the door to see what they were doing. She called them and they did not answer. They were lying down, choked. So Coyote woman opened the door and went in and she too began to cough and sneeze. She dragged the children out. There was no sign of any spot on them. They just lay there blowing, blowing. When they came back to life they said, "Mother, are we spotted?" Their mother said, "No, I see no spots on you." All the Coyotes lived at *pałihainena*, and the deer lived at *pęhaiba*. And they say Coyote wants to do whatever he sees others doing. The deer said, "That's our way of dressing," and they continued to live at *pęhaiba*.

Variant

There lived Bear woman with her husband and children, and Deer woman lived with her husband and children. They were all good friends and they always went out hunting together. Whenever they went hunting, Bear woman would look for bugs in their heads. The deer found out

[1] c'ùn'e?ùnạ (T).
[2] tit'a (T).
[3] ł'a?ù (T).

why Bear woman always wanted to look for bugs. Bear asked why Deer children looked so pretty and spotted. Deer said she burned corncobs (*k'quna*)[1] and put her children in the smoke, that was why they were spotted. Deer woman said to her children that if ever Bear brought them meat they must not eat it because she knew that Bear woman would kill her some time. They should go to their grandfather and grandmother where the sun came up, she said to her children. Deer woman went out hunting, and she found Bear woman and she asked Bear woman to look for bugs. Bear woman told Deer woman first to look over her head. Then Bear woman looked over Deer woman's head and she bit her in the neck and killed her. Before Bear woman went there, she had shut up her children in the corncob smoke. She went and gave meat to the Deer children, she told them their mother was out hunting and she did not see her. When the little deer saw the meat, they ran away to their grandmother. Bear woman went to her house and found her children dead. Bear woman grew very angry. "I will kill her children too," she said. She went to the Deer house, but she did not find the Deer children. She followed the tracks of the little Deer. They got to a river where Beaver lived. Beaver was chopping wood. Beaver said, "*Tiy tiy taki.*" Little Deer said, "Beaver, will you take me across the river." He said again, "*Tiy tiy taki.*" Then he listened to them and told them to look for bugs in his head. Little Deer boy had a bear claw necklace around his neck and Deer girl bit them, instead of the frogs she found in Beaver's head, and she threw the frogs into the river. Then Beaver carried them across the river. Bear old woamn came to where Beaver was chopping wood. She said, "Beaver, will you carry me across the river?" Beaver said, "*Tiy tiy taki,*" and kept saying it, until the little Deer got away. Bear old woman said crossly, "I am asking you if you will let me cross the river?" At last Beaver said, "Yes." Then the little deer came to a place where a bear was lying. The bear said, "What have you with you." And the Deer boy hid the bear claws on his neck, and he said he had some water-fly claws, *po'pyyymqtselene*. Bear asked again, and he said the same thing. "Well, I will carry you across," said the Bear, and he put them across the river. Then the Deer boy put his little sister on his back. Her feet were so red he began to cry[2]. They went along. At last they came to Paköałaana. They asked him to carry him over. Bear woman came to the bear (*köana*) (that took care of the river) and he let her pass and then she

---

[1] k',o?'ona (T).

[2] This part of the story made the little son of the narrator snivel. So in telling the story his father would repeat it, "just to make him cry."

came to Paköałaana. She asked if she could pass; but he did not listen to her, and she asked again. The third time she asked, he let her pass. The little deer came to where their grandfather and grandmother lived. They came out to meet them. "Our grandchildren have come!" they said. The deer went up the ladders and down, and then they saw grey deer and white deer and yellow deer, all kinds, sitting around. Then Bear woman came and climbed up, and just as she was putting her feet in, the deer said, "*Ilili!*[1] Bear woman's paw shows." She asked if the little deer were there. "Yes, they are here, come down and get them!" And both the little deer cried and the other deer told them not to cry. "She won't take you out from here," they said to them. Bear old woman said, "This time I will really come down," and she went down two steps. Again the deer said "*Ilili!* Bear woman's paw shows."—"This time I will come down." And she went down and the deer caught her on their horns and they threw her one to another and tore her to pieces.

53. *Coyote Gets a Hunting Song and Plays Dead*

Coyote, was living at *tu'watöna*,[2] Fox house. He was hunting across the plains. On his way he heard somebody singing,

> yeha ea ea
> yeha yeha yeha
> yeha yeha m! m!

Owl (*kǫwena*)[3] was going to war and he was dressed with a feather in his hair braid such as Apache wear, an eagle tail feather between two hanging split feathers, all tied to a pointed stick, and he carried a war club and an Apache water jar. He was going singing,

> yeha ea ea etc.

Coyote heard Owl singing, and he followed the singing. He met Owl, he said, "*Ankuwam, anpuywaie*[4], you are well, my friend? This is the way we men sometimes meet when we are not expecting it, and we men don't know where we have our beds."—"Yes," said Owl, "that's the way it is." Then Coyote said, "My friend, sing me that song! I have no hunting song." Owl repeated the song:

> yeha ea ea etc.

Coyote learned the song. Then they separated. Owl went on his way and

---

[1] An exclamation of fear, over something strange. See p. 166.

[2] t‚ux‪ᵂat‎'ᵊna (T).

[3] kǫw'ena(T).

[4] ak‎'uwám, ạnp‚uywá?i (T). Same greetings at Isleta.

Coyote, on his way. After parting from Owl Coyote ran on ahead. Then
he stuck arrows into his body and poked up his nose to draw blood, and
lay down as if he had had a big fight.[1] Owl came up. He saw Coyote lying
there. "It is true what my friend Coyote said, when I met him. That is
the way we men meet unexpected enemies. Here he is dead, he must
have been in a big fight." Then Owl bent Coyote up and put him in his
jar and put it on his back and went off. As he started, from inside the jar
came a loud whistle. Then Owl said to himself, "This is what I am most
afraid of." Then he took off his jar and threw it down on the ground, and
his war club and hair feather and ran away. Then Coyote got out of the
jar and took the jar and the war club and the hair feather and said, "My
friend Owl didn't know that I am a wise man." He put the feather in his
hair and went singing:

> yeha ea ea etc.

He was going now to his house and went singing and at the end of every
song he said like the owl, hum! hum! (grunt). Coyote's son was on top
of their house looking for his father. He saw him coming dancing and
singing. He said to his mother, "*łau!* somebody is coming in the road
singing and dancing, in fine clothes. He does not look like my father."
Then the mother came out to see. "That's your father." Then Coyote
neared the house, still dancing. He went up to the top of the house,
jumping and dancing, dancing all the harder when he saw his wife and
his boy. He went inside still dancing, he called to his wife and boy,
"Come on, dance!" So all three danced as hard as they could.

54. *Coyote Gambles with the White-headed Eagles and Plays Dead*

Coyote man (*tow'asöanana*)[2] lived at *pałexonnenyaia*[3]. He went out to
hunt over near the foot of the hill. Then he came to a rocky mountain
point. There two white-headed eagles[4] lived. He was invited to come in.
They looked at him sidewise (as eagles do). They asked him why he came
there. "I was hunting and saw the smoke and came here." They had some
very nice clothing hanging in their room. Coyote man was looking at it

---

[1] Compare Sia, Stevenson 1: 150.

[2] t͜ux^was'əonena, fox-man or coyote-man (T).

[3] *Pałena*, a certain weed which is a foot high, hollow, has no bloom, grows in any dry
place; *xonnenyaia*, root.

[4] *Kuasupalenema*, so called because it is an angry bird and brave; this is its tale name, its
ordinary name is *pasetana*.

and he liked the clothing, buckskin leggings and shirt and other nice things made of the skins of wild animals. He was thinking to himself how he could get that clothing and the mountain lion quiver and the bow and arrows. The White-headed Eagles guessed what Coyote man was thinking about. Then the Eagles said to Coyote man, "If you get us a blue coyote (fine fur) we will give you clothing of all kinds like this, whatever you wish for your dress."—"Yes, my grandsons, I will get you one." So he went away and went down along the plain along the foot-hills. Then he came to a dry spot. There he pulled some sunflower stalks big as arrows. These he stuck in his body and in his head, as if arrows were sticking into him. He poked up his nostrils for blood to run out of his nose. He lay down, pretending he had a hard fight with enemies. He lay there as if he was dead. (He was going to catch that blue coyote.) So as he lay there the blue coyote came around, and saw him lying dead with the arrows sticking in his head and body, and his nose bloody. Blue Coyote stood a little way from Coyote man. Then he hollered, scream-ing very loud, calling to any one who might be near, to Red Coyote, Grey Coyote, Black Coyote, all kinds of coyotes. "Here our grand-father, Coyote man, had a big fight with some enemies and was killed and is lying dead here. Come and see, all kinds of coyotes near here!" So in a short time they gathered near dead Coyote man. First, coyotes of his own kind went to where he was lying, they grabbed him by the head and raised up his head. They shook him with different motions, they tickled and punched him to find out whether he was dead or alive. He made no motion of being alive. The other coyotes said, "Poor man, he is dead." Next Yellow Coyote came to him and said, "I know where he has his life." He pinched him through the ear holes and nose holes and mouth and anus but he never moved. Yellow Coyote said then, "True it is, he is dead." Then Black Fox went up to him and said, "I know where he has his life. Then he went to his head and pulled his whiskers and opened his eyes and tickled him wherever he thought he could make him laugh or speak. But he never gave any sign. "Truly he is dead," he said. Then Blue Fox said, "You don't know what he is trying to do. He is thinking of me. He wants to get me and kill me." Then he went up to him. He reached out his hand with his sharp claws to the dead coyote and, eyeing him carefully, he scratched him hard to make him jump from pain. Then he scratched his back hard. He went in front of his head, scratched his mouth, pulled his lips, pulled his eyelids. Coyote man had his war club under his breast. Then he jumped up with his club and jumped on Blue Fox, clubbed him with his war club and knocked him down dead.[1] Then all the other coyotes ran away in different directions. As they ran they looked back to see what was going on. So Coyote man killed Blue Fox, and he said, "Now I have got what my friends, White-headed Eagles, need." He skinned him and he put the skin of Blue Fox on his back and walked back to White-headed Eagles' home. When he got there, White-headed Eagle said to him, "Come in, grandfather!" He went in and sat down in the house. White-headed Eagle said, "How was your luck, grandfather?"—"I had good luck," he said, "I fought with different enemies, I had a big battle in the plain, I won, and I killed Blue Fox for you. Here it is," he showed them the skin. "Oh, let us see, grandfather! This is what we want, this is what we did not have and badly needed. We are lucky to get it through your bravery. Now we will give you the clothing we promised you for it." So one of them went in the east room and brought out to him a quiver of lion hide full of arrows, and a bow, and buckskin leggings and some nice moccasins beaded with porcupine quills. And Coyote dressed up there and said, "Where can I find very strong enemies to fight with these clothes on, with my bow and lots of arrows? Can you tell me where I can meet such enemies?" And the White-headed Eagles spread out their wings and shook themselves. One of them said, "We don't know where you can find the one you would like to fight." Coyote pulled his bow with one draw. "I can fight," he said, "Suppose I try you, both of you. If you kill me, I bet you my clothing, and if I kill you, you bet me that blue coyote."—"We will fight you tomorrow, in the daytime." So Coyote started out and said to them, "I will wait for you down there in the plain." So he went down to the plain. He camped there. Morning came. He was watching for them to come, at sunrise. He could not see them. He thought, "I will go back and find them and see why they do not come." When he was about ready to start for the White-headed Eagles' home he saw some birds flying from the north. "I guess they are coming," he said. Then he pulled his bow. "This is the way I am going to shoot," he said to himself. So they came flying. They flew around and around, high up. And he was carrying on a sham battle, running and yelping, war whooping, pulling his bow. "This is the way I am going to do." Pretty soon one of them flew swiftly to where he was—ss——s! He dodged and jumped and gave a war whoop. Then he shot the eagle. Then his feathers, the soft white ones, just spread out, but he flew swiftly up again. Then the second eagle came the same way, swiftly flying. Coyote shot at him and

---

[1] For general incident of playing dead, compare Shumopovi, Wallis, 48-49; Laguna, Paguate, Espinosa, 83, 86-87.

his feathers flew out and he swiftly flew up, way up high. Coyote kept jumping and yelping and war whooping. Then the first came back against him, drawing himself together, and he shot his arrow at Coyote. Coyote turned over on himself and yelled. The bird flew up swiftly into the sky. Coyote could hardly see him. He said, "Oh, I will kill them. They can't get away from me." He did not feel the arrow the eagle shot into him (they were very little, fine arrows in their bodies). Then the other eagle came the same way, drawing himself together, making himself small, and shot at Coyote, and Coyote fell. The eagle went up swiftly into the sky. Coyote man was feeling very tired, he hollered and called out for help. He was tired and mad, he did not know what he was doing. As he called for help, coyotes like himself and Yellow Coyote and Blue Coyote and others came to his help. As he did not know what he was doing he shot his own people and killed every one off. Then there was nobody to help him. Then White-headed Eagle came flying again. Came down swiftly over him, shot him, and he fell down. He got up and ran. The eagle was angry and flew against him and knocked him down. The other eagle came down and both attacked him. He jumped around and did not know what he was doing. He was almost dead. Instead of shooting at the eagles, he shot anywhere. He fell on the ground, they attacked him and gave him no chance to get up. Finally they killed him. They stripped him of his clothing. "Grandfather Coyote is not strong enough to fight us. He did not know who we were. He made a mistake when he challenged us to fight. He did not know we were the strongest of animals against any enemies we might meet." They flew up to their home at Rocky Mountain Point, and Coyote remained cast away in the plain, and the White-headed Eagles remained at their home forever. The eagles are the worst enemies the animals have.

55. Coyote Breaks the Continence Taboo

Coyote old man was living at Coyote place. He was living happily with his wife. The Knife boys (*chiaöwiuna*)[1] were living to the north, at *kualaögǫ,* (up at blackbirds' place)[2]. The bald-headed eagles (*kisupalenemu*) were living northwest at *kualata* (down at blackbirds' place). One day Coyote said to his wife, "Well, my wife, I am going hunting. I am going towards the north." He got his lunch and started out. The Knife boys had been fighting with the bald-headed eagles and they were to fight

[1] c¡ia?'əwyunạ (T).
[2] *Kualadenemu,* blackbirds; *k'edenemu,* red-winged blackbird.

them again. As they sat in their kiva they saw a shadow overhead. "Somebody is trespassing," they said. The older one said, "You better go out and see who is around." When Knife boy went out he said, "What are you doing around here?"—"Knife boy, I am hunting. I have come this far." They invited him to come in. He went in and saw some weapons hanging there. Coyote said, "If I had these weapons I would meet the enemies and fight them." Knife boy said, "We are at war with the bald-headed eagles. You may take the weapons and fight them." So he put on the knife helmet and took a knife and went. "Now let us go and watch," they said. When they went up on top of their house, they could see the dust and the feathers flying. Coyote old man got wounded. They saw him coming. "They did not kill him, but he is walking as if he were very weak." When he got there, they said, "You are badly wounded."—"Yes, I had a hard battle."—"You better go home. Follow our advice and you will get well; if not, you will die."—"All right, Knife boy, whatever you say I will do."—"You must not come near your wife for five days. If you do, you will get blood poison and die." When he got home he was bloody and his wife thought he had some meat. But he told her about his fight and what the Knife boys said. She put him lying down. After three days he felt better and said to his wife, "Let me cover myself with a little bit of your buffalo robe!"—"No, you must do what the Knife boys said." But he went under her cover, and when she was asleep he lay close to her. Next day he swelled up and died. She said, "We are coyotes. We will be watching in the mountains and roaming the earth."

56. Coyote Rapes Gopher Old Woman

Coyote was living (at) *paxöpatsanata*.[1] *Pąłułi*,[2] Gopher old man, *pąłiu*, Gopher old woman, lived at *tołałiabpahöta*[3] (cottonwood tree windfall). Gopher old man went to visit his neighbors to the west. On his way he met Coyote. Coyote said to him, "My friend, where are you going?"—"I am going to visit my neighbors' people. They are coming back from hunting buffalo." Coyote said, "Good, good, *nakuyuma, nakuyuma, anpu-waie*[4] (my friend)! And also I am going to visit my friends." Then Coyote went on with Gopher old man. On his way he studied a joke to

---

[1]　Pumpkin seed floating. p₁ox₁ɔp'òc''aneto, pumpkin-seed-water-stepping-on-at, at floating pumpkin seed (T). In the meadow below the village.

[2]　p₁ǫłʼułi (T).

[3]　t₁ułoł₁iabp'òh'ɔoto, cottonwood-crack-ravine-at (T).

[4]　nặkʼʼuyumạ, ạnp₁uywáʔi (T).

play on Gopher old man's wife. Gopher old woman was blind. Coyote got to Gopher old woman's house. He went in, acting as would Gopher old man when he came back. "*Huwi! anpiugaie*[1] (my daughter), help pull me up!" (He pretended he had a big load.) Gopher old woman felt her way to the ladder. "Where are you?"—"Here," he said. Then she took him by the hand. He had longer claws and longer and thicker hair than Gopher old man. Gopher old woman thought to herself, "My husband has not long hair and long claws." Then Coyote threw down his load and said to Gopher old woman, "Here, grandmother (*litu*)! My people have no buffalo meat this time so I did not get any." She felt around and could find no meat. Coyote said to Gopher old woman, "Grandmother, fix the bed, lie down to sleep!" Then she fixed the place. Then Coyote lay down and told Gopher old woman, "Come on, lie down!" (Then my nephew who was telling the story made a sign of what Coyote did, and we laughed.) Then Gopher old woman felt his body and his long hairs. She said, "This is not the way my husband is. You have long hairs."—"Now, come on, I am Old Man Gopher. Don't be afraid!" Gopher old woman said, "*Unkai!*"[2] Then Coyote grabbed her and pulled her to him. Then Gopher old woman cried. But he did what he wanted to her. Then Coyote got up and ran out. Gopher old woman cried. About that time her husband came. Gopher old man went into the house with his load of buffalo meat from his neighbors. As he started up the ladder he called out, "Why don't you come out to help me up?" She came out and felt him, but she was still crying. Gopher old man asked his wife, "Why are you crying?" She did not want to say, but she kept sobbing. "Stop crying, tell me!" [To his own amusement narrator imitated suppressed sobbing.] "What did he do to you? How can I catch him? He is a fast runner and I am short-legged. Don't cry! Are you not a woman? Don't cry!"

57. *Coyote Pretends he is Big Water Man*

Some Apache were living. The two daughters of the chief went to get water. In the middle of the pond they saw a head sticking up with feathers on it; the face was white. It said, "Put your dresses up! Put your dresses up or the world will end.[3] Higher!" he said, "Higher!" And the girls did it because they believed it was Pakölaana (big water man). Then

---

[1] ạnp'ïwk'oyi (T).

[2] Exclamation of distrust or fear.

[3] *Utö͞pala*, day last. ut'ạp'ollá, it will be finished. u- pronominal prefix, + t'ạ- day + p'ollá- future of p'ola, to finish (T).

some other girls came and Coyote said the same, until all the girls had come. Then Coyote jumped into the middle of the tents and called out, "All the Apache women are mine! I know them all!" Then he ran off to the mountain. The men ran after him, but they did not catch him.

58. Coyote Steals the Apache Girls[1]

There lived some Apache in the plain along the rivers. One Apache man had two daughters and two sons. The Apache advised his daughters not to go for water to a spring near the camp. The father was always out on the hunt. However, the two girls went to the spring for water. When they arrived at the spring, Coyote (*choneh*) came there. He said to the two girls, "Now, my daughters, I must take you to my home." When he arrived at his home, he said to his wife, "Why not call it to the attention of the people?" He took the girls to the house, and the girls got married to his sons. Coyote said to his sons, "Now, my sons, take your wives to the east side where the grandfathers—Fire Coyote (*batu choneh*)[2]—live."

When the Apache father came home from hunting, his daughters always used to come out and meet him, but this time the girls did not meet their father. The father put the deer on top of the house and called for his daughters. They were not there. He could not find them. He took the deer in and asked the boys where their sisters were. The boys replied, "Over there at the spring where you told them not to go, they went for water. We went, we saw the footprint of a man. Now you go and see."—"It is nobody else but Coyote. I used to see him about here once in a while." The boys went to the spring and saw the fooptrint and told their father. The father said to his boys, "Now you make your bow and arrows." The boys made their arrows and followed the tracks.

Coyote went to his grandmother, old Gopher, and asked her if there was any way she could get him out from there. "Yes," said grandmother Gopher. So she spat in the four directions with her medicine to cut a deep hole across the way of the two Apache boys for them to sink down into and not reach their sisters. Coyote went back to the home of Fire Coyote and told them he had killed them (the Apache boys). He was asked if he took their scalps to make the dance. He said, "No, we must go to scalp them, so we can dance the war dance."

---

[1] Written by townsman.
[2] p'atuc'ùn'e, fire (burnt) coyote (T).

59. Coyote Tricks his Daughter[1]

Coyote told his daughter that if she ever met a man with a patch over one eye and speaking Comanche she must marry him. So Coyote put a patch over one eye and met his daughter in the road and began to speak Comanche. She said, "My father told me that when I met a man blind in one eye and speaking Comanche I must marry him." So she married him. He would never let her touch his eye. One day he put his head on her knees for her to look for lice. He felt good and went to sleep. Then she looked at his eye and she saw that he was her father and she killed him.

Variant

Hamen′matömxa[2] Coyote was living where the coyote live. He had three daughters. The eldest was very pretty, and he liked her. So he went away and dressed up different and whitened his face and he came back to his house and asked his eldest daughter to marry him. His eldest daughter said yes. So they were married. After that they sat down in a warm place and he put his head in her lap. He had a pimple on his neck. When she told him to turn over on the other side, he would not turn. When he went to sleep she turned him over and saw the pimple and recognized her father. She laid him gently on the floor and got a big stone and dropped it on his head and killed him.

Tenk köiwẹkim,[3] so then you have a tail.

60. Coyote Brings the Buffalo to Taos

Coyote was roaming about the big plain in the east, in the buffalo country. He went about from place to place in the plain. One day he found a bunch of buffalo. Then he made up his mind that he would take them to the people (of Taos)[4]. So he kept on rounding them up, herding them, for three or four days. On the fifth day he began to drive them slowly toward the west. They went walking slowly and gently when he

---

[1] Compare Jicarilla Apache, Opler 1: 280-282; Lipan Apache, Opler 2: 135-139; Ute, Kroeber 2: 268-269.

[2] xǫm‚enmạt‛‛əmxǫ, "once upon a time" (T).

[3] tẹng kǫyxᵂ‛ẹkim(a) (T).

[4] The general idea of Coyote releasing or conveying the buffalo is widespread: Lipan Apache, Opler 2: 122-125; Kiowa, Parsons 6: 26.

wanted them to go. Several days they went, stopping at different places for water. He was thinking that he would take them first to *kankaba*[1] (when the buffalo stands.) He arrived there, he stayed there some time. Then he thought he would take them a little farther west where the people of Taos lived. Morning came, he began to drive them toward the village. He sang,

> hia hia a a
> yaia eya eya
> heya heya

Then the buffalo went dancing, turning their bodies, they went forward and back again, while Coyote sang. Then he would stop at places and dance a while, then at the end of his song he hollered,

> kanchö'chilowe[2]
> buffalo-hunt-cry-out-that one hollering
> a a a -a
> a a au'
> a au'

Then he began to sing, and the buffalo danced. When he hollered, the people of Taos heard him and they went on top of their houses to see if Coyote was bringing buffalo to them. He was just a little way off on the east side of the village and he sang,

> hia hia a a
> yaia eya eya
> heya heya

and the buffalo were dancing. They danced harder when the Taos people were looking at them. Then he started down, still singing, and the buffalo were still dancing. Then he came to the village and took the buffalo to *fialuła t'aine*,[3] Big Earring People (chief), to his kiva, meaning that in the future he (this chief) would make buffalo songs and dances. He presented them to him. From there he took them to the next, to be companion in the dance, to *töt'aine*,[4] Day People (chief). Also he told him he was to accompany the first in the dance. *Töt'aine* said *t'aa* (thanks) to him. Then he went to the next, to *kwałauuna*,[5] Axe-chief, and told him the same, that the buffalo would be theirs, and to take part in the dance with the first man. So he made presentation to the three

[1] k'ongabo, buffalo-when-at (T).
[2] k̦oncəc'ilu̧ʔi (T).
[3] p'ial̦ułot'ʻoynema̦ (T).
[4] t'ət'ʻoynema̦ (T).
[5] kʷ̦oł̦owaʔ'ana (T).

kivas, to make buffalo dances henceforward. Then Coyote went back to his home in the eastern plain in the buffalo country.

61. Coyote Calls for a Scalp Dance

Coyote was living at *tuw'atöaya,*[1] Coyote house. From there he went down into the plain toward the west. He went travelling and learning about different peoples in the western plain. Then he reached the mountain of the backbone of the Sun's rays.[2] He saw the country, the nice springs, all kinds of flowers. He picked the flowers he liked. Then he made a head-band (*pichiina*)[3] of sunflowers[4] (*tultipamena*).[5] Then he picked other flowers, blue, white, red. He bundled them up. He went singing and shouting. He started to dance, with the armful of flowers, and the wreath on his head. As he went along every flower he saw he picked, he had a big bunch, but still he went on picking. Then he said, "Now I will go back. I will take all these flowers to my wife and tell her I found a beautiful new country, full of flowers, with a nice lake in the mountain." So he went back to his home, carrying the flowers. When he got home, he told his wife to make wreaths for herself and their children and all to hold the flowers, while they danced. He went out from his house, he found a dead castaway hawk. Then he thought he would go to the village and call on the people and tell them he had found dead something which from way back in the old times used to be their great enemy, killing the people. "Come people, join with me in a scalp dance (*itu'hutoiya,* mocking dance)[6]! Shut up your doors tight and windows and chimney holes and mouse holes, and dance!" So everybody went out with him to dance. Everybody was in the dance. He sang,

> ki i i sana oiya
> ki i i sana oiya

He had tied the dead hawk to a stick, like a scalp. As he sang and danced, he began to whip the dancers with the dead hawk. The dancers scattered, running away from him. But he went after them and whenever he caught one, he whipped him. The feathers flew all about, and he kept whipping them hard. The people said, "That is not the way to dance a

[1] t̩uxʷat'̩ə?oyą̇ (T).
[2] Tultönpianana, Sun-house Mountain, see p. 70.
[3] (pòb) p'̩ic̩i?'ine, (flower) head-band (T).
[4] These flowers are smaller than the American sunflower, with a red or black centre and yellow petals.
[5] t'ùłipòb'enemą̇ (T).
[6] To make fun of the enemy scalp, spitting on it, hitting it, shooting at it.

scalp dance. Coyote old man is too mean. That is not the scalp dance."
So they ran away to their homes; everybody went away from his dance.
He was left alone. Then he went back to his home.

62. Coyote Visits Underground

Coyote lives at *tuw'atö'aya*,[1] Coyote house. Coyote said to his children
at night, while they were sitting around, that he was going out to hunt
next day, to make him a loaf of bread. And he made a bow and arrows.
His wife made the bread. And they lay down. In the morning he put
his quiver on his back and took his lunch. There was a lot of snow.
Nobody lived near him, he knew nobody. He passed three hills; he
could find nothing, and he was just coming back when he saw smoke on
another hill. It seemed very far away, but he went on. "I did not know
any one was living around here. It seems far to me, but I will go," he said
to himself, "no matter how big he is or how mean he is. I have bow and
arrows, I will go and see who he is," he said. "I am ready for anything."
He got to another hill. It seemed nearer; but he was afraid and was
thinking over whether to go or not. "If I should go back from here and
tell my wife about it, she would say I am not a man. So I better go and
see what it is," he said. So he went. He got there and found a place surrounded with piñon wood, a fire in the middle. He went to the door,
and they told him to come in. There was a man sitting there. He never
had seen him before, but that man knew him very well. "Why are you
coming around here while you are living well with your wife and
children at Coyote house, you hunting and not needing anything? There
is so much snow here and yet here you have come," he said. "Yes, I am
living well; but as I am a man I went out hunting and did not find anything and saw your smoke and came here," he said. He said, "I am
papöpuyuna (above whistle)[2] and I came to live here. I better do something while I have a friend here." He brought out a medicine bag (*tuimuuna*)
and he brought out a hollow cane. He took out his medicine and put it
in his mouth and spat in the directions, east, north, west, south, above
(*k'ita*)[3], below (*nata*)[4]. He stuck the cane into the ground and said to
Coyote, "Men do as their friends tell them to do. If you are not afraid to

---

[1] The same term as in the preceding tale which was told by a different narrator.
[2] Translated as the bird from above, i.e., the bird of the zenith, said to be the name of
an actual bird. p'uyuna is a mythical bird (T).
[3] k'ʼit'o (T).
[4] n'at'o (T).

go with me I will take you down."—"Yes, I will not be afraid," said Coyote. The bird went first into the cane, and Coyote followed him. And they came to a place where things were just beginning to grow, and then to a place where the crops were still higher, then to a place where they were ripening. Coyote began to eat, but the bird said, "Wait until we come to the place where everything is ripe. Of these things that belong to them we are afraid." In a little while they came to a place where everything was ripe, and the bird told Coyote to pick everything he wanted—corn and chokecherries and plums. He picked them for his bag and he made a crown of chokecherries, and when they had enough, they came out. They came to the place they went in and they went through the cane, up into the house. He told Coyote to go home and take the things to his wife. There was a lot of snow, and he was eating all the things he was carrying. He said, "How glad my children will be to get the things I am carrying in this snow. How glad my wife will be!" When his children came to meet him all that was left was the crown he wore, and they ate that. That night he told his wife and children to make big sacks to go and see that bird again. He said to himself that his friend had told him to visit him again. In the morning they were all ready and they went. When he reached the place where he had seen the smoke, he saw no smoke. "This is the place I saw the smoke," he said to his wife, "but there is no smoke now; but we will go," he said. The bird was angry that Coyote had come again, so he had hidden himself in a place where nobody would find him, but he forgot to take his medicine bag in which were the things he used to go down with. Coyote got there and he found the bag. The youngest child said, "Father, maybe he is here." Coyote said, "I do not care if he is here or not, I have found his things and I know what to do." He took out the cane and, just as the bird said, he said, "If you are not afraid to go down with me, I will take you." He said this to his children and he spat out the medicine and put down the cane. And he went down and his children followed him, and they got to the same place, and he said to his children, "Do not eat much! It belongs to those fearful people of the zenith (*k'ita itöin nöpia,*[1] above, live, we are afraid)." But here in this first place everything was ripe. So he told his children to fill their sacks. When they got all they wanted, they turned back and were going up when the bird came home and saw the cane and said, "*Rapti!* Rascals!" and filliped the cane, and the coyotes all fell down and were killed. Then the bird lived happily with nobody to trouble him.

[1] k'ͅit'ot'ˡəʔin(ạ) kạpˡia, above-live-the ones who we are afraid (T).

63. Coyote the Credulous

Coyote went out to hunt. He went to *pięyapqoya*[1] (road earth) and there
was Puakauuna[2] sleeping there. Coyote said to him, "Grandchild, you
are fat and pretty!" Puakauuna was afraid of Coyote and did not say anything when Coyote spoke to him. Coyote said, "Why don't you speak?"
And the little Puakauuna said, "Wait! Wait, grandfather, listen to what
the people who live way below (*kwinata itöin*)[3] are saying."—"What,
grandchild?" said Coyote. "Now, grandfather, I will tell you what they
are saying below. They are saying, 'All who have been urinating and
defecating on the road or on top of the stones anywhere in the world are
going to die.'" Coyote was scared, and said, "*Pia'simo!*[4] Grandchild, you
must not tell, just a little while ago I urinated and defecated in the road.
You must not tell." He jumped and ran away. And he never came back
there. Puakauuna said, "Coyote always gets scared at any little thing.
And he won't come back and I shall live well."

64. Coyote Tries to Grind[5]

People were living in the joyful ancient town of Ahtiadah (grinding
stone town). One day two turtle doves happened to be out pleasure
walking along the mountain valley country. They came to Ahtiadah. As
they sat there, out came two girls of the place. They were invited to come
in to the underground house. There they saw a great many young girls
and a great number of metates (*haneh*)[6] on which they were grinding
their grain. They themselves (the Turtledoves) began to grind on the
stones. Coyote man came close around there. He heard the sound of
grinding in the joyful town. He called in, "*Yan makonah*[7], now grandchildren! I shall join you." And he went to the metate to grind. While
grinding, Coyote scratched off the side of the metate with his long claws
and mixed the corn flour with the crust of the metate that was pealing
off. The girls cried out, "Stop, stop, grandfather! You are too rough."
So they gave him some corn meal in his buffalo hide bag and he went
away to his house.

[1] p'ౖ,ię- road + yo ? + pǫ̀ʔoyą, earth-on (T).
[2] A ratlike animal, (ù ʔ'una, little one. T).
[3] kʷ'inąt̓o it''əm(ą), below they lived (T).
[4] p'iasi, much, many. p'iasimą, ʔ it's too much (T).
[5] Written by townsman.
[6] 'one (T).
[7] yąn, m'ąkuną (T).

65. Coyote Asks for a Grinding-song[1]

There lived some girls at *gaumawiehlo kwilinahmaa*[2]. They had all in a row the grinding stones with which to grind their corn, five stones. They alway ground every day 'til their bowls were full of corn meal. They sang a grinding-song:

achilgo chilgo achilg chilgo
kakimai oh kakimai oh oh

Coyote heard the song from up the hill. He came down toward the sounds of the echo of the song. Arrived at the place, Coyote said, "My grandchildren, may I join in?"—"Coyote always meddles in what does not concern him. We are doing it in our own way." Coyote jumped into the grinding stones and began to grind as the girls did. Coyote asked the girls to sing for him. The girls gave him only *achilgo*. "This is the way it goes."—"My children, sing me the way it is. You look nice and fat, I will eat you up if you do not sing me that song well." The girls got angry and said, "This will be the last time we shall sing."

achilgo chilgo

Then the girls ran and flew away. Coyote kept on grinding:

chilg chilgo chilgo.

66. Coyote Believes the World is on Fire[3]

Bafayounah[4] (plain flycatcher bird) was living in the dry plain. She had her nest on the ground. As usual old Coyote was hunting along the plain. As he was going along across the plain he saw the young squab lying on the ground without any nest. He stopped and looked at them and said, "*Yao*, grandchild, what are you doing?" They replied, "*Heowanah*, nothing!" Coyote said to them, "You look fat and nice. I will eat you up if you do not tell me where your mother is." Before their mother left them they were told that if Coyote should happen to come to them and ask them where their mother was they should open their mouth as wide as they could so as to scare him away. The squabs opened their mouth. Coyote ran away and off to his home at Coyote house. As he descended,

---

[1] Written by a townsman.

[2] ? Owl pollen sprinkling place. Owl, k̜ǫw; corn pollen, m'a̧wi̧ena; spill, kw'ili; -na̧mo, relative suffix -na̧ + locative particle -mo (T., suggested, not identified).

[3] Written by a townsman. Compare Jicarilla Apache, Opler 1: 276-277.

[4] Perhaps p'ǒp'ˌayʔùʔ'una < p'ǒ- water, p'ay- red, ùʔ'una, little one (T).

he looked back and still saw the spot where the squab were in their nest with their mouths still wide open, as red as a flame of fire. As Coyote arrived at his home he made believe to the other coyotes that the world was on fire, that the world was at an end. He told his people to be on the lookout. Then he ran towards his own home where his family was. He told his children and their mother that the world was coming to an end, that the whole world was on fire. Then he said to the mother and children, "Mother and sons, we must go, come on to the big lake where we shall be safe from being burned up!" He took his family to the big lake. As they arrived old Coyote jumped in to the lake, first, then he made all his family jump in to the lake, thinking that so they would be safe from the fire of the burning world. They swam until they all became exhausted and were drowned. The other coyotes were waiting to see the burning of the world. Nothing was to be seen of the burning world, so the rest of the coyotes decided to go and see where old man Coyote and his family were. They followed their footprints .They arrived at the big lake where old man Coyote and his family were floating on the lake with their stomachs full of water. Then they said, "He is always very timid and he scares people about unforeseen things. That is why he put an end to the life of himself and his family forever."

67. Coyote Finds a Baby[1]

Once there lived a band of Apache at *kanbadah*[2] (buffalo river). As the Indians were always happiest in moving around from place to place, the head chief decided to move from Buffalo River to *daibaabaa*, [people-creek-at]. The band prepared in the usual way. The day came to start, quiet hustling, packing up of things, quiet long string hastening along the prairie. As they got out of sight a woman who was pregnant was left behind, she followed behind her people. On the second day of her journey she had her baby boy as best she could. She started again on her journey. She packed her baby in a buffalo hide bag made to carry babies. She hung the baby from the saddle horn. She proceeded sadly on the journey, being all alone, worried and tired. Unluckily it happened that the tie string of the bag gave way without her noticing it. She lost the baby on the prairie. Old Coyote was coming along the prairie and found the baby. Wise Coyote took the baby to his home in the cave. As soon as he arrived at his home, he yelled and cried out, calling to the

1 Written by a townsman.
2 k'onp'òto, buffalo-water-at (T).

different kinds of wild animals and of Indians. They quickly gathered. The animals in each kind inspected the baby who was unknown to them. Then the Indians inspected and found the baby was Apache. So they took the baby to their new home on Indian River. Then the chief asked if any one knew who lost the baby. Finally the mother of the baby appeared and took the baby.

68. Eye Jugglers[1]

Chi'paɫana[2] were about the field, they were saying, "*Chibiibi*." Coyote heard them and went to where they were and said to them, "What are you doing, my grandchildren?"—"We are hanging our eyes on the willows." They jumped around, from one willow to another. They threw their eyes to hang on the willows, and their eyes came back to them. Coyote was looking at them. He said, "My grandchildren, I will do the same as you are doing." He said, "*Chibiibi!*" very loud, and he took out his right eye and threw it on the willow. "*Chibiibi!*" He took out his left eye and threw it on the willow. His eyes hung there on the willow, and Coyote stayed without eyes, and the little birds laughed at him. "Grandfather Coyote, he always wants to do what others do, when he doesn't know how. It is our game." So they flew away laughing at him. Those are the little balls on the willows, Coyote's eyes.

69. Bungling Host[3]

There were many coyotes. This coyote went out in the plains in buffalo country. As he was going along from place to place he found Buffalo and his family. He was invited to come to the house. When Coyote arrived at the house, Buffalo stuck his nose hole with a sharp stick and after doing that he drew out through his nose hole a big stick of marrow. Then again he stuck the other hole and drew out another piece of marrow. Buffalo put the marrow in a wooden dish (*ɫatina*)[4] and told Coyote to eat. Coyote

---

[1] Compare Sia, Stevenson 1: 153; Oraibi, Voth, 194-195; Shumopovi, Wallis, 57-58; Zuni, Cushing, 262-268; Zuni and comparative, Handy, 461; Cheyenne, Kroeber 1: 168-169; Jicarilla Apache, Opler 1: 277-278; Lipan Apache, Opler 2: 171-172; Kiowa, Parsons 6: 33-34.

[2] cᵢip'oɫ'ana (sing.) (T). c'ine, eyes (T). A very small grey bird.

[3] Compare Shupaulovi, Voth, 202-204; Zuni, Benedict 2: II, 211 ff.; Zuni and comparative, Handy, 459; Jicarilla Apache, Opler 1: 275; Ute, Kroeber 2: 265-266; Pawnee, Dorsey 2: 267-268.

[4] ɫòt'ˀiȩnạ (T).

started to eat. That was the dinner he gave his friend. After he ate, they separated. Coyote thought to himself he had something to tell his family (*umuwaine*)[1] when he went back. When he got back, he told what he had seen at the Buffalo house. So he thought that he would do the same to himself. So he asked his wife for two very sharp pointed sticks. Then he stuck one up his nose hole and the blood ran out from his nose hole. No marrow came out. Then he tried the other stick in the other hole. No marrow came out. More blood ran out from his nose, and no marrow. Then he said to his wife, "You try!" Then his wife tried the same way with the sharp sticks, first one stick in one nose hole, then with the other stick in the other hole. Blood ran fast through her nose holes. They saw no marrow. Coyote old man's nose was badly swollen, and Coyote old woman's too. Then they both died and rotted away, and nobody made any use of them.

Variant[2]

Once there lived a buffalo on the mountain plain. Coyote was on the hunt. He came to the Buffalo home. Buffalo said to Coyote, "Where you going? Come in! Come in!" Coyote went in and sat down. Buffalo stuck his nose with a sharp stick and got out some of his brains and put them in a wooden dish. He went in the east room and brought out some wafer bread. He went north and brought him out clothing; west, and brought out plums; south, and brought out all kinds of fruit. Coyote went back home loaded with good things. He told Buffalo to come to his home, too. The next day Buffalo went to Coyote's home. When Buffalo arrived, Coyote said, "Come in! Come in!" Buffalo went in. He sat down. Coyote did the same things as Buffalo did at his home. He took a sharp stick and stuck it up his nose, but he failed to bring out any brains. Then Coyote old woman tried. She took the sharp stick and stuck it up her nose. No brains came. Coyote's nose was badly swollen, also Coyote old woman's nose. Now he tried to have his children poke the sharp stick up their noses. The children began to cry, "Oh, it hurts!" Every one had a sore nose. They were so badly hurt, all of them cried and cried. Coyote old man said to his children, "Hush, do not cry! It makes me ashamed." Then Coyote old man gave to Buffalo some of the fruit he got from Buffalo. Buffalo said to himself, "Coyote old man is always doing things he does not know about."

[1] ạmʔùwáʔiną (T).
[2] Written by a townsman.

70. *Blue Fox Eats up Coyote's Rabbits: Crows as Chickens:*[1] *Cheese in the Water:*[2] *Hailstorm Coming*[3]

One day Coyote was out hunting. He got lots of rabbits. Blue Fox was around. They met each other. Blue Fox said, "Grandfather, what are you doing here?" Coyote said, "Grandchild, I am hunting here. You don't have to hunt, I have got plenty of rabbits. Get wood and make a big fire. Make a hole and cover it with ashes. Watch it, grandchild!" Blue Fox said, "Grandfather, I am going to hunt." He hid behind a tree. Coyote went to sleep and said to his stomach, "When anybody comes round here, let me know!" Coyote went sound asleep. Blue Fox came and uncovered the rabbits. They were nice, well done. Blue Fox ate up all the rabbits. His stomach never told Coyote. Blue Fox ran away, he left only the bones. At last his stomach told Coyote by making wind. Coyote jumped up in the air. "Ah, ah, my rabbits are cooked!" He went to the fire and found only the bones.

He got mad. "I know who did that. Blue Fox did that. He can't escape me. I am going to catch him." He followed him. When he came near, Blue Fox began to pick up rocks and throw them at a cottonwood tree. "Ah, I have caught you! You ate up all my rabbits, I will kill you."—"No, no, grandfather! I am taking care of these chickens. (They were crows.) Some Navaho are having a marriage. I have to kill chickens for the fiesta."—"Yes, I would like to go to the fiesta, too."—"Grandfather, watch these chickens until I come back! I am going to see the boss about the dance." He left Coyote herding those crows, he ran away and did not come back.

Coyote got mad. "I am going to catch that Blue Fox and put him in the coals and eat him." He tracked him, going slowly. When Blue Fox saw Coyote he began to throw stones at the cottonwood trees. "Ah, ah, I have caught you now! I am going to throw you on the coals, going to eat you."—"Oh, no, grandfather! I am throwing stones at that bundle hanging in the tree. There is a great big cheese down in the spring. Go down, try to get it!" That was the moonlight in the water. "Come on,

---

[1] Compare Isleta, Lummis, 223 ff.; Isleta, Taos, Espinosa, 177, 121-122.

[2] Compare Isleta, Lummis, 228 ff.; San Juan, De Huff, 6-7; Tesuque, Parsons 4: 159; Paguate, Isleta, Sandía, Taos, Espinosa, 86, 117, 120, 122; Cochiti, Benedict 1: 147-148; Zuni, Handy, 454; Zuni, Benedict 2: II, 214; Jicarilla Apache, Opler 1: 332.

[3] Compare Taos, Espinosa, 122; Isleta, Lummis, 27 ff.; San Juan, Tesuque, Parsons 4: 158, 159; Laguna, Parsons and Boas, 49.

grandfather! Here is a cheese in the water." Coyote went down, he scratched about in all the rocks, he could not get the cheese.

Blue Fox ran away. "That liar! Never will I believe him again. I am going to catch him and kill him." Coyote overtook him in the cotton-wood trees. "I am going to kill you. I am going to throw you into the coals and eat you."—"Grandfather, today is the last day of the world. There is going to be a hailstorm. I had better save you. Grandfather, get into this sack! I'll hang you in the tree and save your life." So Coyote got into the sack and Blue Fox hung the sack in the tree. He went down, picked up lots of stones, threw them at the sack. He said, "Grandfather, lower your head! There are lots of hailstones." He threw bigger rocks. "Now bigger hailstones are coming. Lower your head!" Then he killed his grandfather with the rocks.

71. The Dance for the Blind: Hailstorm Coming:[1] Crows as Chickens: Holding up the Cliff[2]

Coyote was living at Coyote place. He thought he would go hunting at the edge of the wiregrass (*paⱡihanenai*)[3]. Little Yellow Fox (*tuwaʻchuliuuna*)[4] was hunting in the same place. He saw Coyote coming but it was too late for him to run. "Grandfather Coyote!"—"My grandson, where are you going?"—"I am going to the feast."—"Where are you going to the feast?"—"To the settlers, they have a big feast today. They will feed you in any house."—"Let us go together!"—"All right, grandfather!" After they had started Yellow Fox said, "They treat the blind better than those with sight. They are very kind people."—"What shall we do?"—"Better I put some piñon gum on your eyes."—"All right, grandson!" So Yellow Fox ran up to the mountain and got some gum. "Put it on well!" said Coyote. Yellow Fox began to lead Coyote. As they came close to the settlement they heard some dogs barking. "What is that?" asked Coyote. "At the feast they make a noise and talk loud," said Yellow Fox. They went closer and the dogs barked at them and Coyote was snapping at

---

[1] Compare San Juan, Parsons 4: 158.

[2] Compare Isleta, Lummis, 227 ff.; San Juan, Parsons 4: 158-159; (?) San Juan, De Huff, 3-4, 5-6; Laguna, Isleta, Sandía, Taos, Espinosa, 84, 117, 120, 121; Hopi, Voth, 212; Jicarilla Apache, Opler 1: 279; Lipan Apache, Opler 2: 149-150; comparative and (?) Acoma, Parsons 1: 227 n.2, 229; Vandau and comparative, Boas and Simango, 175, 177.

[3] Perhaps pòⱡ̣ih'uolonʔoy, plains-grass-wireweed-at (T).

[4] ṭuxʷacʼ̣uleʔùʔ'una (T).

them. Yellow Fox ran away. Coyote got his eyes open and saw he was among a pack of dogs.

"Well, grandson, I will get you yet," and he went after him. Yellow Fox saw Coyote following him. He came to a yellow tree. "What shall I tell him now? I will tell him that a big hailstorm is coming," and as Coyote came up he said, "Hurry up, grandfather! This is the only shelter we have. A big hailstorm is coming and it will kill all the roaming animals and the world will come to an end. The best thing I can do for you is to put you in this buffalo sack and hang you to a limb of the tree and I will take refuge in this little hole at the foot of the tree because I am small."—"Hurry up, grandchild! It is getting dark." So he tied up Coyote in the bag and began to collect rocks. He threw a rock at him. "It is coming, grandfather."—"It feels like rocks," said Coyote. Then Yellow Fox ran away.

Coyote tore the bag with his teeth and got out and saw the sun shining. He saw rocks all around him and he was wounded all over. "I will go after him and eat him up," said Coyote. Yellow Fox saw him coming. He came to where they were threshing wheat, the crows were alighting on the ground. "I will tell him I am watching those chickens which belong to a pretty girl who will bring me lunch." He called out, "Hurry up, dear grandfather! Hurry up!"—"What are you doing?"—"I am watching those chickens which belong to a pretty girl who will bring me lunch."—"Let us watch together!" Then the crows began to fly away. Yellow Fox said, "Grandfather, I must go and relieve myself."—"Grandson, do it here!"—"No, grandfather, because when that pretty girl comes there will be a bad odor." So he went off to some brush and from there ran away. All the crows flew away and no girl came. "He has fooled me again," said Coyote. "I don't care what he says. When I get him I will eat him up."

Yellow Fox saw him coming up the mountain. He went under a rock and, as he looked up, it seemed that the cliff was falling down. He began to push it. "Hurry up, grandfather, help me! If this cliff falls down it will be the end of the world for all the roaming animals!" So Coyote pushed; they were both pushing. Whenever he looked up, it seemed as if it were coming down. Yellow Fox said, "Grandfather, I have to relieve myself."—"Do it here!"—"No, grandfather, we are breathing hard. I must go a little distance."—"Well, go!" Coyote stayed holding it. "What shall I do? I will jump. One, two, three!" And he jumped and looked up and the cliff was still there. "Yellow Fox fooled me. It is no use for me to follow him any more. I am Coyote and I am to roam around to watch over the mountains." Yellow Fox said, "I am the little yellow fox, and so the people will always call me, and I am roaming in the mountains to watch over them."

Variant

There were Yellow Fox and Coyote. Yellow Fox saw Coyote coming and he was afraid and he said, "Grandfather, I am taking care of these chickens. (They were crows.) A very rich man owns them and he was good to me and I am taking care of them." Coyote said, "I will stay with you and have a good dinner today." Yellow Fox said, "I will go and get the dinner and you wait here!" And Yellow Fox ran away and hid in a bush. In the evening the crows were flying away and Coyote ran after them and could not catch them.

Then he followed the tracks of Yellow Fox and found him in the bushes, and Yellow Fox said, "Oh, grandfather, there is going to be a dance tonight. They want only the blind. Let me paste up your eyes and take you to the dance!" Then Yellow Fox got piñon gum and pasted his eyes and led him by the hand. "You stand here and when the dance begins I will tell you." He went a little way and burned some weeds which sounded like the dance. "Now, grandfather, you dance." The fire came closer to where he was dancing and melted away the gum. And he grew angry and followed the tracks of Yellow Fox.

And when Yellow Fox saw Coyote coming, he stood close to the mountain and said, "Oh, grandfather, this mountain is going to fall. I am holding it up."—"Let me help you!" said Coyote. "Look up at the clouds!" said Yellow Fox. "Let me go and get a big stick to prop it up, too." Then he ran away.

Coyote got mad and ran after Yellow Fox. He found him making a sack. Yellow Fox said, "There is going to be a big hailstorm and I am going to put myself in the sack. You are so small you can hide yourself anywhere in the woods or under the stones. I am too big. Put me in the sack! It is nearly time for the hail to come."—"Put me in!" said Coyote. So he put him in and hung him up in the tree. He gathered up lots of stones. He said to Coyote he would hide himself close to him. He threw the stones at the sack, one by one. "Now the hail are coming, one by one. Be very still!" he said to Coyote. "Don't move whatever comes. I, too, will be still." Then he threw big stones and the blood of Coyote ran out of the sack, and he took down the sack and Coyote was dead.

72. Coyote Forgets the Song[1]

Tahętau[2], little cotton seed, lived at *muelapięnta*[3] (at the middle of the race track). He said he would hoe the cotton, he sang,

> tahęta munde
> tahęta munde
> munde munde
> tahęta munde
> tahęta munde
> munde munde

While Cotton Seed was working and singing, Coyote heard the song and followed the sound. By and by he came near where Cotton Seed was hoeing cotton. Coyote said to him, "Grandson, what pretty songs you are singing! I have no hunting song.

> tahęta munde, etc.

That's the way it is." Coyote sang,

> tahęta munde, etc.

"Now, my grandson, I have a new hunting song. Now I can sing when I go hunting." So he went away singing, repeating the song over and over. As he was going on his way a flock of quails (*huwaʼlana*)[4] flew away —rr—r. Coyote got scared and forgot the song. Then he said, "I am sorry the stiff-wing quail scared me and lost me my hunting song. I must go back now to my grandson, he will sing for me again." So he went back to Cotton Seed who was still working away at his cotton field. "Grandson, Cotton Seed, the quails made me lose my song. Sing it to me again!" Then he sang,

> tahęta munde, etc.

"Sing it to me good!" said Coyote. "You look nice and fat. If you don't sing for me, I will swallow you up." He would not sing to him. So

---

[1] Compare Isleta, Lummis, 84 ff.; Shupaulovi, Voth, 195-196; Shumopovi, Wallis, 50-52; Tewa (First Mesa) Parsons 4: 295-298; Zuni, Parsons 1: 222-225; Zuni, Benedict 2: II, 217-218, 220-221; Zuni, Cushing, 255 ff.; Laguna, De Huff, 46-49; Acoma, Parsons 1: 225-226; Ute, Kroeber 2: 266-267; for Negro parallels see Jamaica or Antigua, Folk-Lore Record, III, Pt. I, 53-54; Nigeria (Fjort), Publications of the Folk-Lore Society, XLI, 35-38; ? Santal, Bulletin de Folklore, III, 46, Brussels, 1898.

[2] t'ˌoxęt'oʔù (T).

[3] mˌuolipʼ'ięnto, turn-track-at (T).

[4] hùoloną (T).

Coyote jumped on Cotton Seed and swallowed him. Then he went away. On his way he came to a shady tree. He lay down there to sleep. While lying there asleep, he heard somebody singing inside his stomach, tahęta munde, etc.

He woke up and went to look for some stones to break into pieces for a knife to cut open his stomach. He lay down on his back and cut his stomach open. There Cotton Seed came out, all bloody, shaking off the blood. Then he said, "Coyote is never firm about what he has done or said and he goes about to scare people, but he does not persist, he always gives up what he is doing. Now he has killed himself and nobody will make use of him. He is castaway on the ground because nobody will make use of him. I am Cotton Seed and I live in the middle of the race track. I remain living there."

73. Water Spiller[1]

At Coyote house was living Coyote old man. One day his children were thirsty and he went to *pawagaą*[2] (on the Lucero River, *pahöatöalpa'ana*[3], water canyon river). As he went along he passed by *kuwaw'ichuuna*[4], white-breasted swallow.[5] Coyote drank his water and filled his mouth with water to carry to his children. When he passed by Swallow's place, Swallow hid himself and started to laugh and sing: "Coyote old man is carrying water." Then Coyote laughed and the water fell out. Coyote went back for more water and as he came back by Swallow's, again Swallow said, "Coyote is packing water a long way," and started to laugh. Then Coyote laughed and dropped the water. "I don't care what he says, I will not laugh." He packed his water and ran fast by Swallow's place. When he got home, his children were dead. "Well, my wife, we are coyotes and our pleasure is to roam in the plains and mountains, that is where we belong." So today coyotes are roamers of the plains and watchers in the mountains.

---

[1] Compare San Juan, Santa Clara, Parsons 4: 160-161; Cochiti, Benedict 1: 150-151; Cochiti and Siama, De Huff, 135-140; Acoma, Espinosa, 71-72; Zuni and Laguna, Parsons 1: 226-227; Hopi, Voth, 193, 198-199.

[2] p''owagą, water-along (T).

[3] p'òhəot'ˌəolp'ò?'ona, canyon-flying-river ? (T).

[4] k'uowˌoxᵂˌicu?'una (T).

[5] "There are two or three varieties of swallows, maybe *five*."

Variant

Coyote was living where the coyotes live. Her children got thirsty. She went to the river to get water. When she came to the river she heard some one singing:

kulu hu tu tu wi

Coyote had the water in her mouth and she laughed:

a a ha i i hi

"What a nice song!" she said. When she laughed, the water dropped out of her mouth and she had to go back again for water. When she had some more water in her mouth, again she heard the same song and she laughed again, and the water dropped out. "This time when I hear it, I won't laugh," she said to herself. "I will go and carry the water to my children." Bobwhite (*hualaana*)[1] said, "I guess Coyote's children are all dead. Let us not sing any more!" Next time Coyote listened and listened, but she heard nothing. She went to her house and found all her children dead. Bobwhite said, "Let us go and see what Coyote is doing!" They went to her house and found all the children dead. They cut them up and measured collars and gloves for themselves and put them under the water.

74. Coyote Kills his Wife[2]

There was *kwępuuna*[3], bed bug. When she saw Coyote coming along, in order that he should not eat her, she started to dance with a bag of sand on her back. Coyote came and said, "What are you doing, grandchild?" Bedbug said, "Oh, grandfather, I killed my grandmother and I have her on my back and I am dancing," she said. Coyote said, "I better go and kill mine and dance with you." He went and killed his wife as she sat by the fire and put her in a sack and went to dance with the bug. While he was dancing the bug threw the sand into his eyes. He was angry and he took back the sack to his house and put his wife down by the fire. He was very sad and he went out and never came back to his house where his wife was sitting dead.

---

[1] hùol'ona (T).
[2] Compare Zuni, Cushing, 203 ff.; Zuni, Parsons 1: 216-127; Zuni, Handy, 455-456; Zuni, Benedict 2: II, 219, 220; Jicarilla Apache, Opler 1: 331-332.
[3] kʷ͔ęp'una (T).

75. Gum Baby[1]

Rabbit was stealing in the garden.[2] So they made a gum man. Rabbit came and found him. First, Rabbit's hands stuck, then his feet stuck. The man who owned the garden caught the rabbit and gave him to his wife to cook. He told her not to let a drop of blood fall to the ground. But as she was fixing the rabbit, some blood dropped and the rabbit came to life and ran away.[3]

Variant 1

There was an old Mexican, her husband was living, and they had a very pretty girl. Rabbit was making a lot of damage in their garden. They did not know what to do. Rabbit never came out for the old man. He put down traps, he could not catch him. He found the rabbit hole. "My wife, I don't know what to do, this rabbit is damaging our garden so much. But tomorrow I am going after wood and I will get some piñon gum." Next morning early he went and got some gum, he made a little image and put it in the garden at night. Rabbit came out and saw this piñon gum image. "Who are you? Who are you? If you don't talk, I am going to hit you. I am going to hit you." He hit him with his right hand. It stuck. "What do you think? That I got only this one?" He hit with his left hand. It stuck. He hit with his feet, they stuck. He hit with his head, and it stuck. Now he was stuck all together. The old man got up early and found Rabbit caught. He told his wife to put on hot water to clean the rabbit and cook it with chile. "I want it cooked tender, very well done." The old woman put the dish on the table. They began to eat. "Be careful, don't drop any soup from your mouth!" As they were eating, the old woman dropped some soup from her mouth, and Rabbit came to life and ran away, upsetting all the dishes. "I told you not to drop any soup," said the old man, and they fell to quarreling over it.

[1] "Every Taos child knows this story." Cp. Taos, De Huff, 61-64; Santa Clara, Parsons 4: 165; Laguna, Paguate, San Juan, Isleta, Taos, Espinosa, 82-83, 85-86, 92, 117, 121; Jicarilla Apache, Opler 1: 310-312. For bibliography of Tar Baby among other Indian tribes see Parsons 2: 227 n. 1, 228 n. 1, n. 4. Notice the distinctive conclusion of Taos variants and compare Stevenson 2: 443; Parsons 4: 157. See Appendix.

[2] Variant: onion patch.

[3] Variant: Woman tells her children not to let a drop of gravy fall to the ground, else rabbits will run out of the house. The youngest child drops the gravy and rabbits **run out.**

Variant 2[1]

Black Cane old man (*tawehfoneyłułi*) and Round Chunky Corn old woman (*iamałołio*)[2] lived on Cotton Tree Creek. Their plantation was of pumpkins and corn. The old man would get up early in the morning and go to see his little field. He discovered that some animals were damaging or eating his plants, the corn was half husked and the pumpkins almost all had holes in them. He decided that he would watch and find out who it was and catch him. So he went down the early part of the evening to stand guard and watch. By and by Black Cane old man heard a voice—chiz chiz chiz (animal language). He flew up to the tip of the corn. Black Cane old man threw a piece of buffalo hide at the marauding animal and caught him. It was Bat or Flying Mouse. He took him up to his house and told his wife to cook him, which the old woman did. After it was finished cooking, Black Cane old man ordered his wife to serve it. He told her not to drop any gravy for fear something might happen. While eating, the old woman spilled some gravy from her mouth. From the cooking jar out ran Bat. And wherever bats were in jars out they ran. If the old woman had kept to the order of the old man there would not have been any bats.

Variant 3

There lived a Mexican (*kwęna*)[3] and a little rabbit would come to steal the cabbage and onions in his garden. The Mexican got some piñon gum and made it look like a man and put a bow and arrow in his hand. The little rabbit came along and said, "What are you doing in my road?" And the stick gum did not say anything. And the little rabbit said, "I will knock you with my right hand if you do not speak," and his hand stuck. "You think I have only one hand. I will knock you with my left hand if you do not let me go. You think I have only two hands. I will knock you with my right foot." It stuck. And he knocked him with his left foot. He knocked him with his head, and it stuck. And the Mexican man came out and found the rabbit. Then the Mexican said, "You are the one stealing my vegetables," and he took him into the house. He told his wife to take and cook him with chili, but when they were eating not to

---

[1] Written by a townsman.
[2] Cp. Isleta *iemaparu* for corn fetich.
[3] kʷ'ęna (T).

spill any of it or the rabbit would run away. But when they were eating his wife spilled some, and the rabbit ran away.

76. Coyote Cooks Baby Bear: Holding up the Rock

Bears were living at *köałolta* (bear cooked)[1], and Coyote was roaming about the plain. Coyote was always out hunting. One day he went out toward the mountain, came to Cooked Bear. There he found some bears and he studied over a joke to play on the bears. Then he said this to them, "You, lazy Bear old man (*köałułi maiła*), lazy Bear old woman (*köałiu maiła*)[2], the wild berries, chokeberries, all kinds of berries, are just falling ripe and plentiful a little way from here, why don't you go to pick them?" (He knew the bears were very fond of the berries.) Then Bear said to him, "Where, grandfather?"—"Go a little way from here!" and he pointed in the direction. So the bears got ready to go next day to pick the berries. They had a little wee bear. Then they asked Coyote if he could stay there and watch the baby bear (*köaona*)[3]. He said, "Yes, I can stay and watch while you are gone." So Coyote stayed at the Bear's home. Then Bear old man and Bear old woman and the little ones went to pick the berries. When they were gone, Coyote stayed and watched the baby bear. So Coyote went about the house looking for something to cook for the bears to eat when they came back. Coyote did not find anything to cook for them. Then he went to the cradle board and took out the baby bear and killed him. Then he skinned him and after skinning he chopped him up to small pieces to boil in the pot. So he made a big fire and boiled the meat. Late in the afternoon, Bear old man and Bear old woman and the other little bears came back very disappointed from not finding any berries. Coyote old man was still there. He said to them, "You look very tired. Did you find the berries?"—"Yes, we have the berries in branches in our packs." Coyote said, "I have been out hunting and got a deer and I have cooked it for you to eat." Then he served them out of the pot. They sat all around to eat. They never thought of their baby. While they were still sitting down eating, Coyote old man made up his mind and told them that he wanted to go outside to make water. Bear old man said to him, "Just make water right there!"— "Oh, but I'll make a job, it is not decent, while you are eating."—"Just

---

[1] k̡ɔoł'ǫlto, bear-cook-at (T). On Rosero Creek north of Taos. Coyote named the place, Cooked Bear.

[2] k̡ɔołˌułim'ayła, bear-old-man-lazy, k̡ɔołìwm'ayła, bear-(old) woman-lazy (T).

[3] k̡ɔoʔùʔ'una, bear-little-one (T).

drop it outdoors while I hold you by the tail."—"No," he said, "the smell would be too strong. I'll just drop it away from the door." He went out, he ran off. Then Bear old man exclaimed, "Hurry up! Come in!" No answer. The little bear said, "This meat smells just like the meat of my younger brother (*unpaiuna*)[1]." Then Bear old woman went to the cradle, looking for her baby. She did not find anything. They left the dishes and ran out after Coyote, but he was gone. They pursued him.

As the bears were coming after him Coyote came to a high rock. He stood there looking up. He saw the clouds flying in the air and the rock looked like it was going to fall. He got a long pole and put it against the side of the rock as a prop, and with his hands he was pushing against the rock lest it fall. At that time the bears got where he was, and he told the bears, "If this fall to the ground, the world (*pa'ana*)[2] will end. Come and help me!" So the bears came to the rock and pushed against it with their hands, all of them. Coyote said, "Be strong, my children! I will go and get another prop to help." While the bears were holding up the rock, he ran away again. When the cloud passed, the rock was still standing. Coyote ran away and they never caught him. They went back to their home at Cooked Bear, very disappointed and tired. The people say that the bears still live at Cooked Bear.

77. Coyote Steals the Cheese and is Caught by Burro[3]

Coyote lived in the plain. He was always out searching for food. As he was going along, travelling eastward, near a Mexican town some sheep herders were camping. As he went along he saw a burro coming on the road with a heavy load. The burro before leaving the sheep camp was told by his master, "On your way home you have only to look out for Coyote. He is a bad man, he is a man who can never be trusted. If he comes out when you are on the road, don't let him ride!" When Coyote saw Burro coming he began to limp. The burro went to meet Coyote. Coyote said, "My friend, take me on your back, I am very lame, I want to get home quickly. Give me a ride part of the way!" Burro said, "No, my master said not to give you a ride. You are a bad man. I am carrying cheese to my master's house. If I give you a ride, you will eat it all up."— "No, no, my friend, I am a good man, I won't do that! I don't like cheese," he said. Then Burro believed him and agreed to let him ride.

[1] ạnp'ʾọyna (T).
[2] pòʾʾ'ona (T).
[3] Compare Isleta, Lummis, 103 ff.; Cochiti, Benedict 1: 152-153; Lipan Apache, Opler 2: 167-168.

"Come on then, jump on my back!" Then he jumped on top of the load. Then Burro went along on the road. Coyote was working to get the cheese out of the bag. Burro felt that Coyote was pulling at the string, Burro said, "Pedro, what are you doing? Don't take the cheese out of the sack! My master will scold me."—"No, I just pulled the string, I am not taking anything out." But he was tearing the sack, and he took out the cheese and threw it on the roadside. Finally when Burro arrived at his master's house, his load was light. Burro said, "Pedro, I guess you have eaten up all my cheese."—"No, look at my teeth! I am a good man. I don't eat cheese." Then Coyote jumped off his back, off the roadside and Burro went up to the house. All the cheese was gone and the sack was torn. Then his master's wife said, "What did you do with the cheese?" He said, "Coyote met me on the road, he told me he was lame and that he was a good man and would not eat my cheese; but he is the one ate all my cheese." Then his master came home and asked his wife, "Did the burro bring the cheese all right?"—"No, he did not bring any cheese." He gave Coyote a ride on his back and Coyote ate all the cheese." Then his master was angry. "I told you to look out for Pedro and you did not obey me. Now you go near to Pedro's house and just this side of his house you lie down as if dead, and put out your tört (?). Then in the morning Pedro's wife, Coyote woman, got up first and went on top of the house. She saw something lying dead and something red. Coyote woman screamed and said, "Father, get up, get up, hurry! Here near the house lies a dead buffalo, go and get the meat before anybody gets it!" He got up in a hurry naked and was pulling on his clothes and ran up to the top of the house and asked, "Where?" Then he ran down to the dead animal. Coyote woman stayed on top of the house screaming, "*Hijo! hígado!* Son! the liver!" (That is what she wanted first.) As Coyote got up to the burro he did not wait a moment, but put his head up into the anus of the burro to get the liver. Then Burro shot out. Then Burro got up and dragged him up to his master's house. He said to his master, "I caught him. Here he is." Then they killed Coyote and skinned him and left only the hair on the tip end of his tail, and on his paws and on his nose. They cut his ears. Then Burro opened his hind end again and turned him loose. Then he went back without a coat. Coyote old woman was watching for her husband and she saw him coming and she screamed, "*Hijo! hijo! quien te quitó tu catón?* Who took away your [?] coat?" He just shook his head. Then the old woman took him up to the house. He lay down alongside the fireplace, the fire was blazing. Then he began to roast. In whatever part he was cooking his children began to eat him up.

78. The Faithful Wife and the Woman Warrior

A long time ago a band of Apache lived at *namtsuleta*[1], yellow earth. In the band were two young men; one was living as son-in-law (*taana*)[2] to the tribe, married to a nice girl, daughter of the head chief, and he and the other young man were friends. They had some enemies living far off, fearful and dangerous tribes, people they used to fight with. The young men talked of going to that tribe to get some scalps. So they packed up their horses and they started. So they went, at nightfall they camped. In the camp they were talking of their journey. Then the unmarried boy said to his friend, "My friend, as women always are, I bet your wife is tonight sleeping with another young man."—"No," he said, "you may think that, but I would never think that. My wife is very true to me and honest, she will never do that."—"Anyway, I bet you, I will go back tonight and sleep with your wife."—"Yes, my friend, you can go back, but she will never take you. She will not want you."—"I bet you she will want me."—"Well, go and try!" He was very sure of his wife, so he was not afraid. They bet their pack horses and food and everything they had with them and everything they had at home. Then the other boy went back. When he got back he hung around where the girl lived. He saw the girl sitting outside of the tipi. But she never looked at him. He kept smiling at her, but she never looked at him. So the boy thought, "It must be as my friend told me." So he was afraid to go and speak to her. So he got the notion of going to an old woman. He went in the old woman's house and said to her, "My grandmother, my name is Red Hawk (*ta'kiapaiena*)[3]. I was going with my friend to fight with our fiercest enemy. On our journey the first night in camp I told my friend that his wife would be sleeping with another young man. He said, 'She is honest and true to me. She won't do that.'—'I'll go back and sleep with her,' I told my friend. 'Go back if you like and try!' he said. So, my grandmother, we bet all we owned. So I came back. I went around to the girl's tipi, she was sitting there, but she would pay no attention to me, so I got ashamed to talk to her. Have you any way for me to see the girl? I want her tonight. Otherwise, in some way I want to prove to my friend that I stayed in bed with her tonight. Could you find out what her body is like? I'll pay you all the money you ask." The old woman said, "Yes, my grandson, I will

---

[1] n̦amc"'uleto, earth-yellow-at, near Antonito, Colorado (T). See p. 78.
[2] ța?'ana (T).
[3] țokep"ayena (T).

do that. I will find out for you how she looks, if she has any mark on her body. I will go over to her tipi." And the boy remained at the old woman's house. She went over to the girl's tipi, she was ragged and her toes stuck out of her shoes. She took her cane and walked lame. The girl saw the old woman and said, "Poor old grandmother!" She said to someone in the house, "Go out and bring in that poor old woman." So they brought her in and fixed a place in the corner for her to sleep. She made her bed of skins and laid her there to sleep. "Poor old grand- mother, you are tired, go to sleep, there is your bed." Late at night the girl undressed to go to bed. She put on a night dress. While she was taking off all her clothing, the old woman was looking through a hole of her blanket and saw the girl undressing. She had some golden hairs in the centre of her abdomen, long braided hair. She unbraided the hair and brushed it out and braided it up again. Then she wound it around her body, five times. Then on the back of her body, on the backbone, she had a kind of black mark. The old woman noticed all that. Then the girl went to sleep. At daybreak the old woman got up and said to the girl, "Granddaughter, I am going home, I have to feed my turkeys."— "No, grandmother, don't go yet, stay and have breakfast with me!"— "No," she said, "I must go." So she went back to her house. The boy, Red Hawk, was there. He asked, "How did you make out, grandmother?"— "My grandson, I saw the girl, she has golden hairs in the centre of her abdomen and she unbraided them and brushed them and braided them up again and wound the braid five times around her body; and on the backbone she has a black mark." Then the boy was pleased to know that. "Now, grandmother, you shall have the money." Then Red Hawk went back to his friend, to their camp. "What luck had you?"—"I slept with your wife." The boy did not believe it. "Well, to prove it I will tell you what your wife looks like and what she has on the body."—"What is it?"—"She has long golden hair on the centre of her abdomen and a black mark on her backbone." He said nothing, he dropped his head. Red Hawk said, "My friend, the words of a man are worth a great deal." The other boy said, "There are my pack horses and my money and everything I was taking. Take all. We will go back, and I will give you everything, money, horses, cattle, and house." So they went back and he turned everything over to his friend. He never said anything to his wife. His wife kept asking, "What are you doing? Why are you giving everything to that boy?" But he never said anything. He went to work quietly and made a long, big, rawhide trunk and in it he put all kinds of food and money and cooking outfit. He told his wife to dress up in her finest clothes. He put his wife in that trunk. He was going to take a trip on the plains a long way, a pleasure trip to the seashore. "I made this trunk to put you in, to keep you from the heat of the sun, so you would not get burned." He had a cart with wheels all of one piece of wood. He put the trunk on the cart and hitched up the horses, and they went on their trip, to the seashore. When they got to the seashore, he threw the trunk into the big river. Then he went back to his tribe. Then he was asked where he had taken his wife and why he had given all his property to the boy, Red Hawk, but he would not say. So the chief of the tribe worked to make a hole into the underworld. Then he worked for his son-in-law to fall into that hole.

On that big river there was a fisherman fishing. He threw his hook into the river and caught something that pulled heavy. Then he pulled slowly. "A big fish," he said. He pulled and gradually he brought something to the edge of the river. He pulled it out, and it was a big rawhide trunk. He drew it up on land and looked at it. He found a place where he could open it. So he opened it. There was a nice girl inside, a very pretty girl. He took her to his camp. He took her to the chief. Before going to the camp, the girl said, "I will dress in your clothes, and dress you in my clothes." The band of Apache were getting ready to go to war. The girl, dressed in man's clothes, joined the warriors who were going to war. She went with the young warriors. They started in the morning. On their journey the young men noticed the handsome, well dressed young man. They said, "He is not a man, his eyes look like a girl's."— "His movements are like a girl's." Then at nightfall in camp a boy said, "I will make friends with the young man and see if I can find out if he is boy or girl." The young man said he was a medicine man (*toiwaiyena*) and he always put his tent at night apart from the others. His medicine was the Sun, and he always carried a white eagle feather with him. So one of the young warriors went over to his tent, wanting to stay there to sleep. They went to bed. The visitor kept awake all night, waiting for the young man to sleep, but he never slept. When the visitor thought he was asleep, he moved slowly over to him and tried to find out if he was boy or girl; but every time he put his arm over him, he said, "Don't put your arm over me!" After a time again he reached out his arm. The other said, "Go to sleep! Why don't you sleep?" That way they passed the night. At daylight the boy went back to the other boys and said, "I could not find out anything, he never went to sleep." The next night another young man tried, and they passed the night the same way. Throughout their journey a young warrior would try every night; but never did they find out anything about him. Then they reached the country of their enemies. The next day they were going to fight. Then he told his friends to set his tent a little distance from them and to stay very silent in their tents, not to go out. Then the young man spat out his medicine towards where the enemies were coming. He killed off all the enemies. Then he yelled a war whoop and all the young warriors lifted their tent door and came out. He said to them, "I had a big fight and killed them all off. I will go now to the dead and cut off their ears, every one, and take their shields and spears and bows and arrows and war clubs." So he took them all and took their scalps, too. Then they went back, taking all the weapons. They got home and took the scalps to the chief. The chief picked out the young warrior to send as a guard, to take the girl warrior back to her home. She refused a guard. She asked only for a good horse. Now she showed herself. She took off her man's clothes. There she was, the nice young girl who was taken by her husband and thrown into the big river. She said, "I am a girl, I did all the fighting for your young warriors and I killed all the enemies and here you have their scalps and ears and weapons. Formerly my husband was Blue Hawk, and you have my husband shut up in the dark during my absence on account of the trick the young man Red Hawk played on him. Now bring my husband from where he is!" Then they brought Blue Hawk, and she went to meet him and she embraced him and cried. The young man looked thin and sad. She told him, "You were beaten by making you believe that the young man Red Hawk knew my person. He deceived you. You know I love you honestly, truly. Now go and get Red Hawk and the old woman!" So the band of warriors went to search for Red Hawk and the old woman and brought them before her husband and her and the big chief. The girl said to the chief, "You tell your boys to get the wildest ponies in the camp!" So they brought them, two of them. She ordered them to tie Red Hawk to the tail of one horse, and to tie the old woman to the tail of the other horse. Then they turned the horses loose. Off they went, kicking and jumping, and tore them to pieces, away from the camp. (That's the way the Indians used to do, to punish.)

Variant

Mexicans were living. Two boys were good friends. One got married. After he married he said to his friend, "I bet you can not know my wife." The other said, "I bet I can know her." The married boy knew his wife did not care to look at any man. The unmarried boy went to the house of an old woman and said to her, "Grandmother, will you go to that lady's house tonight and ask her to let you sleep with her one night, since her husband is away. You must see what she looks like when she goes to bed," he said. "My friend and I were talking today and he said I could not know his wife and I said I could know her. I went around there twice; but she would not look at me." The old woman said, "I will try." She sat down and looked for bugs in her dress and she put them in a little cane with a hole in the middle and she carried it to that girl's house. She knocked on the door. The girl said, "What do you want?" The old woman said, "Will you let me sleep here just for tonight?" And the girl was kind and let her in. The girl told her to sleep in the next room. "No, I want to sleep in your room," said the old woman. So the girl let her sleep in her room. When they went to bed, at midnight the old woman blew the tube on to the girl where she slept. In a little while the girl woke up and took off her dress to see what was biting her. And the old woman peeked out to see what she looked like. She had golden hair at her navel. It was braided and wound around her waist and tied in front with a red ribbon. In the morning the old woman went away happy because she knew how the girl looked, and she told the boy, "Grandson, she looks just like other women except she has golden hair at her navel which is braided around her waist and tied with a red ribbon." The boy went out very happy. When his friend met him, he said, "I know your wife." The man said, "How does she look?"—"She is just like other women, only she has golden hair at the navel, and the braid is tied with a red ribbon." That made the other man very mad and without a word he went back to his house and he did not say a word to his wife. Then he told the carpenter to make a box as large as his wife. His wife spoke to him, but he would not say a word. The next day they brought him the box and he told his wife to lie down in it. He fastened it up and put it in a wagon and he drove it to the ocean. Then he went back. He had been very rich, but after he threw away his wife he got very poor. He went around very dirty, he would lie in the ash piles.

When a man was fishing he saw a box and he caught it with his hook and brought it to the shore. He opened the box and in it was a very pretty girl. She was so pretty that he did not want any one to take her away from him. So he dressed her up like a man. Where the box was found lived the king and he was fighting with Horned Water Serpent in the ocean. The woman wanted to go with the soldiers to fight. She had to go because she was dressed as a man. "The old fisherman has a pretty son," they said. "We must go and get her." "No, he is not a man. Her eyes look like a woman's." But they took her. When they came to the ocean, she told the soldiers she would go on ahead. She did not see any soldiers. She wondered what they were fighting. She went close to the shore. The water rose up high and from it peeped out that Horned Water Serpent. He did not want to fight a woman, so, gently, he came close up to her. She said, "Father, is it you they are fighting," and she stroked his head. Horned Water Serpent nodded his head, when she spoke to him. She tied him by a red ribbon around her neck and took him with her to the king. Every day they had to feed him. On the *fifth* day the soldiers wanted to kill him. They said to the girl, "If you do not make your Horned Water Serpent talk, we will burn him." She cried and she said to Horned Water Serpent, "They say if you do not talk, they will burn you. Will you talk?" He nodded his head. On the *fifth* day they took him out, and people were gathered from all over to hear him talk. They told the girl to make him talk. "Now, father, for the sake of your life you have to talk," she said. Horned Water Serpent said, "Yes, for the sake of your life, I will talk." The people said, "What did he say? What did he say? Make him say it again!" Horned Water Serpent said, "Yes, I will talk because you are a woman." So he showed she was a woman. They did not burn him, they let him go. She unbraided her hair and dressed it like a woman. After that she wanted to go back to her house and she dressed again as a man. When she got home she asked what was going on. They said that a man who was very rich was going around like a crazy man. She knew it was her husband. She told them to bring him to her. She was dressed like the king. When they brought the man, he said, "*Akuwqmu,* you are well, father!" he said. She asked him why he was around like that. He told her his friend had told him how he knew his wife and how he had got mad and threw her into the ocean and after that he did not care to keep himself clean. And the girl's tears were running down her face. She told the soldiers to get her husband's friend. They got him and she asked him what he said. He said he did not know his friend's wife, but the old woman had worked for him and had thrown bugs and the girl had undressed, then the old woman saw her and told him what she looked like. They told the soldiers to get the old woman too. They asked her what the boy had said to her, and she said the boy had asked her to help him to learn about that girl. So she had gone and thrown bugs in her bed and had seen how she looked. Her husband heard and felt very badly for throwing away his wife and he wept. She said, "Do not weep! Here I am." And she showed him she was his wife. He told the soldiers to pile up the wood to burn the boy and the old woman for telling a lie. She told the soldiers to wash her husband and dress him in good clothes. And after that they lived happily.

79. *Without Fear :*[1] *The Division :*[2] *Rescue from Wind*

In a city lived the *padre* [*ta'pe'kahna*[3] < *ta'pena,* skull, shaved] and he had a godson, he brought him up in his house. This boy looked after everything in the house and after the chickens and he helped the priest in saying the mass, as *sakristano.* He got mad easily at anything. When he fed the chickens, the chickens were fighting for their feed, and he did not like that, so he took a stick and threw it at them and broke the legs of some of them and killed some of them. But he did not tell the *padre.* When the *padre* would go out to the chicken yard he always found some hens dead, but he never asked about it. Finally he asked the boy what was the matter with the chickens. He said, "They were fighting for their feed and I did not like to see it and I killed them." The *padre* said, "You must not do that!" The boy said, "They had better learn to be quiet, then I won't club them." The *padre* said nothing more and went into the house. At nightfall, he called the boy to his room—his name was Pedro, he went into the room. The *padre* said, "My son, tonight at midnight, I will eat my supper, and then you will have to go and ring the big bell in the church tower." The boy said, "*Bueno!*" Then he went out. Then the priest went to work, he fixed a place with a long ladder outside the church, and dug a grave at the foot of the ladder, and set there an exhumed dead body, and another dead body he set at the top of the ladder, and another at the tower bell. Then at midnight, the boy ran out to ring the bell. He was late and he ran to the church and came to the ladder to go up. He saw somebody standing at the foot of the ladder, and the grave dug there close. He crossed over the grave and said, "Who are you? What business have you here? Get away!" But the dead stood still, no answer. "Don't you hear what I say? Get away, I am in a hurry, I am going to ring the bell, for the *padre* to eat his supper." Saying that, he went up to the dead body and pushed it. The dead body fell over on him and knocked him down inside the grave, and fell on top of him. It was heavy and he tried to turn it over. Finally he succeeded and he stood the dead body up for him to climb on to get out of the grave. Then he went up the ladder. The priest was saying, "Now I guess Pedro will never

[1] Compare Zuni, Boas 1: 84-92. A widespread European tale.
[2] Compare San Juan, Parsons 4: 120-121. A widespread European tale.
[3] t'ₒopek'ana (T).

come back. He is a bad boy and I will get rid of him." As he got to the top of the ladder there was another dead body. Pedro said, "What kind of people are you anyhow, standing around here at this time of night?" He pushed him over. Then he went to the bell in the tower. There was another dead body. "What are you doing here anyway, so many of you? I am getting late. The priest is going to have his supper and I must ring the bell." When he pushed it over, it fell over on him and knocked him down. He turned it over and got up and threw it down from the top of the church to the ground. Then he rang the bell. Then the priest heard the bell ring. He said, "Oh this boy, I can not do anything with him. I thought I sent him whence he could never come back. There he is ringing the bell. He is a terrible boy." After ringing the bell, the boy went down and into the *padre's* room. "All right, *padre,* I rang the bell. When I got to the ladder there was a person there. I told him to get away, he did not mind me. I knocked him over and he fell on me inside the grave, I turned him over and used him for a ladder and got out of the grave. I went up the ladder and there was another and I pushed him over, I went to the bell, there was another. I pushed him over and he fell on top of me. I turned him over and got up and threw him down from the top of the church to the ground. I told him, 'You are *bagamundo* (vagabond), standing round here.' So I rang the bell." The priest said to the boy, "Pedro, you must not do that! You hurt those people. If they find you, they might kill you. Don't do that again!"—"I will do it, if I find them at the ladder where they have no business." So Pedro went to bed. Next day, he did worse and worse, killing chickens and doing other mischief. Then the *padre* said, "I guess I must tell this boy to hit the road." He found lots of chickens dead. He said, "Pedro, gather up those chickens and pick them to roast!" So Pedro brought them in and picked them and threw the feathers all over the kitchen. The priest went to the kitchen and called Pedro, "Now my son, I am tired of you. I let you go, to start out in the world. Take the chickens for your lunch!"—"All right," he said, "I am glad, *padre,* I will go." So he started off with his load on his back. He came to a big white house. It was vacant, so he thought he would stay at that house that night. He went in, it had a nice fireplace, he built a fire. Then he put the two roasted chickens on the edge of the fire, to warm them up, for supper. He was lying down on his back by the side of the fireplace. Somebody from the top of the chimney hole said, "*Cairé* (*caeré*), I am going to drop." He got up and listened. A second time, "*Cairé.*"—"Who are you anyway? What are you doing up there? There is a door, come in by the doorway! Don't drop in that way, you will get burned." Then he said, "*Cairé.*"—"What are you anyway that you want to come in by the chimney where there is a big blaze to burn you"? Said again, "*Cairé.*"—"*Caite (cáete), diabolo!* Drop, devil!" Then he dropped down. He scattered the coals and he jumped out. He sat down, with his back to the fireplace. Then Pedro pulled the chickens from the fireplace and told him, "If you are hungry, come on and eat"! The dead body did not turn around to him. Another one whispered from the top of the chimney, "*Cairé.*"—"What kind of people are you, anyway, to come down through the chimney? Come in through the door!"—"*Cairé.*"—"Don't you understand, come by the doorway"!— "*Cairé.*"—"*Caite, diabolo!*" He dropped down. He sat down like the first one, facing towards the dark. Then another one said, "*Cairé,*" three times. "*Caite, diabolo, tonto,* drop, devil, fool, I guess you are not human the way you come down through the blazing fireplace." Then he dropped and sat like the other two. Then Pedro laid the two chickens where they were sitting. "I guess you are hungry, that is why you came down through the chimney when you saw the chickens. Go and eat!" But they seemed not to want to eat. The first one who dropped down said, "When I was in the world, I was justice of the peace. When people brought me a case, in a quarrel, in deciding the case, I decided against the one who was in the right. That is why I am suffering in *el enferno upai'me'naka* (burning always)." The second one said, "When in the world I was a *teniente*. I decided against the one who was in the right. That is why I am suffering in hell." The third one said, "I was a *capitán de la guerra* (*humłauwa t'unena*)[1]. I fined people who were innocent. That is why I am suffering in hell." The first said, "You tell my people to pay the priest to say mass for me to be pardoned." The second said the same thing and the third, the same thing. In the morning they all disappeared. Pedro started out on his journey. Then on the road he came to a dead body lying on top of the earth where they had dug the grave. He was lying there because he was very poor and had nobody to help him to be buried. So the *padre* did not want to bury him. So Pedro made up his mind he would go to the *padre*. So he went to the *padre* and said, "*Padre,* there is a poor dead body lying by the grave. I will pay you five dollars for you to bury him." The *padre* said angrily, "Oh you Indian, you have no money to pay me!" Then he drew out the five dollars and threw them down near the *padre*. "Here are the five dollars! You go and bury that poor body!" Then the *padre* took the money and went to the grave and buried the dead body.

From there Pedro went on his journey and came to a city. When he

[1] x͟umł͟owat'ʼ͟unena (T).

got there he saw three Mexican boys. They were quarreling over the inheritance from their father. Their father had a cane of virtue (*bastón de la suerte*) [*toayenemu*,[1] cane, *inahqwaina*,[2] *suerte*]. So they said, "Brother Pedro, can you decide in some way for us to keep us from quarreling. I am the eldest and I want the cane."—"Yes, if you do what I say, I will decide. I will stand here. Give me the cane! What virtue (*suerte*) has this cane?"—"This cane has this virtue, our father used to raise it up and hit with it on the ground and say, 'Turn me to an eagle!' He would raise it again and say, 'Turn me to an ant!' Lastly, 'Turn me to people (*gente*).' Then it turned him, according to what he asked for. Anything he needed and asked for when he raised it and lowered it he got."—"Now then I will do this for you, the only way to stop your quarreling. You three go a few hundred yards from me and race and whoever comes ahead will get the cane." So they took off their hats and shoes and went into the road. They turned around and asked, "From here?"—"No, go a little farther!" Then they went a little farther and they said, "From here?"— "No, go a little farther, I will tell you." They kept going farther and looking back and he kept them going farther. Then he raised his hat for the start. Then they ran. As they came running, he raised the cane up and lowered it and said, "Turn me to an eagle!" Then he was turned into an eagle and slowly he flew up and circled about. "Oh Brother Pedro, have pity on us! We will divide up equally with you, we will give you a share." But he flew way up and paid no attention to them.

He went to another city. He raised his stick up and down and turned back into a person. He went into the city, where the king lived. The king had three daughters. They were lost. The king advertised among the people, whoever found them could marry the first daughter. So Pedro heard that, and that none of the young men looking for the girls could find them. He went around searching for them; but he could not find any footprints. Some one would have taken them to another country, he had the idea, up in the sky. The whirlwind had come very strong, and found the three girls alone out in the field and carried them up into the sky. Pedro thought he would go up in the sky. He got out his cane, raised it and lowered it and said, "Turn me to eagle!" Then he flew up in the air. He flew up and around and around and around til he was far up. Then he came to a country, where he raised up and down his cane and turned into a person. He raised the cane up and down and said, "Turn me to an ant!" Then he went to the first house. Wind woman was there,

---

[1] tu- stick + ? + enema, suffix (T).
[2] inah͜owáʔina, its luck (T).

making *buñuelo* (bread fried in lard) and putting it in a jucca basket. Ant man was very hungry, he went through the crack of the door and began to eat the *buñuelo*. He kept on eating, and the *buñuelo* was disappearing out of the basket. Wind old woman said, "What is the matter with this basket that I can not fill it with *buñuelo?* My daughters are getting very hungry." It was about noon. So she picked up the basket and threw it away. She put another one there. Ant had got enough to satisfy him. He went through the crack of the door into another room, and there was the eldest of those girls. He raised his cane up and down and turned to a person. He spoke to the girl, and she was very much afraid. She told him that Wind old man was their father and Wind old woman their mother, if they found him in the room, they would blow him away and kill him. "I have come here anyway. Your father advertised you were lost and did not know where you had gone. Your father said whoever found his daughters, could marry the eldest." Then he went into the second room and found the second girl. He said, "Do not be afraid! I will take you out." Then he went in the third room and found the younger sister. He said the same thing to her. He raised the cane up and down and turned to Wind. Then he blew the doors open. He took the first girl out, then the second, then the third. He raised his cane up and down and said, "Turn me to eagle!" Then he put the girls on his back. Then he went flying down to the earth. He got them down to the city where their father lived and took them to their father's house. The king was very glad to recover his daughters. Pedro married the first girl. They made a big feast and had a dance. The king said, "Turn everything over to him!" The king was old, he was to take the place of the king, And so Indians are entitled to be king. For Pedro was an Indian boy and became king.

80. The King's Son Becomes a Deer: The Stolen Mirror

People were living at *töata*[1] (Taos). The war chief (*humławaana*)[2] called out for all the men to go hunting and to meet at the spring, *patsiwilita*[3] (it is toward the east). So they went and with them went the king's son (*laiyokaiye*)[4]. They turned him into a deer, and he did not come back. The king was very sad. All the people died, and just one woman was left. She had a little son. The little boy asked his mother how they used

[1] t'əot'o (T).
[2] x͜umł͜owa?'ana (T).
[3] p'òc͜iw'ilito, water-eye- ?-at (T).
[4] l'ay a̦?ùk"oyi, king his son (lay < Sp. rey) (T).

to live and why she was living alone. The mother said to her son, "A sickness came and all the people died and I alone was left." She did not know from whom she got that boy. He asked her about his grandfather and grandmother and all his relations. She told him how the war chief called the men to the spring to hunt and the king's son went with them and he turned to a deer. "I have heard that that deer always comes to that spring," she said. The little boy said, "Mother, make me a bow and arrows so I can go to that spring and hunt that deer." His mother made him a bow and arrows and baked him some bread, and he went to hunt. When he got to *patsiwilita* there were deer tracks. He followed them a little way and then he returned to the spring and did as his mother told him to do. She had given him a sack of medicine and told him when he saw the tracks of a big deer he was to take earth from *five* footprints and put medicine on that earth and sit and wait for the deer to come. While he was sitting there a big deer came just at sunrise. He drank from the spring. The boy shot at the deer. The deer ran, and he followed. He ran after the deer all day. At last at evening the deer came back to the spring and his deer hide fell off and he was a very young boy and on his head were three stars and a *banda* was tied over them. He exclaimed, "*Huwi*"! The deer boy said, "Through you I am myself again, by your help. You must not ask for money. If my father asks you what you want for bringing me back, you must ask for a looking-glass which will give you anything you want. If my father loves me, he will give it to you." They went to the little boy's mother. She went out to meet her son and said, "I wonder who my son is bringing." She was very glad to see her son. She let them in and gave them supper. They slept there and in the morning he took the boy to his father. When they got to his father's house his father did not know him, but when he untied his forehead his father saw the three stars and knew him. The father asked the little boy what he wanted for bringing his son. The boy said, "I want nothing except your little looking-glass." So they gave it to him.

He went to another country. He had only a deerhide kilt and a mantle of buckskin. There in the other country he found the bones of a dead person. He gathered up the bones and said, "Poor thing! I will tell the priest to give you a mass and bury you." He took the bones to the priest and told him to tell the people to bury him. And he paid him to make a mass. Then he went on. He got to a country where a king lived. There were lots of people working on a bridge across a big river. He asked for work, and they gave him work. In the night he measured the bridge and he said to his glass, "My glass, put a golden bridge here." And in the morning there was a long bridge shining with gold. The king made his daughter marry him. The next night he measured for the house where he wanted to live with his wife. He said to his glass that he wanted a house prettier than his father-in-law's, with a gold roof, and men to wait on them, and cows and chickens. In the morning there were lots of cows in the barn, and chickens, and waiters. An old woman was taking care of his looking-glass. His wife did not like the way he was dressed. She asked him how he could make things so quickly. He told her he had a looking-glass which an old lady took care of. "That glass gives me whatever I want." That night his wife pushed him into a hole where big rats ate people up. When they threw him down, a white cat jumped in and caught all the rats, except one white rat who said, "Brother, do not kill us all, we will help your brother get his glass back." So the cat stopped killing them. The rats made a hole to where the old woman was sitting looking after the glass. They got the glass and took it to the cat. The cat gave the glass to the boy. The cat said he was the one whose bones had been lying in the road, and which he had gathered up. He said, "I came to help you because you were in such trouble, because you helped me, too." Then the boy thanked the cat and he said to his glass, "My glass, burn up all these people!" Then the fire began to burn them up.

81. The Four Brothers

Some Utes (*tahana*)[1] were living at *puan'palaka*[2] (war finished). Some Apache lived at *tun'yaba*[3]. One of the Utes was a very rich man. This Ute had four daughters and he had many guards. One day his four daughters went out to bathe in the lake *paṭipawena*[4]. They were going to bathe one by one. While the first one took off her clothes and went to bathe, the giant came. He called to the girl to come out, "Give me my clothes so I can come out."—"No, you come out, embrace me, then I will give you your clothes." So the girl went to him at the edge of the lake, she stretched out her arms to embrace the giant. Then the giant grabbed the girl and dragged her out. He gave her her clothes and put the girl into his water jar and carried her off, to the mountain where he had a hole, way down to the other world underneath (*kuinata*)[5]. He took her to a

---

[1] t'ohonạ (T).
[2] p'ˌuonp‘ol?ogạ, war-finish-at (T).
[3] t'‘əmyobo, morning-song-at. A place on the Raton road (T).
[4] p'ȯłi + ?, water-grass + ? (T).
[5] k'ˌuyn'ạt‘o (T).

white house where a big white bull lived, to be the wife of that bull. He left her there. Then the next day he went up again to the top world (*k'ʾitʾo*, up above). Then he sat there, watching. Then the second girl came to the same lake to bathe. She got to the lake and took off her clothes. Then the giant went to the lake again, he took her clothes and called to her to come out. She told the giant to give her her clothes to come out. "No, you come and embrace me, then I will give you your clothes." So the girl went to the edge of the lake and reached to him with her arms. The giant grabbed at the girl and pulled her out, gave her her clothes and put her into the water jar. He took her up the mountain to his hole, took her down into the other world. He took her to a house next to the first one, where the big bear lived, and gave the girl to the bear to be his wife. Then he went back again to the upper world. He sat there watching for the next girl to come. The third one came to the same lake, took off her clothes and went to bathe. The giant took her clothes and told her to come out. She said, "Give me my clothes and I will come out." He put her in the jar, took her up to the hole and down into the underworld. He took her to the third house where lived a lion. He gave him the girl for his wife. He went up again to the upper world. He sat watching for the fourth girl to come. The fourth girl came to the lake to bathe, took off her clothes. Then the giant went to where her clothes were and told her to come out. "Give me my clothes!"—"You come and embrace me and I will give you your clothes." She stretched out her arms, the giant grabbed her, gave her her clothes, put her in the water jar, took her to his hole and down into the lower world. She was to be his wife. He took her to his house. All four girls had disappeared, the chief of the Utes missed them after four days. So the Ute chief went to the Apache camp and called out notifying them that his four daughters had gone somewhere he did not know. "Now, you Apache young men, if you search for my daughters, whoever finds them, they will be your wives." So four Apache young men, brothers, went to look for the girls, in the mountains. They found the hole, but they found no tracks from it. "Somebody who lives in this hole took them in." They thought they would find the girls there. So the eldest boy told the others to get a long rope, long enough to reach to the underworld. So they brought some rawhide ropes. The eldest brother said, "Now, brothers, you tie me around my waist. I will go down first." Then they tied him and they lowered him into the hole. They tied the end of the rope to a tree. Before he went down he told his brothers, "If I can not reach, I will shake the rope, and you draw me up." Before the rope was all out, it shook. So they drew him up. And he said, "It was very cold, the wind was very cold. I could not stand going down further." Then the second brother said, "I tell you now if I find the four girls I will bring them to the hole and send them up. The first girl will be my eldest brother's wife and the second, my second brother's, and the third, my third brother's, the fourth one will be mine." They lowered him down. Before the rope was half unrolled it shook, they brought him up. "It was very cold. I could not stand it." Then the third brother went down. Before the rope was all out, it shook. So they drew him up. He said, "It is very hard to go down. I don't believe we can go down." Then the youngest brother said, "I will try, I will go down, I will get those girls; but the nicest one will be my wife." So they tied him, the youngest brother, to go down. He went down and the rope unrolled, unrolled as he went down until it was all unrolled. He reached the underworld. He looked all around, it looked very strange to him. He saw a white house. Then he untied the rawhide and walked towards the white house. He got there, he went up to the door. Then the girl came to the door. She said, "Oh, my brother, why have you come into this world? I am married to a white bull and he is a very angry bull."—"Anyway," he said to her, "your father notified us Apache that you disappeared from the house and he did not know where you went and he said that whoever finds you you will marry. We are four brothers and I am the youngest, and I came down the hole the giant brought you down and here I have found you."—"Oh, my brother, come in then!" The girl was crying. "The white bull will kill both of us. No human being ever comes to this house. Whoever comes here, he will kill. See that pile of bones there? They are human bones." He said, "We will do the best we can." So the boy asked the girl, "Do you know where he has his heart or his life? Where in his body"?—"Yes," she said. "He has his life in the middle of his forehead. I have his life in a little box."—"Where is it?"—"I have it."—"Bring it to me!" She brought the little box, he opened it. He saw something white in the shape of an egg in the box. Then he said, "We have it. Don't be afraid, I'll kill him." Then the girl stopped crying. The boy asked the girl what time of day he got back. "He gets home towards the middle of the afternoon."—"What kind of sign appears when he is coming?"—"A very strong wind begins to blow with dust. That is the time he is coming." They stayed all day in the house. Then he watched all morning, about the middle of the afternoon it began to blow a little wind, it blew stronger and stronger until a heavy windstorm came and dust was flying. Then he hid himself behind the entrance of the door. He had the life in his hand.

He saw it was a fearful looking animal throwing the dust with his horns. He said to his wife, "Umm! I smell people." The girl said, "How can that be? Nobody comes here to the house. What do you smell?"—"Anyhow it smells of people, umm!" He tried to butt the door, he was angry, he looked through the door. Then the boy threw that life of his at his forehead and knocked him over to the ground and killed him. Then he cut his right ear off. Then the girl was very happy. "Now, my father," she said to the boy, "I am yours and now I will enjoy myself out in the open air. I have been shut up here since I came here." Then the boy took the girl by the arm and took her to the hole he came down by. He tied her to the rope and shook the rope, and then the brothers on top said, "*Yudǫ!* my younger brothers (*anumpaiyuwaina*)[1]!" Then they pulled the girl up. They saw a nice pretty girl. The eldest brother said, "This is going to be my wife." The second said, "No, she will be mine." The third said, "No, she is mine." Anyway the eldest brother took the girl. Then the brother below went to the second house for the second girl. He got to the house and found the second sister there. The girl came out and said, "My brother, why did you come into this world? I am married to a big bear and he lets no one live. He kills anyone who comes here."—"Anyhow, I came here because your father notified us people that you were lost from your home. We found the hole and I came down and here I find you. Do you know where he has his life?"—"Yes, he has his life in the centre of his paw."—"Have you his life?"—"Yes."—"Where is it?"—"Here it is!" she said and took it out from a handkerchief. It was a very small thing, it looked like a bead. "What time of day does he come back?"—"He comes back when the sun is a little bit down to the west from the middle of the sky."—"What sign appears when he is coming home?"—"It begins to blow very hard and rocks come rolling, blown by the wind." Then he ate. The girl was crying all the time. "Don't cry!" he said. Then the boy sat watching for him to come back. Finally, after the sun went down from the center of the sky, it began to blow hard, rocks came rolling, and finally came the bear. He came running angrily. He said, "Umm! I smell people. What people are here?"—"Nobody is here. It is me you smell." Then he came near the door and put his hands up in the air. Then the boy threw his life at him, in the middle of his paw. He knocked him down, dead. Then he cut off his right ear. Then the girl was crying for joy. "Now, my father, I am free! I was a captive here. Now I will enjoy my life outside." So he took her by the arm and they walked to the hole. He tied the girl and shook the rope. Then his

[1] ạnạmpʼ͈ǫywáʔinạ (T).

three brothers exclaimed, "*Yudǫ!* our younger brother!" So they pulled her up. Then the second brother said, "This will be my wife. She is mine." The third brother said, "No, she is going to be mine." But the second brother took the girl. Now the boy went back to the third house. He went there and the girl came out and saw him. She said, "Why have you come here? My husband is a lion. He is wild and mad. Anybody who comes here he kills them."—"Anyway I came here because your father notified us people that you were lost from your home. We found the hole and I came down and here I find you. Do you know where he has his life?"—"Yes, he has his life in the centre of his paw."—"Have you his life?"—"Yes."—"Where is it?"—"Here it is!" she said, and took it out from a handkerchief. It was a very small one, it looked like a bead. "What time of day does he come back?"—"He comes back when the sun is a little bit down to the west from the middle of the sky."—"What sign appears when he is coming home?"—"It begins to blow very hard and rocks and big timbers come rolling, blown by the wind." It began to blow hard, rocks and big timber came rolling, and finally came the lion. He came running angrily. He said, "Umm! I smell people. What people are here?"—"Nobody is here. It is me you smell." The boy was behind the door. Lion raised up his head, the boy threw the ball that was his life, he killed him. He took the girl up, they walked to the hole. He tied the girl and shook the rope. Then his three brothers exclaimed, "*Yudǫ!* our younger brother." So they pulled her up. "That will be my wife," said the third brother. He went back to the fourth house. The girl came out and said, "My brother, why did you come into this world?"—"Who is your husband?"—"The giant."—"Where is his life? Have you his life?" The girl was crying, she said, "No, my father. I know nothing about his life or where he has it. There is only one thing that he fears, he fears our god (*wahmea*[1], 'the Catholic god')." Then the boy asked the girl when the giant came back. "He comes back when the sun is a little bit down to the west from the middle of the sky."—"What sign appears when he is coming back?"—"It begins to blow very hard and rocks come rolling, blown by the wind." The boy did not know what to do. They were crying, they thought they were going to be killed by the giant. So the boy prayed to all the gods together (*kwientaina*,[2] ? people, "all the Indian gods"). So he sat there. Then the giant came very slowly and gently. He

---

[1] wòmạyaʔˈana, God (T). Compare Isleta Waiide, Weide, Wẹide (Indian god) (wàʔˈide, spirit, life, god [T.]) or *wahtainin*, spirits (Parsons 7: 295).

[2] kʷientˈʼoynạ, ? tˈʼoynạ, variant form of tˈʼoynemạ, people (T). Compare Isleta kẹnim, stones representing animals and birds.

said, "Those are the only ones I am afraid of. I can not do anything, you can take the girl back, she is yours." So he just lay there with his arms folded. Now the giant said to the boy, "You come and cut both my ears." The boy got his stone knife (spear head) and cut off both ears. Giant told the boy, "Wrap them up!" He wrapped them in a corner of his clothes. Giant said, "Whenever you are in great danger you squeeze my ears, very hard, with you finger nails. Then I will appear to help you." So he took the girl out and started to the hole. He tied the girl to the rope, he shook it, but there was no answer. He shook the second time. No answer. Then he said, "I guess they have left me and are gone with their wives. After I risked my life and did the work, they have left me and are gone." They felt sad and both cried. They did not know how to go up. Then he remembered what Giant told him. Then he untied the ears of Giant from his clothing and squeezed hard with his finger nails. Then in front of them appeared Giant. Giant said, "My son, what is the trouble?" He said to him, "I brought the girl to this rope and tied it and shook the rope, but there was no answer. My brothers have left me and gone back home."—"Don't be afraid! I will help you and take you up." So the wind began to blow hard and strong, and raised them up through the hole like a whirlwind, and put them on top. Giant said, "When you get home, to return my ears pray to your gods, and hold the ears up in the air, and they will be returned to me. Your brothers played you a little trick. You do something to them so they never come back." When he got on top, only the tracks of his brothers were seen. So they started toward home, to *tun'yaba*. Thence they went to *puan'palaka,* to the Chief's house, and told him where he had found the girls, in the underworld and how he took them up, and how his brothers had left him and how the giant helped them up through the hole, and "here we are"! The Chief said, "Son, here is your wife." So they prepared a big feast for his marriage. They called all the Indian tribes to come to the marriage. After they were married they lived there, and the Chief sent his soldiers after his brothers and they brought in the three boys. They had told the Chief that they had fought a big fight with the people in the underworld and got the girls. So they lied. The Chief killed them by burning them on a pile of wood. A heavy wind came and blew away the ashes. Then he remained there to live with the Ute Chief and he managed all the business of the chief. People say that the Apache live at *tun'yaba* and the Utes at *puan'palaka*. They live there, enjoying their lives happily.

82. The Brave Boy

There was a Mexican woman living with her son who was very lazy. They were gathering soldiers from everywhere. The lazy boy would sit and kill flies. When he hit them he would kill lots of them. He wrote on his head-band that in one shot he had killed one hundred. A man of the king came and took him, to be a good soldier. "He will kill all our enemies," he said. He gave him his horse and his gun, and he just cried when they put him on the horse. He did not know how to ride. "Tie the gun on one side and the sword," he said, "and tie my legs to the horse, because I do not know how to ride, and tie the reins to the pummel." The soldier laughed, "How can he fight?" he said. He laughed at him and made him go first. The horse ran away and got to the place where the enemy was. His nose was running and his eyes were red from crying, and they laughed at him and laughed so hard that they died of laughing (just as we too may laugh until we are faint). And it came true that he killed many with one shot. When he saw them dead, he wiped his eyes and went back to the soldiers and said he had killed them all. They did not believe him because they heard no shot. But they went back with him and saw them all lying dead. They went back to the king and told him that he had killed all the enemy without fighting, they did not know how. His horse ran ahead so fast, when they got there all were lying dead. The king asked him how he fought? He said to the king that when his horse ran among them they all fell dead. The king said, "You will be the second king from now on." They washed him and dressed him. He married the king's daughter. They had a big wedding, a big dance. They had servants to wait on them. They lived happily together. After a while they went to see his mother, with servants and wagons and presents for his mother. When he got to his mother's house, she did not know him. He told his story to her and she believed him. His servants built a new house for his mother. She was very sorry for the way he had lived, so dirtily, and she used to ask (pray) for him and, because she asked for him, he got rich.

83. Manuelito and the Saints

Some people were living in a little village. A couple had four boys. After they were grown a little boy was born, Manuelito. The four brothers became rich, but they did not care for their parents. Manuelito grew up and asked, "Why are my brothers so rich and we so poor?"—"They are bad boys, they do not care for their parents." One day Manuelito said, "My mother, you are old; but let me go out to work for you!"—"You are so little; you have never been away; we want you to stay with us. However, when your father comes back, I will make a lunch for your journey." So when the father came back with the corn he had begged, she made Manuelito some bread. He knelt down and asked a blessing from his father and mother.

He left and as he was travelling in the desert he saw a beautiful woman coming in a light. He was frightened. She said, "How are you, Manuelito? Where are you going?" He thought, "I am so poor, how is it she knows me?" He said, "I am going to look for work. My father and mother are poor. I am going to work to support them. My brothers do nothing for us."—"Well, Manuelito, go in the direction I came from. You will see a white house and a carpenter who will give you work." He thanked her and he wondered about her. He went on and knocked at a door. Out came a man. "Well, Manuelito, have you come?"—"How does this man know me? I have never been here before." So he said, "I have come to find work to support my father and mother." The man put him to work at carpentry. As he sat to the table tears rolled down his cheeks. The carpenter asked him why he was crying. "If only I had my mother and father here to eat this good food!" The carpenter said not to worry, at that very moment his mother and father were eating the same things.

He worked five years, then he wanted to return to his parents. "All right, my boy, you may go home. You do not know whom you have been working for, but I will tell you. I am Saint Joseph. I am going to pay you for your work, but I won't give you money, you might lose it on your way." He called him into a room where there were lots of little books of all colors and told him to choose one. He gave him a little bottle of water to drink on his way. He wondered how so little water could last him on his way. He gave him the little book as his fortune (Sp., *virtud; pöahanuna,* medicine bundle). He told him if he met his brothers not to give them anything. On his way he met the Virgin again and she gave him lunch. He went on and he was hungry and he said, "I will ask my little book for something to eat," and there was everything he wanted to eat. "Now I am going to ask you for a horse," and before he finished speaking there stood a horse well saddled and bridled, handsomer than any horse his brothers had. Then he asked for a suit of clothes. He passed by his eldest brother's house. His brother admired the horse and asked him to sell it. "No, I won't sell it." He passed by his second brother's house. He asked him to sell his saddle. "No, I won't sell it." He passed by his next brother's house. "That man has the handsomest suit I ever saw." He asked him to sell it. "No, I won't sell it."—"Stop here at my place!"—"No, I am on my way." His mother and father were sitting outside. His mother said, "Good old man, our boy is coming."—"Good old woman, how do you know?"—"I see the dust of his horse." The boy came and kneeled before his mother and father. They fainted on seeing him. As they lay there he took out his little book and asked for a better house than his brothers' house and a better farm.

Saint Joseph had told him, "When you get rich, my boy, treat everybody well who comes to your store or to deal with you, whether they are rich or poor." They lived together happily. After many years he forgot what Saint Joseph told him and he was not doing the right thing by people. Saint Joseph sent Saint Paul and Saint Peter to Manuelito. They were dressed as shepherds. They took away from him his little book. Then he and his parents grew poor, so poor they had to gather up chips for firewood.

Back came Saint Paul and Saint Peter. They reached the house of the eldest brother who came out to meet them. "What do you fellows want?"—"We are hungry and tired and cold. We would like to stay the night with you."—"No, you may be thieves, you can not stay in my house!" They went on to the second brother. He came out to meet them. "What do you fellows want?"—"We are hungry and tired and cold. We would like to stay the night with you."—"No, you can not stay here, go over to the corral." They went on to the house of the third brother. He went out to meet them. "What do you fellows want"?—"We are hungry and tired and cold. We would like to stay the night with you."—"I don't allow any loafers around here. Go to the pigpen!" They went on to Manuelito's house. They knocked at the door. "Manuelito! Open the door!"—"No, I can not open the door. I am lying here as naked as when I came into the world. You took away my fortune." They knocked again. "Manuelito! Open the door!"—"No, I can not open the door. I am lying here as naked as when I came into the world. You took away my fortune." They knocked again. Then Manuelito found himself lying in his bed in his fine house. Said Saint Peter, "You forgot the advice given you to treat everybody right, and so you lost everything. We came to see what your brothers were doing. They are bad." Now Manuelito lived happily again and treated everybody all right, rich and poor. In a few years Saint Peter came back and said he was going to take Manuelito to Heaven. "How about the house and the stock and the place?"—"They are going to remain on earth." They went out and all felt light and they began to go up and up and up. They saw that down below the places of the brothers were all burning up. They reached Heaven, and Manuelito and his father and his mother all became saints.

84. The Snake Intimidated

There lived some people in a village, and Mexicans lived in their own town. A little woman had two daughters. There was a dance, a Mexican dance. Some young men were going to the dance, they had a long way to go. As they were going on the road, one of those boys said to his friends, "I heard people say that about here in this curve of the road around this hill lives a big snake (*pętsułana*)[1] and he comes out on the road and he catches passers-by and beats them and the person dies." Big Snake heard those boys. One of the boys said, "If he comes out now against us, I will knock him in the head with *carajo*." Big Snake heard that word and put it in his mind. When he heard the boys saying that, he got afraid and would not come out to bite them. He stayed hidden. People were picking piñons around that hill, but Big Snake did not show himself. That way they lived many years in that part of the village. So one time another Mexican dance was going on. And there was this old woman with her two daughters, the girls told her they would like to go to the dance. So the mother took them to the dance. As they were going on that road where the boys had gone, at the curve, by the side of the hill, Big Snake came out and said, "*Awelita* (little grandmother), I will ask you if you can tell me something. Once a lot of boys were passing here. One of the boys said, 'Here lives a big snake that bites passers-by,' and one of the others said, 'I am not afraid of him. If he comes out I will club him with *carajo*.'" Then the old woman said, "Yes, my grandson, I tell you what *carajo* means." She stood there in the road and Big Snake was looking at the old woman. "My grandson, I will show you. That is one of the worst clubs there is in the world. I will show you." She raised up her dress. "You see the place where I was shot with *carajo*. I was shot with that. That will never heal up as long as I live. That is the worst club there is. If they hit you with that you will die." Then Big Snake said, "Oh grandmother, is that true? Then I will not dare to bite any one passing by here. I might get killed."[2]

[1] pˌęcułʼona (T).
[2] This story was heard from an Indian, but the narrator thought the story was Mexican on account of the use of the word *carajo*.

85. The Marriage Feast

Three men went from Taos toward the northwest and came to a house where they were getting ready a marriage feast. The people in the house asked the men to chop some wood for them. The men chopped the wood, but after it was chopped the people in the house gave them nothing to eat. The men said nothing, but they were very angry. They went back to Taos, then they returned and on the way they danced. With their power they put the people of that house to sleep, they put the girl in bed with her *padrino,* and the boy with his *madrina,* and mixed up all the people in the house.

86. Witch Dog

Anciently, when the people were afraid of enemies coming, in order to protect themselves and their horses they had young men for watchmen. They used to herd their horses at Panatsu'laya,[1] in the meadows. Maybe six men would herd for one week (*tsuʻtöle*,[2] seven days), another six men another week, and so on. One day this Taos man, a young man, saddled up a good horse, in the evening. He told his friends that he was going to the pueblo. So he went. When he got there, he stayed over night, with his girl. He went back to Taos Junction early at daybreak. He carried his quiver of arrows and his bow. On the road as daylight was coming he saw ahead of him a black dog. Then he went galloping until he came up to the dog. Then the dog turned back and looked at him and started to run faster. Then he started his horse up fast. He overtook the dog. Then the dog sidled out of the road, with his tongue hanging out. He was a great big dog. He shot at him, he shot a second time. Then he killed him. He went to skin him. Then he found a person inside that skin. That's why they say that those people down at Santo Domingo and Tesuque are witches and have the practice of turning into dogs.

87. The Vision

One man was coming from somewhere along the plain. He could not reach the river to make his night camp, so he stopped in the middle of the plain. Then he heard animals growling, all sorts of animals. He listened and could not sleep, as he was alone. In the middle of the night

---

[1] p'ònạc'ʹulʔogạ, water- ? - yellow-at, in Rio Grande canyon on the road to Santa Fé where the Taos Junction road goes off (T).

[2] c'utʹạle (T).

he heard a song, some one was singing. It sounded quite a distance from him. So he listened. It sounded as if the one singing was coming towards him. He got up when he felt he was very near to him. He saw something that looked black, like a shadow of something, and it was singing,

ee ee ya a

ee ya ya a

ai ya a aiya a

aa ee aa a

After it stopped singing, it said, "*Huwi! toawi'ke* (humanly living) *nowia'ka* (some times we have hardship) *nowiku'mu* (such as we can not bear)." The next day the man went on his way. When he got home he told of what he had heard, and sang the song. That is where they learned this song.

88. The Girl Clairvoyant

There was an old man,[1] very jolly, full of jokes, and saying anything to make people laugh. One time he went out with some other Taos men onto the plain to trade with the Comanche and Kiowa. When Taos traders found a band of Kiowa (they took bread and other things to trade with), they would trade with them and they stayed together some time. At the home of one Kiowa woman where the Taos men stopped was a little old woman, very old, Dolorita Juana. She told this old Taos man, "My son, I am going to tell you one of my own stories. When I was a young girl I travelled with young men who were always going to war, I went with them. I saw many strange things among the tribes of our enemies, but the strangest thing of all that I saw was one time I was going along the bank of Arkansas River. Where the water was deep and stagnant along the bank I saw a *pakŏłaana* lying on the edge of the bank. He looked at me. He had one horn and on his body, short spines; his eyes were yellow and round. As he looked at me, he laughed at me, opening his mouth wide." She laughed. "I was afraid he would catch me, but he jumped into the water." Humorous as was the Taos man, he thought, "This Kiowa woman thinks she can beat me telling a story, but I am going to beat her." (They talk broken Mexican, these Kiowa.) The Taos man said, "Well, my mother, Dolorita Juana, you are a woman and I am a man. You seem to say in your story that you have seen many strange things in your young days by going with the warriors and you tell of that animal you saw on the Arkansas. What did he say to you, anything?"—"No," she said, "he just laughed."—"Let's see you laugh again

---

[1] He was a medicine man; he possessed a fetich lion from a medicine deer's stomach.

as he did." She repeated. "Is that all you saw of that animal?"—"Yes, that was all he did."—"Well now, my mother, I am going to tell you something. I also have seen many strange things, but I have never seen in my travels in the plains and elsewhere anything like I have seen at my home, a human being. She can not talk, she can not walk. She is just lying down, on a soft skin. She always knows things before they happen.[1] She knows I am talking with you now. She knows that we are here, we Taos Indians among you. As soon as she knew we were coming out here, she told her people by signs all that we were doing. She is the niece of my wife. She will know when we start back from here and will tell her people, and what we get from you. If your people think they are going to fight us, she will know and tell it. That animal you saw was not your people, only an animal, but this is a real human being born of my wife's sister." The old woman was scared to hear this.

89. Owl Gives Warning

One time a trading party of Taos men went on a trading trip to some Indians of the Plains (*höa'chana,*[2] roamers). When they were about half way, when they were camping at night, Owl old man was talking away in his nook, just as if he was telling something: *hum hunhun hum! ya'nu hat'-mawǫhę,*[3] now indeed you are about to arrive. "Listen," they said, "listen to what *ału* María says"! They did not know where those Plains Indians were camping. "*Ału* María knows where they are. Perhaps we will find them tomorrow." Owl called all night.[4] At daylight they packed their horses and in the afternoon they found the Indians and did their trading. They started back where they lived, and halfway back, the old owl at night began to call out from the tree,

> hum hunhun hum
> chutxiapulu[5]
> old dirty shirt
> ka'wa'kö
> blood deep

[1] This girl was born dumb, her bones were soft, she moved on her chest, and they fed her. She made signs when it was going to rain or when strange peoples were coming. She was called Chiupapa, (c'iwpòbe. T), Eagle flower. She died about fifty years ago.

[2] h'əocianą, Plains Indians (T).

[3] y'onṳ hod mąw'onhę (T).

[4] For a Zuni pictograph of a similar incident see Roberts Jr., H. H. The Village of the Great Kivas on the Zuni Reservation, New Mexico, p. 151, Pl. 62 b. Bull. 111, Bureau of American Ethnology. 1932.

[5] cùd- shirt + h'i?ię- dirty + pulu ? (T).

meaning they were to be in a bloody-shirt fight, that their enemies were coming behind them to fight. "We must look out," they said. So they thought they would take another road, to escape. They did not want to fight. So their enemies missed them.

90. Grasshopper Calls Out

There was living an old woman, she had two sons. One day the two boys went for firewood to bring on their back. As they were going they passed by a rock by the roadside. From the flat top of the rock somebody said, "*Ilili! haulu piska*[1] (grasshopper naked)." Then he ran in under the stone, into his hole. The boys passed on, going for their wood, and brought the wood back to their house.

91. Two Girls Play at Hiding[2]

Yuwanxena i'taitena,[3] formerly people lived. Two young girls were very faithful friends, they always went together. They like to go out in nice places. They searched for nice places in the mountains. They found places in the mountain, with pretty meadow-like openings, with pretty, small lakes and all kinds of pretty flowers. They went around the lakes very happy and talking in a very friendly way, gathering flowers. They were enjoying it. They went from one place to another, and found different kinds of flowers. The boys wanted to talk to them, but they did not want to talk with them. They liked to keep to themselves. They wore flowers in their dresses. That way they were going along over the different mountains, looking for the most beautiful places. Then they said, "Let us play at hiding!" So they played at hiding, one went to hide and the other looked for her. She stood facing backward while her friend hid. When she found a hiding place she called to her friend, "*tǫhǫta,* now ready!" She went to look for her, singing,

> aiyunge aiyunge
> w'iu[4] pahseren'ge
> t'ai'si.

She found her friend saying, "*t'ai'si,* I found."

---

[1] xòwluʔ'una (T).

[2] This little story was told in response to an inquiry about a Taos parallel to the elaborate hide and seek tale told at San Juan and elsewhere. I infer improvisation.

[3] y'uonxenạ it',oyt''əmạ (T).

[4] Rocky Mountain bee-plant, (xᵂ'įwna) (T).

92. The Apache Journey to Basket Mountain[1]

Once there lived a band of Apache at *ebbaba,* Wild Cherry Creek. One early spring the chief of the Apache band notified his people by going around their tipis saying, "My people, five days from now all will prepare to move away from here toward *boadabianpio,*[2] Basket Mountain."[3] Every day the chief talked, telling his people to prepare meals to take along on their trip, for the journey was to be a long one of many days. All these days they were making preparation. The journey was started on the sixth day. At the end of the day's journey the tipis were set up at night. Fires appeared everywhere. They were beating the drum (*mulunah*)[4], singing, hollowing, and yelping. They were very happy in the Indian's way of passing the night. Early before daylight the chief began to make his talk to get ready slowly for another day's journey. Their removal was to be a long journey of about a month, stopping off at suitable places to camp one day or as many days as the chief thought best, to have a good time hunting, as game was abundant. During their journey of many days in the plains they crossed many good rivers and good mountains, but the destination they had chosen was Basket Mountain. After a long journey they reached the place they were to dwell, at Basket Mountain. That's why the Apache make nice baskets of different kinds. They remained there happy, enjoying their good new home.

93. Storm Old Woman Kidnaps Two Children[5]

People were living at *watiahdah* (tree town). As usual, the children were scattered around playing. One day a very strong windstorm carried two little boys off to the top of a high mountain. Storm old woman took them to her cave. The days passed, nowhere could the children be found, by the men who went out hunting or for firewood or other things they needed. Two men went up to a very high mountain peak. They found the footprints of two children. As they knew two children were lost they decided to follow the footprints which led to the cave at the top of the mountain, where the two children were. Then the two

---

[1] Written by a townsman.
[2] puot',ep''ianpiw (toward, -piwą).
[3] Ute Mountain, near the Colorado line (T).
[4] m'uluną, drum, box, jar (T).
[5] Written by a townsman.

men brought the news back to their people how they had found the footprints of the two children and followed them up to the top of the mountain till they led into a cave. The next day as many as could went up to the top of the mountain. There the two children were playing at the edge of the cave. Soon the two children saw their people. They ran into the cave. Then the men waited and hid where the children could not see. After a short time the two children came out from their cave. The nearest one of the spies ran to the entrance of the cave and shut it with a flat stone. Thus the two little boys could not go back into their cave. They caught them. They were naked. They brought them home, they dressed them and cleaned them and made them vomit. They vomited thorns and pieces of old rotten rawhide from refuse. When heavy wind-storm came, the children wanted to go out, but they would not let them go outside. Finally the children died.

94. Why Salt Man Went Away

Salt man (*pa'łesöanena*)[1] was living at the Mouth of Red Willows, also Louse (*piaya'na*)[2]. One day they met each other as they were out walking. As they were talking together in a friendly way about what they were, Louse said to Salt man, "But you were separated (set apart) not to be used in some Indian doings. And I am not separated in any way," said Louse. "I am always with young men, nice young men, and with nice girls. I am not set apart by any one. My place with young men is on the buttocks and side of the neck and in the armpit. So with nice girls. But when there is any entertainment I always hide myself and run into bush where there are pretty flowers. (He meant the hair of the head.) But I am always very silent. Wherever I am, when the person is alone, I always tickle him. Then he scratches, he catches me and beats me, and sometimes at dances I feel funny, no matter how good a time he is having in a crowd or talking away I tickle him, I make him itch. When they take their clothes off I am always in their clothes, their best clothes. You, Salt man, you are not everywhere like me. You are only at meals. So you are set apart, not like me." Salt man felt very sad at this, and so he left and went to live in the south. That's why at the Mouth of Red Willows there is no salt mine.

---

[1] p'òł̣ i̯ęs'əonena (T).
[2] p'i̯ay'ana (T).

Variant[1]

Louse and Salt once lived together. Louse asked Salt why he was so snappish. Salt replied, "Because I always give a good flavor to food wherever I am used." Louse said, "Yes, but you are not carried and kept in the warmest corners of the bodies of nice girls or in the nicest clothes of the young men." So Salt went away angry to a country far south.

95. Jealous Wife[2]

People were living at home.[3] There was a young man who was married, but who had a young girl friend. One summer day the people had a picnic[4] a distance from home. The young man invited his girl friend to go on that picnic. The morning of the picnic day came, they went on the picnic. The young man was followed by his wife. The young man and his girl friend arrived at the picnic ground. They passed on and went on top of a mountain. His wife followed and overtook them. The two women fell to fighting. They went pushing and rolling until they got to the edge of a cliff, a very high rock wall.[5] They both tumbled down the rock and were torn to pieces, nothing was left of them. Their white Moqui clothes remained hanging on the sharp rocks.

96. The Girl who Married a Bear

When the people went out together in the spring there was a girl who did not want to go with them. She would go alone to *paⱡukiba*.[6] Her brothers watched her. They saw her going nicely dressed and carrying bread and meat up the canyon. Soon there came a big bear, and they embraced each other. She spread out the food. The brothers said, "You shoot and I shoot!" Bear fell, and they beat the girl. Soon after she died.

---

[1] Written by the narrator of the preceding version.
[2] Written by townsman.
[3] t'ʼoyeto, people-at (T).
[4] Paraphrase for pilgrimage to the Lake.
[5] There is an actual place to which this legend attaches.
[6] p'òⱡ̦uok'ʼibo, water-arrows-up there (T). A canyon to the westward.

97. Culture Hero[1]

Piankettacholla[2] (mountain point green-blue) was born about one hundred and fifty miles north of Taos and west of the San Luis Valley. His mother had never known a man, but she put some pretty pebbles in her belt, and soon after the child was born.[3] When the people could not find out who was the father of the child they tried to kill him. But they did not succeed, and as he grew older he began to look very beautiful, "like Jeus Christ."

Piankettacholla taught the people to dance, to make clothes, to plant corn, beans, and melons. From different colored stones he made corn, beans, and melons.

He could fly. He fastened to his breech clout an eagle's tail, and to his arms above the elbows wild turkey wings. . . He got within a few feet of the stars, which are birds. They have very green legs and very bright breasts, like a hummingbird, they have a bill like an eagle's, and very dark eyes. The twinkling of the stars is the slow flying of the birds. The shooting stars are birds in quick motion. When you can not see the stars the birds have turned around, so their bright breasts can not be seen. *Piankettacholla* could not find out how the birds lived, nor could he get near enough to the sun and moon to find out about them.

He would go down into the earth and in summer bring up ice and snow, or in winter, green leaves. He got his name from being able to make the mountains green. He could make it rain.

At one time a flood of hot water came and drowned all the people, except *Piankettacholla* who got inside a big pile of cottonwood bark. He looked down and saw where it was green and there he made the waters go down. He came out of the bark pile, took some foam from the waters and made people. From different colored stones he made seeds, which the people planted.

He told the Pueblo people in advance about White men and negroes and other peoples. He said that the Pueblo people would get fewer and fewer and by and by would all be White people.

---

[1] This is a summary of Miller's account (Miller, 44-45). I was unable to get this culture hero story which resembles in many particulars the Poseyemu-Montezuma story of Tewa and Keres.

[2] p'ˌiank'ˌəotoc'ǫle (T).

[3] A story about impregnation through piñon (common among Tewa) had been heard by my informant, but he could not tell it.

Piankettacholla still lives in a lake to the north. One time a noise, like the beating of a dance drum, was heard in the lake. His tracks have been seen about there, too. "He is very old, but does not die."

98. Puyé and Pecos[1]

My mother's father told me about Puyé cliff ruins. He said that the people who once lived there spoke the same language as the Taos people. They had a large snake in the pueblo. They used to give small children to the snake to eat. The families took turns giving the snake a child. After a while the people got tired feeding the snake. They did not feed him any more. Then after a while it did not rain any more. The people did not have corn enough to eat. So finally they moved away. They went to Pecos—you know where those old ruins are east of Santa Fé? Well, that is where they went.

[1] Recorded by Leslie A. White.

APPENDIX

By George L. Trager, Yale University

The following tales are given as they were recorded, except that occasional phonetic notations have been replaced by the final phonemic analysis; normalizations have been introduced only in a few cases of evident error, but many of the accentual indications have been supplied after recording; words appear with the accentual forms they have in isolation except in those cases where these have been changed by sentence sandhi. Commas in the text indicate non-terminal pauses, and periods the terminal pauses; these are the only two sentence types known to me for Taos.

For phonological and grammatical details reference must be made to my *Outline of Taos Grammar,* in a volume whose collection was begun by Edward Sapir and is now being edited by Professor L. Bloomfield. In line with the practise of that *Outline,* the symbol j is used here for the palatal semivowel (rendered by y in the rest of the present volume), and initial glottal stop is written instead of being omitted.

The interlinear translation is literal, but does not always render exactly the order of elements in a Taos word; hyphens are used between elements.

Gum Baby

xǫmˌɛnmǫt‘'ǝmxǫ	*kʷ'ɛnem*	*ʔǫnnit‘'ǝmǫ*	*t‘'olomu-*
Once upon a time	Mexicans	they 2 (narrative)-lived	Ranchos de

no.	*h'uxu*	*ʔǫnnǫwiwˌaltok'ˌujup‘'ihu.*	*h'uxu*	*pìwʔùʔ'una*
Taos-at.	And so	of them 2 (nar.)-garden-is nice.	And so	rabbit-little

wit‘'ǝm	*h'obo.*	*h'uxu*	*kʷˌɛs'ǝonena*	*t‘ˌǝmh'alum*
he (nar.)-lived	also.	And so	Mexican-man	morning-early

c'ǫn.	*hux'ǫ*	*ʔǫnǫwiwˌaltok'olmǫ.*	*h'uxu*
he went out.	And then	his (nar.)-garden-was eaten up.	And so

173

t"ənʔoj   c"əodhu,   ʔᵫmᵫwiɫiwc'iahu.   p'ᵫjuʔu-
house-into he goes in,   he-his own (nar.)-wife-addresses. "Who-might

h'ihu   kᵫnnᵫw̥altok'ol'ahu,   miwwiɫiwʔᵫm'ᵫhu.
it be   of us 2-garden-may be eating?"   it is said-he (nar.)-wife-tells.

p'ᵫw'ᵫm   h'onxu   huwòt'ómᵫ,   pìwʔùʔ'una   hu
"Who-one   so then   indeed-not-is doing; rabbit-little   indeed

t'óhu.   h'onxu   j'on   ʔoɫòt"əomᵫxu,   tikʷᵫp'oj-
is doing.   So then   now   when I-wood-gather-shall go,   I it-pitch-

xʷ'iajá.   h'uonmenᵫ   tikʷᵫp'ojt'ojp'ajimᵫnᵫ   tᵫxiw'ᵢnejá
will get.   Then   when I it-pitch-person-have made I shall stand it

p"olk'əoʔogᵫ.   h'uxu   kʷᵫp'ojk'ᵫlimᵫnᵫ   wi-
hole-mouth-at."   And so   when he-pitch-had brought   he (nar.)-

t'ojp'a.   h'uonmenᵫ   wih'ujihu   pìwʔùʔ'una   ʔᵫp"olnent'o.
person-made.   Then   he (nar.)-takes it   rabbit-little   his-hole-to.

h'uxu   pìwʔùʔ'una   pᵢᵫj'ᵫxonxu   ʔuwiw'əli.   hux'u
And so   rabbit-little   in the evening   he it (nar.) comes out of. And so

                xᵫwit"'ojkʷin.   h'ili,   h'uxu   xᵫwi-
right then-he (nar.)-person is standing. "What?"   And so   right then-

c'iaʔᵫhu.   h'ijod   ʔᵫt'óhu   miwwi-
he (nar.)-addresses it. "What-and   you-are doing?"   it is said-(nar.)-

ʔ'ᵫmᵫ.   h'uxu   h'iwenᵫ   wòʔit'ᵫmᵫ   hu'xu   w'iwa
he said.   And so   anything   not-it-talks.   And so   again

   wic'iaʔᵫ,   pokᵫwòt'ᵫʔi   ʔᵫwá-
he (nar.)-asked,   "(question)-you-not-the one who speaks   you-are-

mᵫ.   j'onten   majwòʔᵫm'ᵫxu   ʔᵫmᵫ̇-
(able)?   Now then   when you me-not-shall speak,   I you-shall hit

t'emmá   mᵫwiʔ'ᵫmᵫ.   h'uonmᵫtenᵫ   wimᵫ̇t'emᵫ.
with my hand,"   thus-he (nar.)-said.   Thereupon   he (nar.)-hit him.

h'uxu   ʔqmimą̀nt̓'əba.   poj'ynemtenų
And so   his own (nar.)-hand-became stuck.   "(question)-this-then (only)

ʔqnqmk'imqmiw   wiʔ'ymę.   h'uxu   wimą̀t'em
I have it-it is said?"   he (nar.)-said.   And so   he (nar.)-hit him

w'ęmhujpi.   h'uxu   poj'ynemtenų   ʔqnqmk'imqmiw
one-on the side.   And so   "(question)-this-then   I have it-it is said,

ʔqp'ienemq.   t'enxu   wiʔįǫsiabq.   h'uxu   ʔqmiʔįę-
you-think?"   Then   he (nar.)-kicked him.   And so   his own (nar.)-

t̓'əba.   poj'ynemtenų   ʔqnqmk'imqmiw   ʔqp'ienemq.
foot-became stuck.   "(?)-this-then   I have it-it is said   you-think?"

wiʔįęsiab   c'alpi.   poj'ynemtenų   ʔqnqmk'imqmiw
he (nar.)-kicked him   on left side.   "(?)-this-then   I have it-it is said

ʔqp'ienemq.   t'enxu   t̓"įębo   wimą̀t'emq.   h'uxu   hob'o
you-think?"   Then   belly-on   he (nar.)-hit him.   And so   also

wit̓'əba.   h'uxu   h'uoto   wit̓'əba.   h'uxu
he (nar.)-got stuck.   And so   all over   he (nar.)-got stuck.   And so

t̓'əmh'alumxu   s'əonena   wiméǥhu   ʔqnqw‚altokʷi-
morning-early-when   man   he (nar.)-goes   his garden-being

n'enpiw.   h'uxu   pìwʔùʔuna   wit̓"q.   h'uxu   h'od
located-where.   And so   rabbit-little   he (n.)-found.   And so   and

wih'ujhu   t̓"ənpiwq.   h'uxu   ʔqwit̓it‚u-
he (n.)-takes him   house-where.   And so   his (n.)-old woman-he

c''əoti.   h'uxu   wit̓iwʔym'ęhu,   j'yna   menh'u
brought it to.   And so   he (nar.)-woman-tells,   "This one   indeed

kqnt̓'įwp'ola,   mépuoʔi   wámq.   j'onu
of us 2-onions-finished;   the one who was going   he is.   Now

ʔoc'ilit̓‚əp'aʔámiw   t̓iwʔym'ęhu.   h'uxu   t̓iw'ena
you-chili-soup-will make-it is said,"   woman-he tells.   And so   woman

wic‚ilił'əpa.   h'uxu   h'od   ʔank'‚olm'ɛxu
she (nar.)-chili-soup-made.   And so   and   when they 2-were eating

witiwʔ‚ym'ɛhu,   kɑnwòc‚ilił‚əł‚ulp'umiw,
he (nar.)-woman-tells,   "We 2-not-chili-soups-let us drop-it is said,"

witiwʔ‚ym'ɛhu.   h'uxu   tiw'ena   ʔqwic‚ilił‚əł'ulɑ.
he (nar.)-woman-tells. And so   woman   her (nar.)-chili-soup-dropped.

h'uxu   ʔqnqwipìwʔùxʷ‚iabw'əla.
And so   of them 2 (nar.)-rabbit-little-run away-she caused to go out.

h'uxu   kʷ'ɛnemɑ   ʔqnwámɑm,   t'enxu   t'olo-
And so   Mexicans   they 2-became-it is told,   thereafter   Ranchos de

muno   ʔqnitˣ'əmɑ.   h'uki   t'olomuno   kʷ'ɛnem
Taos-at   they (nar.)-lived. That's why   Ranchos de Taos-at   Mexicans

ʔiwip‚iał‚ił‚iwhaj'ihu.   h'utɛng   kɑwixʷ'ɛkimɑ.
they (nar.)-root-grass-onions-raise. And thus now you (nar.)-tail have.

Free translation

Once upon a time two Mexicans lived at Ranchos de Taos. They had a
nice garden. A little rabbit lived there also. Early one morning the
Mexican man went out and found his garden all eaten up. So he went
into the house and said to his wife, "Who might it be that is eating up
our garden? No person is doing it, the little rabbit is doing it. So when I
go to gather wood I shall get some pinyon gum pitch. Then when I have
made a pitch-[figure like a] man, I shall stand it at the mouth of the
[rabbit's] hole." And when he had brought the pitch he made a figure
and took it to the little rabbit's hole. And the little rabbit came out in
the evening and there was the figure standing. "What's this?" he said,
and addressed it: "What are you doing here?" But it didn't answer anything. So he asked again, "Aren't you able to speak? If you don't speak to
me, I'll hit you." Then he hit it and his hand became stuck. "Do [you
think] I have only this one?", he said, and hit it on the other side. And
then he said, "Do you think I have only this one?" Then he kicked it and
his foot became stuck. "Do you think I have only this one?" And he
kicked it on the left side. "Do you think I have only this one?" And he hit

it with his belly. And this also got stuck. And so he was stuck all over. And early the next morning the man went to his garden and found the little rabbit. And he took him home and brought him to his old woman and said to her, "This is the one who destroyed our onions and who was running about in our garden. Now make some chili stew with him." And so the old woman made some chili stew. And when they were eating, he told the woman, "We mustn't spill any of our chili." But the woman spilled some, and thereby caused their little rabbit to jump out and run away. And so the two of them were Mexicans thereafter; they lived at Ranchos de Taos. And now you have the [fox-]tail [and it's your turn].[1]

---

[1] Variant: Rabbit lived near Grass Root and his wife (a name for vegetable-growers?), who had a garden. Rabbit came to them pretending to have a toothache; they fed him and he said his toothache stopped; then he came again and a third time, eating all the vegetables. Grass Root went to the forest and got some pinyon gum and made a doll of it. Rabbit came, encountered the figure, struck with one hand and stuck fast, then with the other, then his feet, and then his belly, until all of him was stuck. Grass-Root came out and found him, and brought him to his wife to cook. As they were eating, Grass-Root cautioned his wife against spilling any of the sauce. She spilled some, and Rabbit ran out, rattling the dishes.

Coyote tricks his daughter

xǫm ̩ęnmǫt'ꞌemxǫ   c'ùn'e   ʔǫmʔùp'ialxu   wit'ꞌǫmǫ.
Once upon a time   Coyote   his-family-with   they (nar.)-were living.

j'iane   h'od   c'ǝkitenǫ   c'ùn'e   wiwámǫ.   j'iane   h'od
Then   also   always hunting   Coyote   he (nar.)-was.   Then   also

ʔǫwip'ꞌiwkʷ'ǝlwámǫ.   j'iane h'od   huwip'ianem
he (nar.)-daughter-young girl had.   Then also indeed-(nar.)-he thought

c'ùn'e,   h'utenǫ   ʔǫnmop'ꞌiwk''umǫ.   h'uxu   n'ǫtenǫ
Coyote,   "Now then   my own-daughter-is pretty.   And so   I-indeed

h'i   ti?'ǫmmámụ.   j'iane   h'od   tùƚ'oneg
something   I-her-will do-it is said."   Then   also   in the evening

    ?i?'ęxu   huwiƚiw?ụm'ęhu,   ?ojx'enhi   n'ǫ
when they-were sitting   indeed-he (nar.)-wife-tells,   "If   I

?op'iw?ǫn   j'odti   mǫw'əlijá.   h'uxu   ?ǫnc'ͺubp'iw'ena,
I-die,   here-from   you (pl.)-will go away.   And so   my-first-daughter,

    mǫsͺəonc'ͺub?ͺucum'i?i   pͺuontụm'ę?ojteng,
you (pl.)-man-first-whom you meet   foreign [language]-speaks-if indeed,

hu   ?ǫnp'iwk''oji   ?ǫt''əjámụ.   j'ianexǫ
so   my-daughter   you-will live [with him]-it is said."   Then-indeed

        ?ǫnǫsun'ǫxu   wih'əoltáhu   c'ùn'e.
[that] it might certainly be [so],   he (nar.)-becomes sick   Coyote.

h'uxumͺen   k'ͺəop'ino   ?ǫwip'ͺelk'i?ǫnǫ.   j'iane   h'od   c'ùn'e
And so-now   neck-upon   he (nar.)-mole-had.   Then   also   Coyote

    wic'əmę́.   h'uxu   kͺowpͺiwkujn'ent'o
he (nar.)-hunting-went.   And so   horse-dead-lying-to where

    wiw'onǫ.   h'uxu   ?iwip'ͺot'ubc'ụ
he (nar.)-arrived.   And so   he it (nar.)-hollow flute [plant]-picked

        ?ipͺiant'op'ol'i?inǫ.   hͺunom'enǫ   ?iwip'ͺita-
it-in middle-hollowed-the one that is.   Thereupon   he them (nar.)-

x'əwhu.   j'iane   ?iwit'ojhu   j'iat'o.   hͺuonm'enǫ
worms picks up.   Then   he them (nar.)-places there-in.   Thereupon

?ukʷ'ilimenǫ   wimę́hu   t''ənpiw.   j'iane   h'od
when he it-shut,   he (nar.)-goes   home-toward.   Then   also

        mǫwih'əolkǫlǫ.   h'uxu   h'od   c'ùn'e
he himself (nar.)-sick-brought himself [to be].   And so   also   Coyote

hͺəolp'ͺimęw'oju   mǫw'i?ǫmhu.   j'iane   tͺu-
sick-very much   he himself (n.)-makes.   Then   stick-sewed [ham-

p'elto mąw'ik'uo. h'uxu h'od j'iane h'od
mock]-on he himself (nar.)-laid. And so also then also

w'it'ə̀ nąn'ąxu c'ùn'e h'od ʔitˌuop'ˌitał'ulihu.
two-days when it was, Coyote also he them-meat-worms-spills.

h'uxu h'od hu ʔąwił̀iwt'ųhu linąw'itǫ̀młˌəom,
And so also indeed his(nar.)-wife-says, "Alas, father-is sinking,

j'onų h'od j'uhi pˌǫmąc'ujámų hob'o n'ą
now also maybe world-he will leave-it is said. Also we

ʔimąc'uwaʔá. j'iane h'od c'ùn'e h'od
we-will be left. Then also Coyote indeed [said to himself],

h'ili majwòʔ'ęlumę. j'iane h'od c'ùn'e
"Something you me-not-are shaking." Then also Coyote

ł̀iwʔù ʔąmʔùp''ialxu h'od ʔiwiw'əlihu.
[Old-] Woman-little her-children-with also they (nar.)-go away.

j'iane h'od ʔihˌəomę́hu. j'iane h'od c'ùn'e
Then also they-are travelling. Then also Coyote

mąwitˌəobx^w'iaji, hˌuonm'enteną mąwit'ˌujp'ˌo-
he himself (nar.)-jumped up, thereupon he himself (nar.)-clay-

l'aʔąmą hˌuonm'enteną mąwiʔ'įęlu wˌojc''əopi
white-made. thereupon he (nar.)-ran facing them

ʔąmʔùʔˌęh'ęnpi. h'uxu h'od ʔimǫjʔ'ucu jˌiat''o,
his-family-coming-there. And so also he them (nar.)-met there-at,

h'od c'ùn'e wipˌuont'ųhu. tą
and Coyote (nar.)-speaks in a foreign language. "So then,

ʔąnp'ìwk''ojimų j'onų kitǫ̀mwápuoʔi ʔątˌųwáʔi
my-daughter-it is said, now our-father-that was his-words

mąx'umxu ʔiwòʔ'ųmmámų, j'ųna kus'əon-
untruthfully they-not-will speak-it is said. This one you him-man-

t'əjá.   *j'iane*   *h'od*   *c'ùn'e*   *ʔqpʻiwpʻʻialxu*
will live with."   Then   also   Coyote   his-daughter-with

ʔqnn'itʻ əta.   *j'iane*   *h'od*   *p'oʔogq*   *c'ùn'e*   *ʔqmwip'ˌimə̀huo-*
they 2 (nar.)-lived.   Then   also   legs-on   Coyote   he it (nar.)-head-

k'ujmq̣.   *wimˌabup'iwkujmq̣*   *ʔqwpʻˌu-*
handling-was lying.   He (nar.)-very loving-was lying,   while she them-

mˌqkqm'amegq̣.   *j'iane*   *k'ˌəop'iʔog*   *ʔqmmq̀k'ǫlag,*
lice-was looking for.   Then   neck-on   her-hand-touched-when,

xen'nonu̧   *mq̣wicˌelx'ęhu.*   *j'iane*   *c'ùn'e*   *wi-*
    then   he (nar.)-refuses to be touched.   Then   Coyote   he (nar.)-

ʔˌqsijˌiap'iw.   *j'iane*   *h'od*   *kʷˌəl'ena*   *huwit'u̧hu,*
sweetly-went to sleep.   Then   also   the girl   indeed-(nar.)-says,

x'ǫmhi *h'uxu* *j'u̧na*   *j'u̧g*   *mq̣cˌelx'ęhumu.*
"Why   also   this one   at this point   he refuses to be touched-it is said?"

j'iane   *mù̧miʔojx'enxu*   *ʔqwipʻʻelkimq̣,*   *jˌiatʻoxǫ*
Then   she looked-if-when   he (nar.)-mole-had,   there-indeed

ʔqtǫ̀m'enato   *wiwámq̣.*   *j'iane*   *h'od*   *huwit'u̧hu,*
her own-father   he (nar.)-was.   Then   also   indeed-(nar.)-she says,

j'u̧na   *łˌułihˌiʔįęp'una*   *j'onu̧*   *pˌiwpiw'ojá.*   *j'ianexǫ*   *h'iwʔoxu*
"This   old man-dirty   now   he will be dead."   Then   stone-upon

ʔqmp'ʻik'uo,   *hˌuonm'enq̣*   *ʔqwihˌiwʔ'upʻuo.*
his-head-she put,   thereafter   her (nar.)-stone-she threw down.

jˌiah'uxo   *c'ùn'e*   *wimˌu̧t'apˌujj'iaxǫ.*   *t'en*
There around   Coyote   (nar.)-empty hide-is thrown about.   Now

kq̣wixʷ'ękimq̣.
you (nar.)-tail-have.

Free translation

Once upon a time Coyote was living with his family; he was always hunting. He had an adolescent daughter. Coyote thought, "My daughter is pretty; so I'll play a trick on her." That evening when they were sitting, he said to his wife, "If I die, go away from here; and as for my daughter, the first man whom you meet, if he speaks a foreign language, you will marry him." And so that it might happen in this way, Coyote made himself sick. Now he had a mole on his neck. So Coyote went hunting, and came to a place where a dead horse was lying; and he picked up a hollow-stemmed plant that grew there and gathered some maggots and put them in the hollow. Then he shut it and went home. Then he made believe he was ill, and he looked very ill. Then he lay down on the hammock, and after two days he released the maggots. Then his wife says, "Father is sinking, maybe he is leaving the world and us." Then Coyote said to himself, "You are no longer shaking me." Then Coyote-Woman goes away with her children, and they are travelling. Then Coyote jumped up, covered himself with white clay, and ran so as to meet his family. And he met them there, and Coyote spoke in a foreign language. [And the mother spoke:] "Now, my daughter, our late father's words will not be spoken in vain. You will marry this man." Then Coyote and his daughter lived together. Once Coyote was lying with his head on her lap; he was very amorous, while she was looking for lice. Then when her hand touched his neck, he pushed it away. Then Coyote gently went to sleep. Then the girl said, "Why does he avoid being touched in this place?" When she looked, there was a mole there; it was her own father. Then she said: "This dirty old man will die for sure now." She put his head on a stone, and dropped another stone on him. And Coyote's skeleton is scattered all around there. Now you have the tail.

LIST OF REFERENCES

Benedict   1. Ruth Benedict. Tales of the Cochiti Indians. Bulletin 98, Bureau of American Ethnology. 1931.

2. Zuni Mythology. Columbia University Contributions to Anthropology, XXI. 1935.

Boas   1. Franz Boas. Tales of Spanish Provenience from Zuni. Journal American Folk-Lore, 35: 62-98. 1922.
2. Keresan Texts. Publications, American Ethnological Society, vol. VIII, Pt. I, 1928.

Boas and Simango   F. Boas and C. K. Simango. Tales and Proverbs of the Vandau of Portuguese South Africa. Journal American Folk-Lore, 35: 151-204. 1922.

Cushing   F. H. Cushing. Zuni Folk-Tales. New York and London. 1901.

Dorsey   1. George A. Dorsey. The Mythology of the Wichita. Carnegie Institute of Washington, Publication No. 21. 1904.
2. Traditions of the Skidi Pawnee. Memoirs, American Folk-Lore Society, VIII. 1904.
3. The Cheyenne. Field Columbian Museum, Pub. 99. Anthrop. Series, vol. IX, no. 1, 1905.

Dumarest   Noël Dumarest. Notes on Cochiti, New Mexico. Memoirs, American Anthropological Association, vol. VI, no. 3. 1919.

Espinosa   Aurelio M. Espinosa. Pueblo Indian Folk Tales. Journal American Folk-Lore, 49: 69-133. 1936.

Fewkes   J. W. Fewkes. Hopi Katcinas. XXI (1903) Annual Report Bureau American Ethnology.

Goodwin   Grenville Goodwin. White Mountain Apache Religion. American Anthropologist, 40: 24-37. 1938

Handy   E. S. Handy. Zuni Tales. Journal American Folk-Lore, 31: 451-471. 1918.

Harrington and Roberts   J. P. Harrington and Helen H. Roberts. Picurís Children's Stories. XLIII (1925-26) Annual Report Bureau American Ethnology.

Kroeber

1. A. L. Kroeber. Cheyenne Tales. Journal American Folk-Lore, 13: 161-190. 1900.
2. Ute Tales. Journal American Folk-Lore, 14: 252-285. 1901.

Lowie

R. H. Lowie. Myths and Traditions of the Crow Indians. Anthropological Papers ,American Museum of Natural History, XXI, Pt. I, 1918.

Lummis

C. F. Lummis. Pueblo Indian Folk-Stories. New York, 1910.

Miller

Merton L. Miller. Preliminary Study of the Pueblo of Taos, New Mexico. Chicago, 1898.

Opler

1. M. E. Opler. Myths and Tales of the Jicarilla Apache Indians. Memoirs, American Folk-Lore Society, XXXI, 1938.
2. Myths and Legends of the Lipan Apache Indians, Memoirs, American Folk-Lore Society, XXXVI, 1940.

Parsons

1. Elsie Clews Parsons. Pueblo-Indian Folk-Tales, Probably of Spanish Provenience, Journal American Folk-Lore, 31: 216-255. 1918.
2. The Provenience of Certain Negro Folk Tales: Tar Baby. Folk Lore, XXX: 227-234. 1919.
3. Die Flucht auf den Baum. Zeitschrift für Ethnologie, 54: 1-29. 1922.
4. Tewa Tales. Memoirs, American Folk-Lore Society, XIX. 1926.
5. The Social Organization of the Tewa of New Mexico. Memoirs, American Anthropological Association, XXXVI. 1929.
6. Kiowa Tales. Memoirs, American Folk-Lore Society, XXII. 1929.
7. Isleta, New Mexico, XLVII (1929-30) Annual Report Bureau American Ethnology.
8. Laguna Tales. Journal American Folk-Lore, 44: 137-142. 1931.
9. Mitla: Town of the Souls. University of Chicago Publications in Anthropology, Chicago, 1936.
10. Taos Pueblo. General Series in Anthropology, No. 2. 1936.

Parsons and Boas   E. C. Parsons and Franz Boas. Spanish Tales from Laguna and Zuni, New Mexico. Journal American Folk-Lore, 33: 47-72. 1920.

Stevenson   1. Matilda C. Stevenson. The Sia. XI (1889-90) Annual Report Bureau American Ethnology.
2. The Zuni Indians. XXIII (1901-2) Annual Report Bureau American Ethnology.

Voth   H. R. Voth. The Traditions of the Hopi. Field Columbian Museum, Pub. 96, Anthrop. Series. vol. VIII. 1905.

Wallis   W. D. Wallis. Folk Tales from Shumopovi, Second Mesa. Journal American Folk-Lore, 49: 1-68. 1936.